BAKING AS BIOGRAPHY

Baking As Biography

A Life Story in Recipes

DIANE TYE

McGILL-QUEEN'S UNIVERSITY PRESS

Montreal & Kingston · London · Ithaca

© McGill-Queen's University Press 2010

ISBN 978-0-7735-3724-8 (cloth)
ISBN 978-0-7735-3725-5 (paper)

Legal deposit third quarter 2010
Bibliothèque nationale du Québec

Printed in Canada on acid-free paper that is 100% ancient forest free
(100% post-consumer recycled), processed chlorine free.

This book has been published with the help of a grant from the Canadian Federation
for the Humanities and Social Sciences, through the Aid to Scholarly Publications
Programme, using funds provided by the Social Sciences and Humanities Research
Council of Canada. Funding has also been provided by Memorial University of
Newfoundland.

McGill-Queen's University Press acknowledges the support of the Canada Council
for the Arts for our publishing program. We also acknowledge the financial support
of the Government of Canada through the Canada Book Fund for our publishing
activities.

Library and Archives Canada Cataloguing in Publication

Tye, Diane, 1957–
Baking as biography : a life story in recipes / Diane Tye.

Includes bibliographical references and index.
ISBN 978-0-7735-3724-8 (bound). ISBN 978-0-7735-3725-5 (pbk.)

1. Tye, Laurene, 1931–1989. 2. Spouses of clergy–Biography.
3. Christian women–Biography. 4. Middle class women–Canada–
Biography. 8. Spouses of clergy–Social life and customs. 6. Christian
women–Social life and customs. 7. Middle class women–Canada–Social
life and customs. 8. Baking–Folklore. 9. Food habits–Folklore. I. Title.

TX649.T94T94 2010   641.5092   C2010-902073-1

This book was designed and typeset by studio oneonone in Sabon 10/13

For my parents,
Laurene and Henry Tye

CONTENTS

RECIPES

ILLUSTRATIONS

ACKNOWLEDGMENTS

As I neared the end of writing this book, my son Callum marvelled that such a slim volume could take me so long to finish. I share his incredulity. His comment brought to mind the proverb that it takes a whole village to raise a child. How many people per page, I have to ask, did it take to produce this book?

I have been supported by many good friends during my several years of work on this project. In particular, Jane Burns, Linda Cullum, Pauline Greenhill, Ann Marie Powers, and Mary Ellen Wright offered advice when asked and encouragement when needed. I owe a special thanks to Barbara Rieti, who by now must want never to hear another word about recipes or baking.

Students and colleagues in the Department of Folklore at Memorial University have been more than helpful. Faculty and staff members Bev Diamond, Holly Everett, Jillian Gould, Diane Goldstein, Philip Hiscock, Martin Lovelace, Jerry Pocius, Paul Smith, Cory Thorne, Cindy Turpin, Sharon Cochrane, Pauline Cox, Patricia Fulton, Barb Reddy, and Eileen Collins provided valuable suggestions and willingly shared their personal experiences when I once again steered casual conversation to the subject of food.

I presented parts of this work at meetings of the Folklore Studies Association of Canada, the American Folklore Society, the American Anthropological Association, and the First International Congress of Qualitative Inquiry. On each occasion I benefited from the comments of audience members and was bolstered by their enthusiasm.

McGill-Queen's University Press staff, especially Jonathan Crago, provided wonderful guidance through all stages of the process. I particularly appreciate the thoughtful assessments of the three anonymous readers and the careful editing of Anne Marie Todkill, which helped make this a better book. Publication would not have been possible without the financial assistance of the Aid to Scholarly Publishing Program and Memorial University's publication subvention program.

Extended family members and friends kindly consented to be interviewed: Fred Falconer, Geraldine Falconer, Helen Farrow, Annie Goodyear, Anne Green, Sadie Latimer, Peg Miller, and Helen Ward. Their memories are integral to this work.

Families often help shoulder the burden of a writing project. My family not only supported me in the many usual ways, but also allowed me to make their lives my text. Through the preparation of this book I have developed a fuller appreciation of my mother's life and work as well as the many ways in which my father continues to nurture each family member. The trust and unconditional acceptance that he, along with my brother Mark and sister Cathy, showed at every stage of this project is humbling.

Peter and Callum made all things possible. Their dependable good humour and generous spirits made the experience enjoyable.

BAKING AS BIOGRAPHY

white cookies

Flora MacAskill
Cape North

½ cup shortening
1 cup sugar
1 egg
4 tbsp. hot milk

1 tsp. soda
1 tsp. cr. of tartar
2 cups flour

cream shortening and sugar, add egg well beaten,
soda dissolved in milk, sift cr. tartar with flour
roll and sprinkle with sugar

may add nutmeg and vanilla.

A LIFE IN RECIPES

I have clear a memory of my mother baking. In truth, it is possible that this is actually several memories conflated into one, because while I was growing up I often watched her bake. The time I think I remember is a Saturday morning. I am eighteen years old. It is my first year of university and I am home for a weekend visit. My mother does not take time to sit down with me, so we follow a familiar pattern: we talk as I sit and watch her work. I am not sure why she does not ask for, or seem to want, my help. Maybe because it would take too much time to show me how. Maybe because the kitchen of our 1970s bungalow is not much more than six feet square. The space is cramped with one person, let alone more. Later in my life, I will reflect on how the design of kitchens with enough room for only one person sentences women to lone service, but at the time I am remembering I give this no thought. I am not troubled by the fact that there is no room for me, or that I am not wanted. In fact, I am content not to be involved and make no offer of assistance. I am happy to sit at the table in the "dinette," sampling the finished products and chatting as my mother fills the adjoining kitchen with a blur of activity: mixing batter, spooning cookies onto a cookie sheet, and washing up dishes. In a little more than an hour she produces the bulk of the family's weekly supply of "staples": cookies, squares, biscuits, cinnamon rolls, and an apple pie. None of this productivity impresses me. It is simply how my mother fills every Saturday morning. Today, as always, she places the baked goods into a series of square Tupperware containers and round metal tins that originally held fancy store-bought cookies or candy. Wiping the flour from her hands, my mother pauses. "You know," she says confidentially, "I really don't like to bake."

Sometimes our everyday memories are the most telling. This particular memory stuck with me over the years, and at a certain point I became intrigued by the many possible implications of my mother's simple, surprising disclosure that she did not like to bake. What could this mean? How could it be that she spent so much time at an activity that held – at least apparently – so little importance for her? The more I thought about this, the more I was lured by the idea of telling my mother's life stories through her baking. At first this idea struck me, to say nothing of others in my family, as an unlikely subject in relation to my mother's life: she did not have a wide reputation as a fine cook, nor did she pride herself on culinary accomplishments. If she found some aspects of baking creative or enjoyable, she never said as much. Nor at first glance were the recipes she owned inspiring texts. Her collection shows no signs of being lovingly developed or maintained. Rather, it contains approximately 350 simple recipes for baked goods: cookies, cakes, breads, and squares. Most are recorded on three-by-five cards that she stored in a metal recipe box. Later, after the box was full, recipes spilled over onto scraps of paper and were stuffed into a kitchen drawer. This drawer also held a community cookbook; produced by one of the early women's church groups to which my mother belonged, it was marked by signs of heavy use. These recipes are so strikingly uncomplicated that, when I shared some of my preliminary reflections on the links between my mother's recipes and her life in a paper to the American Folklore Society, another member of the panel was skeptical that such straightforward directions for basic cookies or biscuits could convey very much (Diane Tye, unpublished, 2005). I have discovered, however, that when read closely these recipes reveal hidden messages. And, in part because my mother's baking was obligatory, a response to family and community needs rather than an activity that gave her personal enjoyment, there are subtexts to this collection of recipes that offer insights not only into her life and but also into the realities she shared with other women.

Exploring the contradictions of my mother's life through baking presents certain challenges, now that more than twenty years have passed since her death. Like many other women, she did not leave much in the way of a written record, and the few tangible remains of her life are captured mostly in photograph albums and scrapbooks. These structure and expand my fleeting images of the past into fuller, richer, and more colourful pictures – so that I am often no longer clear as to whether my memories actually happened or if they are thoughts of what might have been. As Ruth Behar reminds us, memory is volatile and slippery and can be tied down only when linked to places and sites (1996, 81). More details from the past emerge in my mother's directions for squares and cookies, breads and cakes. They tell of her youth in a village in northern Nova Scotia during in the 1930s and 1940s, her relationships with her mother, husband and children, and her more than three decades as a minister's wife. The recipes contain stories of her journey through three church congregations in Nova Scotia and Prince Edward Island and of her eventual settling in Amherst, Nova Scotia, when my father left the pulpit for an administrative position. People who were part of my mother's life in all of the places she lived speak through the recipes: some friends and acquaintances come and go over the years, while others are present as life-long connections. These recipes, supplemented by the recollections of those who loved her, offer glimpses beyond the sketchy outline of my mother's life that I am able to piece together. They give substance to my fading memories.

LAURENE

The brief story of my mother's life as I know it, the one that her recipes expand, begins with her birth on 21 July 1931 in Eureka, a small village on the west side of the forks of the East River in north central Nova Scotia.[1] A few miles outside of the town of Stellarton, the area was settled by 1789 by farmers who were part of Pictou County's early waves of Scottish settlers.[2] Mom's father, Fred Falconer (1906–1991), belonged to one of these founding families, while her mother, Isabell or Bell (1905–1983), came from a family of Scottish descent who moved to the village in the late 1800s. Fred and Bell married in 1928 after Bell returned from a two-year stint in Montreal working as a nanny. Her employer was a minister who had formerly served the Methodist congregation in Eureka. Within a few years the couple purchased a house in the centre of the village, and there my mother, Laurene, was born in 1931, followed in 1934 by her brother Fred. My grandparents' Scottish background and rural upbringing underlined their world view, which was expressed in their adherence to Protestantism (the United Church of Canada after its founding in 1925), in folk beliefs, and in a wry sense of humour more often than not conveyed in colourful phrases. It also surfaced in foodways, both in terms of the plainness of food (meat and potatoes, scones and oatcakes) and in the way it was categorized. In their home, there was basic, unpretentious "grub," and slightly more elevated baked goods known as "sweet stuff."

Despite its rural location, Eureka was heavily shaped by industrialization. Farms dotted the area when the Intercolonial Railway went through in about 1866, but the village itself came into being in 1882,

EUREKA, NOVA SCOTIA, c. 1930

when the Eureka Milling Company erected a factory there (Ferguson 1967, 201). When the New Glasgow Iron, Coal and Railway Company selected this as the site for its coke-washing plant, coke ovens, and blast furnace in 1891, the community peaked. By 1898 it boasted the Eureka Woolen Mills, the Ferrona Iron Works, Nova Scotia Telephone, Western Union Telegraph, two halls, three churches, two hotels and seven stores (McAlpine 1898). Unfortunately, prosperity was short-lived. The blast furnace shut down in 1901 (see McCann 1981), and the Eureka Woolen Mills did not fare much better. The mill had a rocky history, going into liquidation soon after 1890 and then experiencing a succession of owners before burning down in 1915. Many of the approximately 150 unemployed workers (Cameron 1983, 152) relocated with the company to Windsor, Nova Scotia. With both the blast furnace and woollen mill gone, Eureka's population stabilized at around 500, its size during my

mother's childhood in the 1930s and 1940s. After Eureka's rapid dein-
dustrialization, most of its remaining labour force found employment
outside the community. By World War II, the village had become a bedroom community for those who worked in industries in nearby towns.
About seventy-five per cent of the wage earners in Eureka worked at
Eastern Car, a manufacturer of railway cars based in Trenton (Laurene
Tye, Interview, 1984). This included my grandfather, who began at thir-
teen as a riveter and rose to general foreman of the steel erection and
construction department of what was Hawker Siddeley when he retired
in 1970.

Mom's journey out of Eureka began when she was sixteen years old.
That summer she met my father, Henry Tye, at a church youth camp
where he was employed for the season as a grounds manager. Born in
1930, Dad was from New Glasgow. There, his father Orval (1907–1970)
and grandfather Charles (1878–1949) worked at the Maritime Steel
foundry. My parents dated through high school and through the seven
years of my father's university education, which earned him a BA and a
divinity degree. After graduating from grade eleven in nearby Stellarton,
my mother completed a commercial course at the Maritime Business
College in New Glasgow and worked in the office of Hoyt's Hardware
store in New Glasgow for a year or two before marrying in 1954.

My father can no longer recall what or who influenced his decision
to enter the ministry. His choice seems to surprise him now when he
thinks of it. Few of his friends considered attending university as an alternative to a factory job, and he cannot remember his parents placing an
emphasis on education. Whatever his reasons, once ordained as a United
Church minister my father was sent to a rural area of Cape Breton Island.
In those days his posting was described as a "three point charge" in that
he served three congregations: a church in the village of Cape North and
smaller churches in nearby Aspey Bay and Pleasant Bay. Located in the
Cape Breton Highlands, this largely Scottish farming area was remote

LAURENE WITH HER MOTHER BELL,
EUREKA, 1931

LAURENE, EUREKA, c. 1953

HENRY AND LAURENE, CAPE NORTH,
c. 1954

(see MacDonald 1980); it was not until the 1930s that one could travel there by car, although by the time my parents moved there in the mid-1950s some of the land had been expropriated for Cape Breton Highlands National Park, and road access was improved to accommodate the increased traffic. Despite this improved access, the area remained isolated, especially in the winter months. Provisions were shipped into the community in the fall, and travel outside the immediate area during the winter was limited. Mom and Dad settled into the church manse in Cape North, where there was also a store and church. My mother's friend Anne Green, although herself from a rural community outside of New Glasgow, was unprepared for the monotony of life in backwoods Cape Breton. Fifty years later, there is still a hint of amazement in her voice when she remembers the isolation she experienced during a visit there: "We spent the whole week and there wasn't a thing to do. And she [Laurene] spent the winter" (Green, Interview, 2004).

When my parents reflected on their time in Cape North, they often recalled arriving that first autumn to discover that the former minister had not put in the winter's wood supply. This was a very serious situation, and with the help of neighbours my father managed to cut, split, and stack enough wood for the winter. However, my parents' inexperience with a wood furnace meant that they were never able to adequately heat the two-storey house. Whenever they shared recollections of Cape North, my parents emphasized the discomfort of living in that manse during their first winter. In fact, the story of the winter's short supply of wood and the tableau of the cold house are indicative of my parent's inexperience, a theme that underlines many of their stories. It encapsulates their inability to look after themselves independently and prompts accounts of how readily others came forward to help. Generosity underlines their stories. They told of being served countless meals in the homes of church members and of how they would frequently return home to find food left for them on their back doorstep – perhaps vegetables, fresh fish, a cut of meat, or a dozen eggs. Women shared their recipes for White Cookies, Chocolate Oatmeal Cookies, and Thimble Cookies with my mother; these were among the first items that she filed in the recipe box she had been given as a wedding-shower gift. And, as my father is still fond of telling, it was a neighbouring woman who gently told my mother after an early unsuccessful attempt at baking that recipes calling for tea required brewed tea, not tea leaves.

In the summer of 1957, when I was only a few weeks old, my parents moved to Parrsboro, a small town in mainland Nova Scotia. First settled by the Acadians in the seventeenth century, the area was populated by New Englanders after the Acadian Expulsion. During the nineteenth century, Parrsboro and several nearby communities, including Port Greville,

CAPE NORTH UNITED CHURCH, c. 1954

PARRSBORO UNITED CHURCH, 1960

boasted significant shipyards. Today, Parrsboro has a population of about 1500, but when my family moved there in the late 1950s it would have been nearly twice this size. Even by that time, however, the former ship building community was in decline, and the town had suffered one of three fires that would devastate its downtown district. During the first year or so that my parents lived there, Parrsboro was the coal shipping port for the Springhill mines, but this ended with the Springhill Mining Disaster in 1958. My father's responsibilities included Trinity United Church in Parrsboro, a congregation of approximately 250 families, as well as a rural congregation of about 50 families in Port Greville, twelve miles away. It was a very heavy workload. There were capital projects, and the forty funerals my father conducted each year were in themselves enough to keep him busy. I don't remember my mother sharing stories of this phase of her life, but her time in Parrsboro was linked inextricably to the church and its functions. She was involved in both congregations and actively supported women's and youth groups.

In 1961, Dad accepted a call to a 500-family congregation in a newly developed suburb of Charlottetown, Prince Edward Island. Living in a modern, upscale manse, my mother revelled in new physical surroundings that presented a welcome contrast to the older, cold, and drab houses she had previously occupied. The congregation represented another contrast: the parishioners were generally much younger than those in Cape North and Parrsboro, and for the first time my mother was able to connect with a large group of young mothers close to her own age. Although my parents were still both involved in church work, their lives began to disentwine. My mother no longer accompanied my father on his regular visits to parishioners. My father turned more of his efforts to ecumenical, community-based work, while my mother's energies were devoted not only to church responsibilities (teaching youth groups, and working with the United Church Women's group), but also to her part-time employment as a kindergarten teacher, her children and her homemaking, and to the flow of neighbourhood life that, in the 1960s, centred on stay-at-home mothers and their children. My mother had added responsibilities when my sister Catherine, or Cathy, was born in 1962. My parents soon realized that she was deaf,[3] and for the next few years my mother devoted part of every day to home schooling, drilling Cathy on sounds and language acquisition. Correspondingly, Mom's recipes from Charlottetown reflect a growing balance of church and neighbourhood networks.

In 1967, my father assumed an administrative position in the United Church regional headquarters in Sackville, New Brunswick. The move was prompted by the fact that Cathy had reached school age, and the

LAURENE, HENRY, DIANE, AND CATHY, CHARLOTTETOWN, c. 1963
PHOTO BY EDITH ROBINSON

Interprovincial School for the Deaf, a regional educational facility, was located in Amherst, Nova Scotia, a few kilometres from Sackville. Although the majority of students were residential, my parents were determined that Cathy not be one of them. For the duration of her schooling, Cathy lived at home.

When my mother relocated there, Amherst was a town of approximately 10,000. Although by the 1960s the community was no longer the important industrial centre it had been at the turn of the century, some industries struggled on. The town retained its working-class character and still felt the influence of the elite families who once controlled the factories. Shortly after her arrival, my mother became involved in the town's newly developed Headstart kindergarten program and for several years was employed as one of two part-time teachers. In 1970, my brother Mark was born, and around this time my parents purchased a home in a newer residential area located near the School for the Deaf. Mom became friends with the neighbourhood women, many of whom she already knew through the United Church. Most also had children of the same age. Until the late 1970s, she worked as a teacher's assistant at the School for the Deaf, at which point she upgraded her secretarial skills. Then, for about the next ten years, she was employed at the high school, first as a secretary in the main office and then as the guidance office secretary. My mother's recipes in Amherst show her increasing independence. She continued her heavy church involvement, but my father travelled extensively. In his absence, she developed her own social outlets.

In 1989, my parents returned to Charlottetown to spend my father's last years before retirement at the same church he had served earlier. My mother died never having fully unpacked from the move. It marked the end of a long battle with breast cancer that, in the last year of her life, had moved into her bones. After eight years as a cancer patient, beginning with a radical mastectomy and progressing through a lengthy course of chemotherapy to a remission that was followed by a recurrence treated with radiation, the cancer returned. This time it was inoperable. She died on 5 October 1989 after a few days' hospitalization.

FOLKLORE AND FOODWAYS: HOW EVERYDAY FOODS TELL UNINTENTIONAL STORIES

In looking to my mother's baking to supplement this incomplete life history, I draw on an understanding that lies at the basis of Folklore as a disciplinary practice: every day, people communicate meaning through ordinary acts and everyday forms, from clothes hung on a line to a casual verbal expression or personal experience story to a hand-fashioned quilt or rug. Sometimes meaning is intentionally placed; at other times its creation is unselfconscious. In my own thinking about folkloric meanings, I rely on Elliott Oring's "orientations." Oring writes that "folklorists seem to pursue reflections of the *communal* (a group or collective), the *common* (the everyday rather than the extraordinary), the *informal* (in relation to the formal or institutional), the *marginal* (in relation to the centers of power and privilege), the *personal* (communication face-to-face), the *traditional* (stable over time), the *aesthetic* (artistic expressions), and the *ideological* (expressions of belief and systems of knowledge)" (1986, 17–18). One richness of folklore is that it often allows those with few other vehicles for expression a valuable opportunity to find a voice. Because of this, it is sometimes subversive and can be a powerful tool not only in bringing people together but in introducing change. Although some of Mom's baking, like birthday cakes and Christmas cookies, was clearly celebratory, other recipes seem to resist the gendered constructions that shaped her life. And, as I have discovered, not all the meanings in her baking are read as uniformly positive by all members of our family.

Folklorists recognize the social nature of folklore and its transmission, locating expression in the group. Barre Toelken writes that "one of the key features of a folk group will always be the extent to which its own dynamics continue to inform and educate its members and define the group" (1996, 57). Henry Glassie further expands on the connections between folkloric text and social group when he writes that "[f]olk and lore link people and expression in a functional circle ... The group exists because its members create communications that call it together and bring it to order. Communications exist because people acting together, telling tales at the hearth, or sending signals though computerized networks, develop significant forms that function at once as signs of identity and forces for cohesion" (1995, 400). Building on the work of writers such as Toelken and Glassie, this book examines ways in which my mother's production of simple types of food positioned her within several overlapping groups or contexts: cultural background (Scots Presbyterian ancestry), socio-economic position (working-class roots and middle-class adulthood), and occupation (mother and minister's wife). Drawing on Michael Owen Jones's claim, in his 2005 presidential address to the American Folklore Society, that "eating practices reproduce as well as construct identity" (2007, 130), here I explore how my mother's baking not only reflected the groups to which she belonged – her family, church, and community – but also helped to shape them.

Although my mother's recipes contain personal subtexts that speak of the unique ways in which her identities intertwined in her life, they also tell larger stories of how women of her generation balanced personal needs against the demands of family and community. My mother's seeming disinterest in food and the simplicity of her recipes frustrated me as a teenager. I felt that she should want to prepare more elaborate dishes, like those women I occasionally saw on television or in magazines "whip up." But she was not alone. The dishes my mother made were shared by many of my friends' mothers in the 1960s, 1970s, and 1980s. Everyone I knew ate plain, economical food, and the fancier squares our mothers took to church or community functions were strikingly similar. My memory is that we consumed these dishes without much comment. Nor do I recall extensive conversation among my mother and her friends about food preparation. Occasionally they exchanged recipes, but it was as if food was to be appreciated by consumption rather than in conversation and to be enjoyed rather than relished. Within a larger cultural context – where food was not viewed as a subject of pleasure, and its preparation was fundamental to the construction of womanhood – my mother's apparent disinterest in food makes more sense to me, even if the fact remains that it makes her a rather unusual subject for a book with food at its focus.

In reflecting on meanings contained in my mother's baking, I think of Margaret Visser's claim that "[t]he extent to which we take everyday objects for granted is the precise extent to which they govern and inform our lives" (1988, 11). For Visser, as for others, notably Roland Barthes, food is a signifier of much larger dynamics. Barthes asks: "For what is food? It is not only a collection of products that can be used for statistical or nutritional studies. It is also, and at the same time, a system of communication, a body of images, a protocol of usages, situations and behavior … When he buys an item of food, consumes it, or serves it, modern man does not manipulate a simple object in a purely transitive fashion; this item of food sums up and transmits a situation; it constitutes an information; it signifies. That is to say that it is not just an indicator of a set of more or less conscious motivations, but that it is a real sign, perhaps the functional unit of a system of communication" (1997, 21). He concludes: "One could say that an entire 'world' (social environment) is present in and signified by food" (Barthes 1997, 23).

Folklorists, too, have shared a long-standing interest in the intersections of food and culture, one that Lucy M. Long argues was embraced by the 1881 inaugural mission statement of the American Folklore Society (2009, 3). As Long explains, however, this interest initially translated into attention to the foods and food practices that existed in the oral traditions of those groups considered "folk," particularly those foods in danger of dying out, and little work on food was published in the *Journal of American Folklore* until the 1970s.

The more comprehensive study of "foodways" evolved from "folkways," a term coined by William Grant Sumner in 1906 "to denote those customs, practices, and ways of thinking shared by members of the same group" (Camp 1989, 24). Foodways entered North American scholarly usage through folklife scholars such as Don Yoder and Warren Roberts, who, as part of a movement to broaden the range of genres studied by folklorists, stressed "the need to study the totality of practices and beliefs surrounding eating and food" (Long 2009, 3). Originally, North American foodways scholarship demonstrated an historical and regional emphasis in part because food provided a bridge between European ethnology, which emphasized the ordinary structures of everyday life, and

American folklore studies. Yoder made this link in his article, "Folk Cookery," published in Richard M. Dorson's 1972 textbook, *Folklore and Folklife: An Introduction*. Characterized as "the first clear 'call to arms' for an intensive study of foodways by Americans interested in folk culture" (Humphrey and Humphrey 1988, 4, cited in McNeil 1989, 14), Yoder's article suggested two directions for future study: regional variation in domestic cookery, and the comparative study of American and European folk patterns of cookery (McNeil 1989). Although Yoder's identification of five potential areas of foodways research – food in folk culture, research problems in American folk cookery, the function of folk cookery, folk cookery and material culture, and traditional cookery in the twentieth century – was groundbreaking for its time, his approach did not differ significantly from that of folklorists studying other genres such as ballad and folktale. He conceptualized foodways research as basically historical and descriptive and was motivated by the belief that regionally based traditional cookery was disappearing and was rapidly being replaced by a national eclectic American cookery (McNeil 1989, 14). Thus, Yoder was most interested in documenting either the past or those "relict areas," such as Appalachia, "where earlier foodways have been preserved in the face of contemporary social change" (Yoder 1972, 332, cited in McNeil 1989, 14). McNeil writes, "foodways scholarship, then, was basically an exercise in cultural archaeology, and those who studied the topic were essentially dealing with survivals" (1989, 14).

By 1971, Jay Anderson was recommending that foodways research adopt a "conceptual model," by which he meant it should consider "the whole interrelated *system* of food conceptualization and evaluation, procurement, distribution, preservation, preparation, consumption, and nutrition shared by all the members of a particular society" (Anderson 1971, 161, cited in McNeil 1989, 14), and in the late 1970s Charles Camp encouraged folklorists to investigate food traditions by emphasizing events rather than the food itself (McNeil 1989, 15). In his review of foodways scholarship, Camp identifies the real contribution as its expanded notion of context and increased appreciation of folk expression as symbol-making, which led folklorists to a revised model of tradition in culture. Camp points out that, unlike other folklore genres, foodways are seldom anonymous. Narratives and songs, shaped over time by multiple performers and audiences, raise questions of ownership, but the intentions of the person producing the food and the expectations of the person consuming the food are easily documented and analyzed. Consequently, almost as soon as foodways was included as part of Folklore, it branched out in many directions. Its explorations of food and identities such as locale, ethnicity, gender, occupation, and religion reflect an underlying folkloristic emphasis on community (Camp 1996).

Since the 1980s, many foodways scholars have explored the cultural significance of food. Located in a number of disciplines in addition to Folklore, including Anthropology, Geography, History, Sociology, and Women's Studies, they have focused on food's symbolic nature, stressing the important and growing role of food in how people go about constructing a meaning and context for themselves in the rapidly changing world of the late twentieth century (Shortridge and Shortridge 1998, 6). In this regard, Barbara G. Shortridge and James R. Shortridge identify several "highly interconnected" areas of scholarship on foodways, including issues of celebration (such as how plum pudding adds meaning to Christmas gatherings) and the evolution of food associations (such as why cereal and orange juice have come to represent breakfast). They also stress food's links with cultural identities, including age, class, gender, race, and regional and ethnic diversity (1998, 6).

In keeping with earlier foodways scholarship, here I focus on the connections of my mother's foodways experience to a particular time and place. In *The Taste of American Place*, Shortridge and Shortridge present regional foodways as an interplay of physical geography and cultural history (1998, 2) so that environmental conditions, especially climatic ones, ethnic heritage, and availability are among the many factors that come together to affect an individual's food choice (1998, 4). The promise of foodways, then, according to Linda Keller Brown and Kay Mussell (who draw on Jones 1976, 118), lies in its ability to explore from the inside "regional identity as 'a process with its own rhetoric.'" Brown and Mussell continue: "Geographical location alone does not define a regional group; as proximity encourages groups to coalesce into subcultures with a self-conscious sense of unity, the markers of group identity often interact with those of other affinity groups and are modified by ethnicity, by time and by ecology" (2001, 6).

Shared foodways can help researchers better understand how groups within a region self-define, how they interact with and are modified by other subcultures, and how they creatively shape their ethnicity (see Jones 2007, 131). As Margaret Bennett's work (1998) on Scottish communities in Canada and Hasia Diner's study (2001) of Italian, Irish, and Jewish immigrants to the United States attest, foodways are adapted in unique ways to new settings. A food that a region or a group within a region identifies as representative – Maine lobster or Louisiana crawfish – can convey complex and sometimes competing messages about "presentation of self" (see Goffman 1959) to residents as well as outsiders (see Gutierrez 1984; Lewis 1989; Long 2004). Drawing on ideas that emerge from analyses of regional and ethnic foodways, in this book I explore how my mother's baking, which grew out of cultural traditions of Maritime Canada, reflects an inextricable intertwining of region, ethnicity, and cultural group.

Other identities intersect with region and ethnicity. Two that were important in my mother's experience are socio-economics and religion. Although most foodways research has explored the everyday foods of ordinary people (e.g., Omohundro 1994, Counihan 2004), some studies have focused on the recontextualization of "peasant food" (e.g., Lewis 1989, Montaño 1997, Lockwood and Lockwood 1998, Tye 2008, Everett

2009) and exposed processes whereby foods of poverty are elevated to iconic markers of regional or national identity. Similarly, links with food and religion extend, as Camp writes, "from dietary rules that limit what a member of a particular faith may eat, to the symbolic connection between nutritional and spiritual sustenance, to the frequent use of food events such as church suppers and bake sales as fund-raisers and social events benefiting religious groups" (Camp 1996, 302). Church women formed an important context, or "folk group," for much of my mother's food production. Their shared ideas of suitability and taste shaped her baking.

Finally, Mom's baking was part of her occupational folklife. Jan Harold Brunvand describes workplace culture as "expressive," for it puts "special emphasis upon informally learned narrative, skill, and ritual used to determine status and membership in the work group" (1996, 519). Although the earliest folklorists concentrated on songs in male-dominated logging camps and fishing vessels or on documenting traditional craft, contemporary research approaches urban and industrial work settings as sites of construction of gender, ethnicity, and power. Folklorists still have not devoted much attention to women and domestic labour, but what they study in other occupations applies: how workers see and organize their world, what is important to them, how their world is classified, and how new workers are incorporated. As I look through my mother's recipes, I discover how as a young woman she equipped herself to be a minister's wife (see Grant 1993).

My mother's recipes and others' recollections of her baking confirm that food is a complex communicative system even for one person. Camp warns that, as a cultural text, food is too diffuse to be easily read: the meanings of food choices are not so easily demonstrated or codified as codes of dress or decor, for example (1989, 23). The shifting meanings in my mother's baking are multivalent and fluid; they are both positive and negative. So, while personal and social meanings come together in food in individual ways, my mother's experiences of domesticity were shared by other women in her family, and by those in her generation, locale, and social position. To understand the individual, or the particular, is to begin to understand the general.

FOOD AS WOMEN'S CARING WORK

"My mother used to make these for me when I was Callum's age," I exclaim to my husband, Peter, as I sample the peanut-butter cookies I take from the oven. With a three year old in the house, I have turned to my mother's recipes, resurrecting tastes and smells and textures of her everyday foods, some of which I have not eaten for decades. Why am I driven to reproduce these tastes for my son? What will they mean to him? These questions preoccupy me, and yet there are no easy answers.

I am very grateful that my Women's Studies students are not witnesses to my weekly baking. These young women are socially aware consumers, many of them conscious of every bite that goes into their bodies. Vegetarians and vegans, proponents of whole food and slow food, they would be appalled by the amounts of white sugar and white flour that form the basis of the food I produce in the name of nurturing my child. They would be even more disapproving of how easily in my motherhood I have reverted to such a conventionally feminine domestic role. But they will not know. Baking for my young son remains my guilty secret. It feels both right and wrong to me, natural and unnatural at the same time. I try to work out these conflicting feelings every Saturday morning as I continue to produce sheets of cookies and pans of cinnamon rolls. It is not lost on me that I am modelling my mother's nurturing not only through the making of her recipes but also by baking at the very same time each week she baked. "Why am I doing this?"

I ask myself aloud so many times that finally Peter replies, "I don't know but I think you need to try to find out."

That I turned to my mother's recipes as a new mother is not surprising, given the findings of a growing literature that documents the centrality of food in women's lives. With the knowledge that women still do most of the domestic cooking, feminist social scientists point to the work of feeding one's family as an area rich for gendered analysis (see Avakian and Haber 2005). Carole M. Counihan is central among feminist anthropologists who have turned their attention to studying food practices. She writes, "One of the most significant domains of meaning embodied in food centers on the relation between the sexes, their gender definitions, and their sexuality" (Counihan 1999, 9). Counihan's important work over several decades has explored the interconnections of food, culture, and gender, particularly the gendered power relations that surround food and that mirror the power relations of the sexes in general (1999, 4). She points to the complexities in these gendered intersections, for while "food provisioning often reproduces female subordination by requiring women to serve, satisfy, and defer to husbands or boyfriends who do not feel a similar need to serve their women" (Counihan 1999, 13), some women have also used food as a path to power, either symbolically – though fasting, for example – or materially, by "exert[ing] power over men by refusing to cook, cooking food men dislike, forcing them to eat, or manipulating the status and meaning systems embodied in foods" (1999, 11). Writing of the American context, Sherrie Inness elaborates: "Gender, in particular, is heavily intertwined with food, since food preparation is so frequently assumed to be women's primary domestic responsibility. In order to understand how gender is created in the United States (and around the world), it is essential to understand how food and food culture have shaped and continue to shape our lives. From grocery shopping, to preparing the food, to cleaning up afterward, every aspect of food is intermingled with issues of gender. We need to understand these gendered messages to understand better the gender differences and inequities in American society" (Inness 2001a, xv). Inness notes that the search for a better understanding of the interconnections between food and gender has led to many thoughtful studies that consider the relationship between women, gender and particular foods, examine how media shape women's relationship to food, look at how food is self-expression, and reflect on how food and its preparation can perpetuate class, ethnic and race divisions (2001a, xiv). She adopts the term "kitchen culture" to refer "to the various discourses about food, cooking, and gender roles that stem from the kitchen but that pervade our society on many levels. Kitchen culture influences advertising, cooking literature, and our daily meals, wherever we might consume them" (Inness 2001b, 3). Laura Shapiro's classic work, *Perfection Salad: Women and Cooking at the Turn of the Century* (1986), illuminates the possibilities of food as a vehicle for understanding more about women and their roles in the past. Her exploration of scientific and religious ideas meeting in the kitchen in the early 1900s holds relevance for women half a century later, and her recent work (2004), which focuses on the 1950s, provides an even closer historical context for my study.

Fundamental to my exploration of my mother's baking is Marjorie DeVault's argument that "it is not just that women do more of the work of feeding, but also that feeding work has become one of the primary ways that women 'do' gender" (1991, 119). More particularly, DeVault locates feeding the family not only as gendered work but as part of women's work of care: "Specific definitions of the work of feeding a family – decisions about what to do when – develop as part of a broader project of care for family members. The work is organized so that it becomes part of a set of social relations that constructs a household group as family" (1991, 137). Grounded in Dorothy E. Smith's feminist sociology of the everyday as problematic (1987), DeVault explores how caring is constructed as women's work, emphasizing the complex ways women themselves are drawn into participation in prevailing relations of inequality (1991, 11). Women's ethic of care is embedded in their concern for relationality. In her study of women in Chicago in the 1980s, DeVault writes: "The women I talked with referred to their activity as something other than 'work' in any conventional sense, as activity embedded in family relations. Many spoke of the activity as emerging from interpersonal ties, part of being a parent" (1991, 10).

Because this work incorporates my memories of my mother and her baking and reflects on the meanings it now holds for our family, I also build on a growing literature that examines food and memory. In his wonderful book, *Remembrance of Repasts*, David Sutton explores con-

white cookies   Flora Macaskiel
                                 Cape North

½ cup shortening   1 tsp. soda
1 cup sugar   1 tsp. cr. of tartar
1 egg   2 cups flour
4 tbsp. hot milk

cream shortening and sugar, add egg well beaten,
soda dissolved in milk, sift cr. tartar with flour
roll and sprinkle with sugar

may add nutmeg and vanilla.

AN EARLY RECIPE, CAPE NORTH, c. 1954

nections between food and strategies of remembering among residents of the Greek island of Kalymnos, arguing that "if 'we are what we eat,' then 'we are what we ate' as well" (2001, 7). Sutton and others show that the links of food and nurturing run deep and can last a lifetime. Food often serves as common ground for families, binding them together through tastes and events such as mealtimes. Adults may remember childhood, or people they knew as children, such as a grandmother, through memories of food (see Berkeley 2000). There is also a strong connection between food and the emotions (Lupton 1996, 32; see Locher et al. 2005). As an adult, one finds that the smell, taste, and even the thought of some foods create nostalgia for or even recreate childhood (Lupton 1996, 50). Meyers recalls eating many meals that evoked thoughts of her mother: "In the decade since her death, I feel closest to my mother when I sit down before a meal I know she would enjoy. It's communion" (2001, 1). Meyers is right. When I use my mother's measuring spoons, my grandmother's cake pan, or one of their recipes, I feel truly connected to them. Food bridges generations of women, and in this book I reach back to my mother and grandmother and out to my sister in my own expression of familial continuity and commonality. This seems natural, for as I remember these women I think of them most often in their kitchens, preparing food, serving food, cleaning up food.

INTERSECTIONS OF FOLKLORE
AND WOMEN'S STUDIES

It is my first year of full-time teaching, and as part of my appointment in Canadian Studies I am assigned an introductory Women's Studies course. This is the first Women's Studies offering at the university, so its progress is closely watched by the program director. At the end of the year, he suggests that the course be collectively evaluated by the guest lecturers I've invited to speak and by other faculty members associated with Canadian Studies. This is a very intimidating prospect for a new teacher hired on a two-year contract, and I dread the meeting from the time the director announces it. When the evaluation actually begins I feel excruciatingly vulnerable. As we move around the room from speaker to speaker, I am terrified that the next person will expose my failures as a teacher. The scrutiny feels very dangerous.

What I don't anticipate is how the revelation of my inadequacies will be life-changing for me. Fortunately, things go better than I fear. I get off lightly in that my colleagues are kind when we talk about what's gone well and gentle when they make suggestions about what might be strengthened next year. My epiphany occurs near the close of the afternoon when a colleague, whom I can no longer remember clearly or even name, turns to me privately. "I notice," she observes, "that you didn't include anything in this course about women's folklore." Her casual comment changes the course of my career. Suddenly I realize that the thought of introducing students to women's traditional culture never even occurred to me. It didn't seem relevant. Then the real reason for my omission hits me. "I can't," I think to myself. "I don't know how." At that moment, I promise myself that this silencing will never happen again. I will find out about women's folklore. For my students and for myself, I will learn what women were singing when their husbands were off in lumber camps or on fishing vessels, sites of earlier folksong collecting. Someday, I vow, I will be able to describe where, when, and how women tell stories. This desire to discover the uses women make of folklore has guided my research and shaped my teaching for more than two decades and finds expression again in the pages that follow.

This book is very much influenced by my experience of more than twenty years of teaching and writing at the intersection of Folklore and Women's

Studies. Although there is no one feminism, I often turn to Chris Weedon's well-known text when introducing feminism to my students. Weedon begins her book: "Feminism is a politics. It is a politics directed at changing existing power relations between women and men in society. These power relations structure all areas of life, the family, education and welfare, the worlds of work and politics, culture and leisure. They determine who does what and for whom, what we are and what we might become" (1994, 1). I agree with Weedon that it is not enough to refer unproblematically to experience. Rather, we need a theory of the relationship between experience, social power, and resistance (Weedon 1994, 8). My decision to examine the recipes used by my mother – a woman who did not like to bake – is not so surprising in this light. While this book celebrates her life and contributions, it also recognizes ways in which the demands of domesticity restrained her.

Chris Weedon's statement above indicates some of the many ways that subjectivity is not fixed but constructed: it is produced in a whole range of discursive practices, whether economic, social, or political (1994, 21). As she reminds us, subjectivity is a site of disunity and conflict rather than being unified or fixed (Weedon 1994, 21). The meaning of gender, therefore, is both socially produced and variable between different forms of discourse (Weedon 1994, 22). Some of my mother's various gendered roles—mother, minster's wife, white middle-class church woman, and female friend – found expression in her baking. As Deborah Lupton notes in her study of food, embodiment, and subjectivity, "We do not necessarily need language and discourse to experience food. However language and discourse are integral to the meanings we construct around food" (1996, 13). My mother constructed her sense of self in the food she produced, just as others – for example, family members – constructed themselves through meanings they assign to that food in consuming it. On a more general level, by recognizing the shaping of different, and sometimes competing, female subjectivities in women's baking and personal recipe

collections, we attend to social spaces and cultural forms that have previously been devalued as female and unimportant.

This study grows out of earlier feminist work in Folklore that calls
into question male-centred disciplinary practices and understandings of
expressive culture (see Hollis, Pershing, and Young 1993, Greenhill and
Tye 1994, and Greenhill and Tye 2001). Here, as elsewhere, I am influenced by feminist writers who recover, recontextualize, and re-examine
women's narratives (see Abu-Lughod 1993). Within the discipline of
Folklore, I think in particular of the applicability of Joan Radner and
Susan Lanser's important work on implicit feminist coding in women's
expressive communication. Radner and Lanser identify ways in which
women resist and subvert patriarchy through what they term "implicit
feminist coding": a "set of signals – words, forms, behaviors, signifiers
of some kind – that protect the creator from the consequences of openly
expressing particular messages." They continue, "Coding occurs in the
context of complex audiences in which some members may be competent and willing to decode the message, but others are not" (Radner and
Lanser 1993, 3). The accounts I collected through personal interviews
tell me that my mother's recipes possess a kind of "bilingual" quality in
that they were understood in one way by women in her friendship and
social circles but might be "read" differently by "outsiders." Some of the
recipes, and my mother's performance of them, can be interpreted as
"critical of some aspect of women's subordination," a characteristic that
Radner and Lanser understand as central to implicit feminist coding
(1993, 3), and as exhibiting many, if not all, of the six forms of implicit
feminist coding that Radner and Lanser identify: appropriation, juxtaposition, distraction, indirection, trivialization, and incompetence. More
recent work on women's narratives, such as Elaine Lawless's *Women
Escaping Violence,* is equally formative. Lawless highlights the ways in
which women's stories of domestic violence are shaped to conform to
master narratives at the same time as she addresses how women's stories often subvert these master narratives. Just as Lawless encourages

readers to hear women's stories of violence in new ways that attend to gaps and silences in the narratives as well to the words spoken, my analysis of my mother's baking looks at what is there and what is not. Finally, this study also extends several aspects of my own earlier work, most centrally the retrospective exploration of subversive texts and subtexts within women's narratives (Tye 1997, 2002) and the recognition of alternative forms of women's narratives (Tye 1996, 2001). In the pages that follow, then, I try not only to consider ways that gendered expectations constrained my mother and other women of her generation, but how these women used informal means – cooking among them – to resist, and at times transform, those limitations.

RECIPES AS AUTOBIOGRAPHY

"I remember her." As I look through my mother's little tin box of recipes, the women's names written on the top right-hand top corner of the three-by-five index cards spark memories: Sadie, Effie, Jean, Winnie, Helen. These women were close to my mother. Their recipes are tangible indicators of their many shared positions; most were middle-class white mothers and wives who belonged to the same United Church congregations in the Maritime provinces as my mother. "I remember these," I say, picking up a recipe for Cherry Surprise Cookies that my mother made only at Christmas. Another – a pineapple dessert – was one she usually served when company visited or when she hosted her bridge club. People, places, and times come flooding back. The names and brief directions in faded handwriting on these cards speak evocatively to me of my mother's life. They chronicle her tastes and travels through various geographical moves and cut across her circles of friends, co-workers, and the church and community organizations she belonged to. These recipes speak to me loudly of who my mother was.

As a folklorist, I use a conceptual tool kit that differs somewhat from that of other social scientists in that my primary research approach is the recorded interview. Since I am no longer able to interview my mother, I look to her recipe collection. In what Barbara Kirshenblatt-Gimblett calls "an object of memory" (1989), I search for clues to her life story. I believe that we can think of women's recipe collections, such as that compiled by my mother, as belonging to a poststructural category that Sidonie Smith and Julia Watson term "everyday autobiography." As Smith and Watson remind us, "We are habitual authenticators of our own lives. Every day we are confessing and constructing personal narratives in every possible format: on the body, on the air, in music, in print, on video, at meetings" (1996, 2). They write that "[o]n a daily basis, then, personal narrators assume the role of the bricoleur who takes up bits and pieces of the identities and narrative forms available and, by disjoining and joining them in excessive ways, creates a history of the subject at a precise point in time and space" (Smith and Watson 1996, 14). However, expression is shaped by form, and Smith and Watson emphasize that all everyday forms of autobiographical practices regulate subjects by reforming them in specific ways (1996, 10). They claim: "In telling their stories, narrators take up models of identity that are culturally available. And by adopting ready-made narrative templates to structure experiential history, they take up culturally designated subjectivities" (Smith and Watson 1996, 9). Although recipes shape women's words by means of cultural notions of what a recipe is and how it should be recorded, as well as through preconceptions of a woman's place in the family, they do represent a site where women are able to tell some of their life stories in their own words.

More specifically, this book is one of a number of recent studies to seriously consider recipes as an important expressive form for women. Typically, recipes have been regarded both as too trivial and too formulaic to merit study, but more recently writers have pointed out that they do not rely only on formula. Although it is true that recipes are never completely new, based as they are on former recipes and coming out of specific culinary traditions, Lisa Heldke emphasizes their flexibility, referring to the "recipe plan" (1992, 259), and Elizabeth Telfer talks about recipes being analogous to musical compositions, the dish cooked on a particular occasion being akin to a performance (1996, 58). Similarly, Debra Castillo argues that a recipe is not a blueprint: "It is less a formula than a general model; less an axiom of unchanging law and more a theory of possibilities that allows the recipe teller the ability to express multiple narratives" (1992, xiii).

Others have emphasized intersections of recipes and recipe collections with women's private writing (e.g., see Bloom 2001). Literary theorist Estelle Jelinek (1980) observes that women's life writing is episodic, anecdotal, nonchronological and disjunctive – as compared with the more linear and progressive narrative style of male autobiographies. These characteristics, as well as others such as fragmentation, also apply to recipes. Recipes are similar to brief diary entries, as Linda Murray Berzok found when she read through her mother's collection of a dozen boxes of index cards spanning a forty-year period (1952–1992): "I discovered that my mother had used her boxes for a complex task – a combination of recipe development, diary/family Bible, and social notes" (2001, 84). She writes: "As I picked my way through the cards, reading each one, I began to realize that there was a story here – one that could be read through the cards. Some women leave diaries, I thought. My mother left recipes" (Berzok 2001, 86).

Women's relationships have provided another direction of inquiry. Most of the recipes in my mother's collection come from other women rather than from popular media, and she often recorded the names of the women who had shared a recipe with her, or noted the family's response: "So and so really likes this." These connections support Anne Bower's observation concerning women's community cookbooks, that "[r]elationships almost always occupy a central place in women's auto-biographies; and in cookbooks too, one finds explicitly stated or subtly implied links to family, friends, and community. And as with auto-biography, in the cookbooks we also sense that the 'self' or 'family' or 'community' projected may be idealized" (1997b, 31).

As Bower suggests, recipes can tell different stories. In her article, "Cooking Up Stories: Narrative Elements in Community Cookbooks" (1997b) Bower identifies several narrative elements, including setting (home, region, historical time, and social milieu); character (mostly collec-tive, in the case of community cookbooks); plot (female plot of ambition and home plot which she breaks down into the categories of integration plot, differentiation plot, plot of religious or moral triumph and histor-ical plot); and dominant themes in community cookbooks (including the breaking of silence, the importance of women's domestic role, and her power within the home as nurturer). Sometimes the stories that are told are fictionalized, idealized representations of self, family, and commun-ity. It is likely, for example, that my mother's collection contains untried recipes. These possibilities would have both mirrored and influenced her view of herself as a good mother.

Other writers identify political and social commentary in cookbooks and recipe collections, for, as Janet Theophano writes, "As much recipes for living as formulae for cooking, cookbooks are forums for discussing the conduct of life. Even the most pragmatic of cookbooks alludes to both a moral world and an aesthetic to be tended. Although the salient function of cookbooks is to provide instruction in the domestic arts, women have used them and household manuals in subtle and ingenious ways. Living within the constraints of their respective eras, they have used these texts to examine and shape their own and others' lives" (2002, 227).

Certainly, recipes represent a way women have passed along their skills and wisdom to one another. As Theophano observes, "Cookbooks,

BELL BAKING IN HER KITCHEN, EUREKA, c. 1960

then, besides describing foods are records of women's social interactions and exchanges ... [W]omen's cookbooks can be maps of the social and cultural worlds they inhabit" (2002, 13). When viewed intergenerationally, as some writers suggest, this transmission amounts to a "feminine culinary genealogy – a matri-lineage based not just on a woman's name but also on her kitchen, her act of cooking, and her body" (Bishop 1997, 102). Recipes remain one means by which women can commune with earlier female kin: they are a tangible connection to a female past. For example, handwritten recipes are now almost the only remaining material legacy of my grandmother, who was barely literate. Despite Theophano's suggestion that readers need to use an imaginative leap into women's worlds in order to read their cookbooks as autobiography (2002, 118), I have come to understand the recipes in my family as partial life stories of women in earlier generations. In reality, my mother did not leave a much larger written record than her mother. Reading her recipes, and reading between the lines of her recipes, reveals to me some of her stories.

SO WHOSE STORY IS THIS?
AN AUTOETHNOGRAPHIC APPROACH

My mother is dying. Now that the end is here, I try to forget this fact, to turn off this bald statement that has been playing in my head like a mantra for weeks. She is lying on her side in the hospital bed, eyes closed. She doesn't appear conscious, but perhaps she is only lulled by the morphine: she seems to respond to our voices. As she moans, my father, sister, and I respond together, reaching out and patting her back with our hands until she moans loader and we realize that, in our anxiety, our pats have become more like thuds than gentle caresses and we immediately pull back. Minutes later she takes her final breath. "That's it" my father says with finality. "She's gone." Only my sister cries. "What am I going to do without a mother?" she asks plaintively. None of us have an answer, because it is our question, too.

An hour or so later I return with my brother, sister, husband, and father to the kitchen of my parents' home. My father, perhaps spurred on my his ministerial sense of duty, rising to what he feels is expected of the family patriarch, or seeking an appropriate sense of closure to this epochal moment in our family's life, addresses my sister, brother, and me: "You people were everything to her. Your mother lived for you." We are silent. There is no response. She was everything to us; she was the glue that held the family together. What will we be without her? Will we be without her?

Suddenly I want to escape this surreal scene. I want to sleep. Before I leave the kitchen, I open the drawer where a few weeks earlier my mother stashed a single chocolate bar. It was her habit to occasionally hide a chocolate bar, and I can remember when I was growing up that from time to time she would produce one as an unexpected treat and we would share its pleasure together. In the last weeks of her life, as my mother was dying in her hospital bed, I found this chocolate bar to be more evocative of loss – both my mother's and my own – than anything else in my parents' home. It screamed to me every time I opened the drawer. She would not eat this chocolate bar, and never again would she and I share such simple pleasures as stashed candy. We would not share anything. The chocolate bar poignantly signalled to me both the end of my mother's life and the end of our relationship. I unwrap it and share it with the others. In an act of communion, which is at the same time my own act of closure, we celebrate my mother's life by breaking chocolate.

In looking to my mother's recipes to narrate her life, I find, like Caroline Brettell (1997, 229), that I must necessarily combine biography and autobiography. Brettell claims that "the lives of a mother and a daughter are inextricably intertwined" (1997, 229), and I find it impossible to separate my mother's story from my own; I cannot grasp the elusive qualities of her character without also reflecting on my own life and mothering. Perhaps in telling my mother's life story I have unintentionally joined a group of contemporary memoirists who explore the loss of a parent because, as Nancy Miller notes, "it tells us something important about who we are" (1996, ix). Perhaps my need to take on this project lies more than I realize in Miller's argument that we write about the dead "to figure out if they were right" (1996, 12). Given the belief that we tell our own stories backward through our mother's and grandmother's stories (see Behar 1996, 94), whose story or stories am I writing? At the beginning of this work I wondered if it was possible for me to write about my mother outside of my relationship with her. I wondered, when I read her recipes, if they would tell me about her life, or if I would be able to recognize only those stories that reflected her relationship with me. Robert Anderson writes, "Death ends a life, but it does not end the relationship which struggles on in the survivor's mind towards some final resolution, some clear meaning, which it perhaps never finds" (1968, 281). I now believe that many stories are told simultaneously in this study.

When I write of my mother I am necessarily working from memory – whether mine or someone else's – and this results in further blurring. Where does one story or memory end and another begin? Writing a remembered life is a complex undertaking for, as Carolyn Ellis notes, "Writing privileges one version of a story, but memories of untold details and alternate story lines still linger" (1995, 336–7).

As I search my mother's recipe collection for clues of gendered cultural expectations and performances, it is impossible to assess fully how much I and the other participants have been influenced by our own cultural scripts. Mary Catherine Bateson reminds us that it is difficult to look back and not see all good or all bad, depending how the experience turned out. She writes:

> We also edit the past to make it more intelligible in cultural terms. As memories blur, we supply details from a pool of general knowledge. With every retelling, words that barely fit begin to seem more appropriate as the meaning slips and slides to fit the stereotype. Was my English nanny as perfectly true to form as I remember her, or has the memory been smoothed and normalized? And what about the smoothing that denies the painful parts of happy memories and even makes nightmares more consistent? What about the

inappropriate emotions denied and the anomalies that drop out of our storytelling? Even for the recent past and in situations where there would seem to be little motivation for distortion, memories are modified and details supplied to fit cultural expectations (1989, 32).

In this she echoes Miller's belief that "[w]e think we remember, we want to remember, and we try. What we can't help doing, though, is connecting the pieces from then that we have housed inside us with the feelings we have about them now. Representing others has everything to do with representing ourselves – over time" (1996, 159).

My recognition of how the story I tell of my mother's life is intertwined with my own comes from my reading of recent autoethnographic work by Carolyn Ellis and others (see Ellis 1995, Ellis and Bochner 1996). Autoethnographic texts take many forms: short stories, poetry, fiction, novels, photographic essays, scripts, personal essays, journals, fragmented and layered writing, and social science prose (Ellis 2004, 38), but all autoethnographic writing is located at the intersection of autobiography and ethnography in that the focus is at once on the self and on culture (Ellis 2004, 31). In the most general sense, it is "writing about the personal and its relationship to culture" (Ellis 2004, 37). This "autobiographical genre of writing and research that displays multiple layers of consciousness, connects personal and cultural experience" (Ellis and Bochner 2000, 739) dates from the 1970s.[4] It grew out of feminist and social-scientific questioning of relationships between researchers and subjects, along with a growing commitment on the part of many ethnographers to make their own presence, values, and biases known in the writing of research (Berger and Ellis 2002, 156). According to Deborah Reed-Danahay, autoethnography reflects changing conceptions of the self and society in the late twentieth century in that it synthesizes both postmodern ethnography, in which realist conventions and the objective-observer position of standard ethnography have been called into question, and postmodern autobiography, in which the notion of a coherent, individual self has similarly been called into question (1997, 2).

Finally, autoethnographic writing also recognizes the importance of the reader in the process of constructing meaning. Leigh Berger and Carolyn Ellis write:

> Autoethnography encourages ethnographers to develop a relationship with those studied, to treat them as co-researchers, to share authority, and to assist participants to author their own lives in their own voices. Readers, too, take a more active role as they are invited into the author's world, asked to respond to and discuss the events being described, and are stimulated to use what they learn to reflect on, understand, and cope with their own lives.
>
> Essentially, autoethnography opens a dialogue among the researcher, participant, and reader. In the sharing and co-creation of stories, the goal of this conversation is for researcher and participants to understand one another better and for readers to interpret and form opinions about what they are reading. Autoethnography invites readers to accompany the author on a journey and to add their own emotions and reactions as they travel into worlds of new discoveries and possibilities (2002, 156).

Ellis and Bochner emphasize that, during the autoethnographic process, the researcher's gaze zooms backward and forward, inward and outward; distinctions between the personal and cultural become blurred, sometimes beyond recognition (2000, 739).

Autoethnographers have been valuable guides as I reflect both on my mother's life and on my dual position as researcher and daughter. They have helped shape the questions I ask and how I think about my subject. As I worked my way through this project, I came to agree with Ellis and

Bochner that a primary concern in autoethnographic (or, I would add, even autoethnographic-inspired) exploration is what consequences it might produce (2000, 746). In recent decades ethnographers have become increasingly sensitive to the impact of their work on participants, and it is a commitment of autoethnographers to work collaboratively with the people they interview and write about. When one's own family is the site of ethnographic study, the feeling of risk is great. How I experience life and understand my family is different from how other family members experience and then remember the same people and events. For me to share those thoughts feels dangerous, for both me and for others in my family. Nancy Miller reflects that "[i]n some way, every memoir of a parent's life is an act of exposure, making the private public, telling family secrets, violating decorum" (1996, 147). My mother, the woman at the centre of this study, is no longer alive, but I have been aware that sharing my reflections with others in my family might not only affect their memories but also alter my relationships with them. To remain faithful to my own memories and experiences without hurting those closest to me is an ongoing struggle. This fascinating but delicate process demands that I tread carefully. As I have shared my reflections with my family throughout the research and writing process, comparing my memories and interpretations with theirs, I am sure they have been as aware as I have that our discussions of recipes – seemingly inconsequential chocolate chip cookies – thinly mask a much deeper subject: how we construct ourselves and how we place my mother within the family we constitute.

Ruth Behar emphasizes that memory is a form of knowing that always takes place somewhere else (1996, 82), and my efforts to understand my mother's life are clouded by my own imperfect lens. As my own memory of her baking reminds me, she had identities other than that of being my mother, as central as that relationship was for me. Her baking is an important link to my own long-ago childhood and a connection that I now share with my son, but of course this is not what it meant to her. Ironically, in reading her recipes as life stories, I am choosing a means that she did not consciously use to define herself. I know that she would not want to be read through her recipes.

* * *

In that this book explores the foodways of a white, middle-class woman in Maritime Canada, it is an unusual Folklore study. Although scholars have explored the culinary traditions of many groups, including those of middle-class or white communities (e.g., see Shapiro 2004), it is most common, as Brown and Mussell indicate, for folklorists to approach foodways as an identifying marker of culturally or ethnically defined subgroups (2001, 3). Foodways is often a means to establish boundaries and to distinguish those who are "other": as Roland Barthes says, "we do not see our own food, or worse, we assume that it is insignificant" (1997, 20–1). In its attempt to reveal what may be invisible and to problematize what is overlooked or even made fun of – everyday, mundane, middle-class food – this book challenges that "othering" of distinctive food practices.

An exploration of stories embedded in everyday food and its preparation points to the potential richness that disciplines like Folklore and Women's Studies have to offer one another. Only relatively recently has Folklore turned its attention to women's issues, and feminist folkloristics is a burgeoning subdiscipline. On the other hand, Women's Studies has been criticized as being theoretically "top down," and Folklore, with its close lens on the everyday, brings with it a useful empirical focus. Viewed under this lens, one woman's baking offers a contextually situated example of how a generation constructed and managed identity roles; it offers new possibilities for seeing meanings in everyday food. Some of the stories contained in my mother's recipes speak loudly of what it was to be a minister's wife and to move in several female social circles. They arise from networks of both obligation and friendship. Other recipes show signs of resistance. They suggest that women like my mother did not unselfconsciously assume restrictive social roles. Although these are some of the most difficult subtexts to interpret, the recipes hold clues to my mother's challenges to the social expectations that shaped her life: expectations of what it was to be a good wife and mother, what it meant to be a good hostess, and what it was to be a good neighbour, church supporter, and community member. I also find stories in my mother's recipes that are definitely more mine than hers. Many of her recipes are no longer made; they are not being not reproduced by the next generation. That I have chosen to resurrect them here and to make them the centre of this study perhaps speaks of my own longing for a mother and a long-ago childhood. Some of these stories of loss are shared by my father, sister, and brother; some of them are mine alone. Many of the most powerful stories I read in my mother's recipes, however, are the ones I turn to next. These tell of her homemaking and of her nurturing.

2

FEEDING OUR FAMILY WELL

This Saturday night is like many others I remember from high school. I return home around midnight after an evening out with friends. I no longer recall the specifics of the occasion, where I have been or with whom, but I do have a clear image of my return home. Everyone is asleep. I lock the back door, hang up my coat, and head quietly but deliberately to the cupboard that holds the baking. I briefly consider the possibilities: molasses cookies, chocolate chip cookies, brownies, cinnamon rolls, and biscuits. I choose the tea biscuits. Biscuits are always on this kitchen shelf, the soul of our house. In a square, worn, plastic container, they sit beside the assortment of flowered tins that originally held fancy store-bought cookies and now contain my mother's home baking.

Biscuits are solid and reassuring. From the time I was a small child, biscuits have been a common bedtime lunch. On countless nights I have seen my parents or my mother's parents eat biscuits before bed. "What's for lunch?" my grandfather bellows in his deep voice every night at ten – if it has not already been set before him.[1] My mother or grandmother responds quickly, jumping up to put on the kettle for tea and more often than not taking out the tin of biscuits. Biscuits with butter accompany all our meals, but biscuits with strawberry jam, or buttered biscuits with sliced cheddar cheese on top, are most often the stuff of bedtime lunches.

Tonight I take two biscuits out of the container and slice them in half. I generously slather the sides of one with peanut butter. On the other, I smear cheese spread. The familiarity of these biscuits connects me with my family. Their taste instantly tells me that I am home.

Perhaps this memory of eating biscuits remains because it was part of a familiar pattern of eating upon entering the house. On these occasions, hunger did not drive me to my mother's baking. Rather, it was the act of consuming something homemade that was important. It was my ritual return from the outside world and symbolically represented my re-entry into the family.

To taste a biscuit, cinnamon roll or cookie – molasses, chocolate chip, oatmeal, or peanut butter – was immediately to be enveloped by all that our family was. These specific tastes and textures instantly integrated me into its past and present and signalled my belonging to *this* family. Made by my mother for the rest of us – my father, sister, brother, and me – baked goods spoke not only of my membership, but of the roles we all assumed and our familial dynamics more generally. In his discussion of food and power in prehistoric Europe, Michael Dietler argues that "food is a pervasive and critical element in the articulation and manipulation of social relations" (Dietler 1996, 91, cited in Long 2000, 156). My mother's baking certainly functioned this way, embodying our "commensal politics." As I think back to my childhood, I now imagine our family as fixed, but of course our relationships were dynamic and ever-shifting, affected by day-to-day events as well as by larger factors such as moves, my parents' employment, health issues, and growing children. Significantly, my mother's baking cupboard held enough mystery that one was never sure exactly what tastes lay behind the doors – or what exactly, therefore, it meant to be home. What sat beside the ever-present biscuits, cinnamon rolls, and cookies? Old favourites, like banana bread or date squares? Some days were less certain. Possibilities emerged from a larger, more fluid baking repertoire: rarer tastes that included seasonal offerings such as rhubarb pie, or an entry into a more exotic realm with coconut squares. As I think back on this cupboard, I realize that, like our family itself, the shelves and its contents were reassuringly familiar yet never completely predictable.

GOOD FOOD

Looking back, my father, brother, sister, and I best remember my mother's biscuits and her familiar, everyday baking, rather than more occasional or special dishes. Underscoring David Sutton's observation that "it is not simply at 'loud' ritual occasions that food and memory come together, but in the pragmatic and ritualized aspects of everyday life" (2001, 28), Mark can recall Mom's everyday baking in detail: "She'd always bake cinnamon rolls and chocolate chip cookies and then there would be probably some biscuits she would bake. Those would be the staples I guess ... I mean she made jelly rolls and [different kinds of] cookies, I guess, like peanut butter cookies and chocolate squares ... She'd make all kinds of pies. She'd make apple pies and whatever was going, I guess. She wouldn't make a cake very often" (Mark Tye, Interview, 1999). His recollection of Christmas specialties is more tentative: [She'd make] shortbreads ... and she decorated them up and she made all kinds of different things at Christmas. I don't remember what they were. But I mean, fudge. I remember chocolate balls. She would make those. She would make fruitcake, wouldn't she?" (Mark Tye, Interview, 1999). For Mark, the familiar tastes of ever-present biscuits, cinnamon rolls, and chocolate chip cookies are the most meaningful. When he was a child, they gave him comfort and a sense of continuity; as an adult, he is grounded by their memory. In contrast, the richer, more occasional tastes have slipped away.

I wonder about the roots of these everyday tastes that are so important to our family that they remain in our minds decades after we relied on them. What binds us so strongly to these foods? What is their genealogy? Certainly, some can be traced back at least three generations: both my mother and grandmother served biscuits with every meal and often before bed, and apple pie was a staple. It makes me think that in making what she considered to be good food for her family, my mother at least partly reproduced the tastes of her childhood,[2] and that these tastes provided her with a sense of continuity.

BISCUITS, OATCAKES, AND SOFT MOLASSES COOKIES

Probably one of the first recipes my mother acquired was for biscuits. Reflecting Mom's polished skills as a stenographer and her new portable typewriter, it appears very neatly typed on its index card:

Biscuits

2 cups sifted flour
4 tsp baking powder
1/2 tsp salt

LAURENE'S FATHER, FRED, WITH BEDTIME LUNCH OF BISCUIT AND JAM,
DURING A CHRISTMAS VISIT, CHARLOTTETOWN, c. 1965

3 to 5 tbsp shortening
Add: ²/₃ cup of milk
Bake 450 for 12 minutes, yield 16 Biscuits

Sometime later she wrote the ingredients of a variation in pencil across the bottom:

½ tsp baking soda
1 tsp cream tartar
Sometimes an egg

On another card is a third recipe, recorded in pen and in firm handwriting:

Biscuits

2 cups sifted flour
$1/4$ cup white sugar
$1/3$ cup powdered milk
shortening
2 tsp cream tartar
1 tsp soda
1 tsp salt
moisten with water

My mother passed on a final variant to me when I moved away from home and asked for her biscuit recipe. This is the one that I remember most from my childhood but for some reason it now survives only in my own recipe box, entered carefully and proudly in my twenty-year-old handwriting, having either been dictated to me by my mother or copied from her original:

Biscuits

2 cups sifted flour
1 tbsp white sugar
4 tsp baking powder
1 tsp salt
Cut in: $1/2$ cup shortening
Add: 1 beaten egg
$2/3$ cup milk
Knead about 20 strokes. Roll out $3/4''$ thick. Bake 450 for 1–14 min.

These simple recipes for biscuits trace my mother's life through time and place. They read like souvenirs of her childhood home in rural Pictou

County and of her journey through Nova Scotia to the remote Cape Breton farming community of her first years of marriage in the 1950s, to small-town life in Amherst in the 1970s and 1980s. At the same time, they indicate the centrality of biscuits to my mother's baking. Throughout her lifetime they remained a core item, but their evolution reflects a shift in preference toward lighter, sweeter baking.

Biscuits are equivalent to, or a variation of, scones, which Davidson notes as widespread throughout the British Isles but a Scottish specialty in particular (2002, 844). The *Concise Oxford English Dictionary* defines *scone* as "a soft cake of barley-meal or oatmeal or wheat-flour of size for single portion usually baked quickly in oven or on griddle" and Davidson notes that "the term is mainly a British one, and covers a wide range of small, fairly plain cakes." He notes that in the United States "the term 'biscuit' may denote more or less what in Britain would be called a scone – though the term 'scone' has also come into limited use in North America" (Davidson 2002, 844).

Margaret Bennett identifies scones as the keystone of the Scottish baking traditions she encountered in Quebec. When Bennett did her fieldwork in 1976–77 and during the summers of 1991 to 1995, she discovered that baking scones[3] "needed no special occasion – 'there's not too many left' was enough of a prompt. As is the case with most home-baking, however, the anticipation of visitors was an added incentive to have 'freshly baked' ones for that day" (Bennett 1998, 175). She expands: "Quebec's Hebridean kitchens are renowned in the Eastern Townships for turning out a variety of scones – white flour, whole wheat flour, rolled oats, oatmeal, or a combination of any two. Some are made in the oven, though most are made directly on top of the stove or occasionally on a griddle. Although individual recipes vary, the basic ingredients are flour, salt, a small amount of sugar, baking soda and sour milk. If fresh milk is used, the baking soda is replaced by baking powder. Most recipes are not written down, though in recent years a number of parish cookery books have included scone recipes contributed by women of various church groups" (1998, 172). In Bennett's study, scones embody Scottish heritage; she claims they are considered the most characteristic food of the Scottish in Quebec (1998, 173).[4]

Many of the observations that Bennett makes in the context of Quebec apply to biscuit-baking in Pictou County, where they were also a staple and women were judged on the quality of the biscuits they made. Helen Ward, who was in her eighties when I talked to her, had lived in rural Pictou Country all her life and in Eureka for all of her adult years. In describing local baking traditions, she singled out one of her friends as the community's best biscuit maker: "And Ann Bell, she is noted for her biscuits. Of course she's down at the home now. But she made the nicest biscuits and she'd give you the recipe but they would never turn out the same. I don't know why" (Ward, Interview, 2004). My mother's regular production of biscuits and their daily consumption in our home tied her to the village where she grew up and to her Scottish roots.

In his entry on scones, Davidson cautions that "[t]his recipe, so simple and excellent, should not be messed around with." However, he allows that "[i]nstead of making small individual scones, the dough can be baked as one large flat cake and split into wedges later. These large scones were probably the norm in previous centuries" (Davidson 2002, 844). He also underscores their connection to "the closely related bannock," which Davidson describes as "a griddle-baked flatbread from the highland zones of Britain, made from barley, oats, or even peasemeal, water or buttermilk" (2002, 66). Davidson relates bannock to both scones and oatcakes: "It is thicker than the oatcake, and larger than a scone" (2002, 66).

It is consistent with Davidson's comments that, when my mother was growing up, biscuits were not always cut out individually but were sometimes baked in a cake pan. "Cake bread," as this was called, was a staple in many households. My mother's brother, Fred, remembers cake bread being served in their home when he and my mother were children. Asked to recall the baking of his childhood, Fred first names biscuits and pie. He then attempts to describe cake bread, although clearly it has been a long time since he has eaten or even thought of it, since he cannot conjure the name. His wife, Geraldine, originally from New Brunswick, tries to prompt him but is unfamiliar with cake bread. Fred recalls:

> And she [Mom] had, what do you call it? Not shortbread but it would be like a biscuit in a big pan – and you would cut those. What do you call those?
>
> [Geraldine:] Scotch cakes? Shortbread?
>
> [Diane:] Is it called biscuit cake or cake bread or something like that? Is it like biscuits?
>
> I can't remember. It's like a biscuit exactly, only you cut them.
>
> [Geraldine:] It wasn't cornbread?
>
> No, no. Well, it was exactly like a biscuit anyway. And I'm sure it was exactly the same mix.
>
> (Fred and Geraldine Falconer, Interview, 2003)

When I asked my father about the baking of his childhood in Pictou County, he offered what was for him an extensive description of the making and eating of cake bread:

> Three or four dishes stand out. One was cake bread. You know cake bread? Well, it's like an unleavened bread and you put it in a big pan. It's a big long rectangular pan but you didn't fill it up.

You just put the batter in there and the corners of the pan would be empty and the batter would sort of just swell out as it baked. And it was like, it was a biscuit material of some kind. It substituted for biscuits. And you cut this in a square and you cut them in two and put jam, butter, whatever you want in between them. It was just, it didn't rise a lot. Cake bread. We called it cake bread. That was a staple. And my mother made biscuits fairly regularly but the cake bread was several times a week. That would be number one (Henry Tye, Interview, 1999a).

Although some residents of Pictou County refer to cake bread as bannock,[5] a recipe from around the 1940s attests to cake bread's close relationship to biscuits. A few years ago I purchased a second-hand copy of Fannie Farmer's *The Boston Cooking School Cook Book*. The book's original owner, Jean R. Humphries, signed the copy on 6 April 1944. She also recorded a recipe on the flyleaf that bears both the titles "Biscuit Cake" and "Aunt Laura's Good Biscuits." The two names, as well as the recipe text itself, support my uncle's and father's recollections of biscuits and cake bread as interchangeable. Humphries's recipe bears the marks of frequent use; reading it, one can imagine Humphries's Aunt Laura struggling to reproduce the recipe for cake bread for her niece. It is clear that she made it so often that she worked by feel. This effort to record the recipe may well be the first time it was committed to paper:

Biscuit Cake (Aunt Laura's Good Biscuits)

Sifter of flour (her sifter is small little over 2 cups)
2 tsp cream tartar
1 tsp soda
1 tsp salt
Piece of shortening (size of an egg)

Piece of butter (size of an egg)
Mix with milk till soft. Hot oven!!!

It seems that by the time I was growing up, cake bread had been replaced almost completely with individually cut-out biscuits. I encountered it only in the last few years, when a rural Pictou County bakery began to produce it. Perhaps this is in part because, as my mother's recipes show, biscuits have become increasingly lighter fare. The biscuits I associate with my mother are the later ones: light and fluffy, calling for more shortening and incorporating baking powder and an egg. Their texture was removed from the harder, drier biscuits that Mom might have made in the early days and were still produced by other women in the region, including my grandmother. Those more closely resembled the biscuits of their Scottish roots. By the 1970s, light biscuits were a valued commodity in Amherst, and I can remember conversations with older women at that time about the virtues of adding an egg to one's biscuits. These biscuits were also sweeter than their predecessors, and my mother's later recipe calls for more sugar than the earlier three. Despite the fact that Mom's biscuits were not reproduced from a recipe that had been handed down, their taste, as well as their constant presence, would have conjured memories of a number of closely related baked goods from her own childhood, including biscuits and cake bread.

As Davidson indicates, biscuits are also closely related to oatcakes. My mother grew up with oatcakes, for which there are two recipes among my grandmother's handwritten collection. My grandmother got the first of these from her neighbour, Christie Fraser, who had the reputation of being an excellent baker:

Oatcakes

2 cups oatmeal
¾ cup white flour

⅓ cup brown sugar
1 tsp salt, soda
½ cup shortening

Mix with little milk or water

These directions conform to Davidson's description of oatcakes as "made from oats (in the form of oatmeal), salt, and water, sometimes with a little fat added" (2002, 654). He goes on to declare oatcakes "the staple food of the inhabitants of the Pennines and the Lake District in England and of the Scottish Highlands for centuries" (Davidson 2002, 654).

Oatcakes are the food most associated with Scottish roots in Pictou County, and a good recipe for oatcakes is much sought after. Helen Ward spoke to me of her granddaughter's recent request for a "good" recipe for oatcakes: "And I said well I have one I always make but I said the best person to ask to get a good recipe is Catherine Haslam … [She] makes the nicest oatcakes around here. I don't know where she got her recipe but she does make beautiful oatcakes" (Ward, Interview, 2004). This, and a second recipe my grandmother owned for oatcakes, were both added to her collection in mid-life, suggesting that, like Helen's granddaughter, she also may have been in search of the perfect oatcake. In addition to the oatcake recipe from her neighbour, Christie Fraser, she had one from "Mrs. John A. McNaughton, Stellarton," a fellow member of the Rebecca Lodge:

Oat Cakes

1 cup shortening
1 cup brown sugar
1 egg
Cream that
2½ cups oatmeal

1 cup flour

1 tsp salt, soda, vanilla

Cut as you want, bake 8 minutes, 375 oven. If made of rolled oats, add ½ tsp nutmeg with vanilla. Makes good cookies filled with date filling or icing.

Undoubtedly, my grandmother would have sampled these oatcakes during one of the lunches that was served after each Lodge meeting and asked for the recipe. Although both recipes call for similar ingredients – oatmeal, flour, a little shortening, and sugar – Mrs. McNaughton's oatcakes are sweeter, with a lighter texture. They blur another line: that between cake and cookie. The interchangeability of recipes for oatcakes or cookies is reflected in the closing directive: "Makes good cookies filled with date filling or icing."

Biscuits, cake bread, and oatcakes all lie at the intersection of cake and bread, illustrating Davidson's point that the frontiers between cake and bread, biscuit and bun are indistinct (2002, 147). Oatcakes, which Davidson refers to as a "modern survivor" of the earliest form of cake, were "made from roughly crushed grains, moistened, compacted, and cooked on a hot stone." Davidson points out that, although they are called oat*cakes*, these are now considered to be more closely related to biscuits because of their flat, thin shape and brittle texture. He writes that "from the basic method for making what was essentially desiccated porridge, leavened and unleavened cereal mixtures evolved into breads, cakes and pastries" (Davidson 2002, 147). Although Davidson links the oatcake to forms of cake as well as bread or biscuits, its low sugar content and dense texture leads my father, who is expansive on the limitations of the oatcake, to classify it among the latter rather than the former. He considers oatcakes as a "food" rather than as a "sweet" or "treat," implying that one ate it to "fill up" and gain needed energy. Oatcakes were not to be enjoyed; their flavour was not to be savoured:

They were not treats, they were almost a staple like potatoes. You don't go to Tim Horton's and order a potato ... they were almost food. Sweets are supposed to be a treat. And if you like the taste of grain, I can imagine that this is what a horse would eat when it eats grain. But we like sugar, don't we? ... There was no flavour added to it ... [When you eat a sweet] you don't taste flour, do you? Well in oatcakes, you tasted the basic ingredient, which was ground up oats. You wouldn't think of that as a treat, would you? (Henry Tye, Interview, 2005)

My father remembers oatcakes not from his childhood but from Cape Breton during his early days as an minister:

I do recall that ... your mother tried to make oatcakes a couple of times and they were hard as rocks and I made it known to her that oatmeal cookies were not my favorite ... I eat them but you know but every farm house [in Cape North] you went to, you got these oatcakes and if they gave you butter, they would slide down the back of your throat. The oats hadn't been transformed in the cook-ing. It was just like picking up raw oatmeal and eating it. When you buy oatcakes in the stores, there is sugar added. That was not the case in Cape North. I did not grow up with oatcakes ... And then when we went to Cape North [oatcakes] were a staple of that community ... So your mother tried to produce those because simply people might expect to have them when they came into our house, it was normal. When you had tea there, they would give you a small plate and on that plate would be a staple such as a homemade biscuit and oatcake ... plus cheese and some other sweet. So it was expected when you went in the oatcake would be on the plate as a filler. And your mother was not a cook when she went there. She was not a baker. She never went in the kitchen when she was in Eureka to my knowledge so she tried to make oatcakes. I don't recall whether this was one time or many times, but this is my impression that they were totally dry and hard as iron (Henry Tye, Interview, 1999b).

It is perhaps not surprising, given my father's negative assessment, that my mother did not regularly bake oatcakes, although I know that she ate them if someone else served them. Although she occasionally made oatmeal porridge, it was not something she relished. This might have been because, as I remember her telling me, she ate porridge every day as a girl in the 1930s. Perhaps by adulthood she'd had her fill. Perhaps her tastes, like my father's, had moved in other directions. Certainly she would not have been encouraged to make oatcakes by my father, who stresses that when he was growing up his family preferred molasses-based cookies:

They [oatcakes] were in the house, in the family, but they weren't a staple. But molasses cookies were and ginger cookies were. And that kind of thing. There was always those in the house when I was growing up. We kept the cookie jar dry but they were in the house. The molasses were bigger and the ginger smaller, that's how I distinguish them (Henry Tye, Interview, 1999b).

My mother's solution was to replace oatcakes, and the thick, substantial oatmeal cookies of her youth, with something called Cruncky Cookies:

Cruncky Cookies

| ½ cup shortening | 1 egg |
| ¾ cup Rolled Oats | ¾ cup flour |

¼ tsp soda	¾ cup Brown sugar
1 cup cocoanut	¼ tsp salt
1 tsp baking powder	

Roll in small balls and flatten with fork.

This was one of several recipes that helped Mom refashion the dry, heavy oatcake into a sweet cookie with a light, crisp texture through the addition of sweeteners, such as brown sugar and coconut, and/or richer ingredients like margarine, or even butter, instead of shortening. Such transformations traversed the family's food categories. As Mary Douglas demonstrated in her now-classic exploration of what constitutes a meal, families are governed by internal structures that allow them to develop their own classificatory systems. In producing her Cruncky Cookies, Mom replaced what my father saw as a questionable "food" or "filler" with something he regarded as an acceptable "treat." Although our family's categories of "filler" and "treat" sometimes overlapped, texture (dense and dry versus light and/or crisp), and sweetness were defining factors, categories Barthes points to as relevant for North Americans within their conceptualization of food as "a system of communication" (1997, 23, 21). Barthes argues that food is so intricately linked with its context that it *"has a constant tendency to transform itself into situation"* (26); for example, coffee is now not so much a substance as a circumstance (1997, 26). According to the grammar that structured my mother's baking, fillers and treats could be linked with different situations. Fillers were associated with the most mundane and meanest of food events: they could be eaten at any time of day on their own or served at a meal to provide more substance. Treats tended to be consumed later in the day; they often accompanied tea or coffee or marked the end of a meal. In terms of Barthes's dichotomy of activity and leisure, which he suggests underlies the contemporary signifying nature of food

– rather than work and celebration, which formerly structured food events – treats were more closely associated with leisure, and fillers with activity. To some extent, these categories also reflect Mary Douglas's distinction of intimacy and distance (1997, 41). Fillers represented the most economically made foods and were made primarily for the family. Although fillers could be shared with guests, company were more likely to be offered treats that required fancier, more expensive ingredients such as chocolate or dried fruit. Together, "fillers" and "treats" made up my mother's supply of "staples," those foods such as biscuits that were almost always on hand.

Thinking back to these staples, Dad remembers items such as ginger snaps: "One of her staples was ginger snaps, made in the rolls, and I cut them for her many times because she wanted them thin and uniform. Most times when you came into the house you'd run into them" (Henry Tye, Interview, 1999b).

Ginger Snaps

½ cup shortening
½ cup brown sugar
½ cup molasses
1 egg
3 cup flour
2 tsp soda in ⅓ c. hot water
½ tsp salt
1 tsp ginger
1 tsp cinnamon
1 tsp allspice

Mix ingredients well. Knead on flour board. Roll real thin. Cook 375 oven. Cooks in a few minutes. Don't let brown.

I share his memory. Gingerbread, ginger snaps, and molasses cookies were common in our home and, like biscuits and oatcakes, were linked to the regional baking traditions my mother grew up with. Historically, Atlantic Canadian cooks had many uses for molasses. My grandmother's recipe collection contains lots of these recipes, including molasses squares, ginger cookies, hermit drop cookies, molasses taffy, and molasses drop cookies. Some, like instructions for her mother's mince meat and cakes – Christmas fruit cake, marble cake, ginger cake, and war cake[6] – were special holiday foods that would have lent cachet and special meaning to other, more ordinary, molasses-based foods. As Mary Douglas showed, meals are interconnected and derive meaning from all others: "Meals are ordered in scale of importance and grandeur through the week and year. The smallest, meanest meal metonymically figures the structure of the grandest, and each unit of the grand meal figures again the whole meal – or the meanest meal" (1997, 42). The common add-ins of raisins or dates and the well-known combination of spices used when baking with molasses – cinnamon and ginger, and sometimes nutmeg or mace, which also have long histories – connected families like ours to what Rozin describes as shared "flavor principles" that "provide powerful and characteristic flavor profiles that are familiar and pleasing to those within the system" (2000, 135).[7] So familiar was this combination of spices in both festive and everyday baking that some of my grandmother's recipes simple indicate "spices," leaving the exact combination and amounts to individual discretion.

Molasses Drop Cookies

½ cup shortening
½ cup white sugar
½ cup molasses
1 egg

2 tsp soda in 2 tbsp boiling water
1 tbsp vinegar

2¼ cup flour
1 tsp ginger, cinnamon, salt & vanilla
6 tbsp or ⅓ cup cold water added last
Add walnuts if desired

Jean Proudfoot

As I have argued elsewhere (Tye 2008), molasses provides, perhaps more than any other food, a culinary entry-point to cultural dynamics in Atlantic Canada.[8] Important to the early economy of the Atlantic region, molasses formed part of a trade exchange between the North American colonies and the West Indies that dates back to the seventeenth century. Settlers traded lumber, salt fish, and salt beef for sugar, molasses, and rum. Records show that this trade was important to the prosperity of the Fortress of Louisbourg, and Simeon Perkins' diary entries from the 1770s indicate an exchange of products, including molasses from the West Indies, for lumber and other goods in Liverpool, Nova Scotia (Innis 1948). Molasses was essential to the survival of some groups of settlers, including a band of Black Loyalists who arrived in Birchtown, Nova Scotia, in 1783. The new residents found themselves without the land they had been promised and facing a winter without adequate food or shelter. Their provisions of "meal and molasses" saw them through. Nova Scotia historian A. A. MacKenzie provides another example from 1816: "In Halifax then, poor Newfoundlanders were arriving, many of them half-frozen and sick. To keep them alive the government had to supply cornmeal, molasses, spruce beer, coffee, tea, beef and rice" (2003, 3). Throughout the nineteenth and early twentieth century, molasses was eaten daily by most Atlantic Canadians. In 1947, just prior to New-foundland joining Canada in 1949, 8,000 to 10,000 puncheons (or 560,000 to 700,000 gallons) were imported annually from Barbados (Anonymous 1948, 45). According to the entry for bread in the *Dictionary of Newfoundland English* (1999), a winter's supply for a family in outport Newfoundland "would be possibly 20 or 30 barrels of flour, so many bags of bread (hard tack), a puncheon of molasses, tea, sugar, beans etc."

In the early days, residents incorporated molasses into nearly every meal. Gingerbread with cream, or hot steamed brown bread made from cornmeal and molasses, was served as breakfast (Robertson 1991, 151); bread or buns sweetened with molasses, known as lassybread or lassie buns, might serve as lunch, while baked beans and molasses constituted Saturday night supper in most parts of the Maritime provinces. Molasses on bread and biscuits accompanied each meal, and if there was no other food, it could be *the* meal, which was sometimes referred to as "a poor man's meal" (Weale 1992, 24). It was also used as a sweetener for tea. Molasses was feature of some regional specialities, including the Acadian dishes *poutine rappée*, a mixture of raw grated potato, cooked potato and salt pork formed into a ball, simmered, and served with molasses or brown sugar, and rappie pie, a stewed chicken potato dish, also served with molasses. As my grandmother's recipe collection indicates, molasses was also an ingredient in a wide variety of cookies, from thin ginger snaps to large plump molasses cookies (known in Cape Breton during my parents' time there as "Fat Archies" or "Moose Hunters"). It flavoured cakes and desserts: gingerbread, raisin, date and other fruitcakes, mincemeat pie and tarts, and molasses pudding. Finally, molasses was the basis of many home remedies aimed at curing a wide range of ailments, including sore throat, earache, colds and coughs, bronchitis, croup, flu, diphtheria, and constipation. It was used as a blood purifier, to treat cuts and minor skin ailments, to rid worms, cure digestive ailments, and to serve as a spring tonic.[9]

By the late nineteenth century, brown sugar and molasses became the sole property of the less sophisticated – the rural or working class – as new methods of refining sugar brought down the price of white sugar. Harvey Levenstein reports how a monopoly of sugar manufacturers successfully managed to denigrate brown sugar so that, by the twentieth century, most sophisticated cooks relied almost solely on white sugar (Levenstein 1988, 33). Notwithstanding sugar's rise in popularity, molasses continued to be used in Atlantic Canada throughout the twentieth century, becoming more associated with working-class households in rural parts of the region until eventually even there it was replaced by other foods. During both my mother's childhood and my own, however, workers routinely relied on molasses for energy. Lassie buns, also known as jay buns or lassie mogs, made with molasses and fat back pork or salt pork were a staple lunch for woodsmen and fishers (Jesperson 1974, 48), farmers in part of the Maritimes drank a molasses-based drink known as switchel or stenchel while haying, and baked beans were standard fare in lumber camps through the Atlantic region.

In the last few decades molasses has taken on symbolic meanings. As Weismantal writes, "It is because they are ordinarily immersed in everyday practice in a material way that foods, abstracted as symbols from this material process, can condense in themselves a wealth of ideological meanings" (1988, 7–8). Molasses has become synonymous with Atlantic Canadian identity, as reflected in its presence in popular culture forms from fridge magnets representing molasses cartons to songs such as Dick Nolan's "Newfoundland Good Times," which signals molasses on doughboys and molasses in tea as markers of Newfoundland identity.[10] Meanwhile, manufacturers capitalize on nostalgic consumers: the Canadian grocery-store label Presidents Choice introduced a molasses cookies under the brand name "Lassy Mogs" in 2004.

During my mother's lifetime, the public regional nostalgia for molasses products had not yet taken hold. Its meanings were still being constructed for individuals or families within domestic settings. Although my mother did not have as many recipes as my grandmother that called for molasses in combination with the spices mentioned above, this ingredient figured in her instructions for mincemeat, for some cakes and, more often, for cookies. Her collection of ten cookie recipes includes instructions for a variety of textures from big, soft, "bear paws" to hard "crinkles" sprinkled with white sugar. There are molasses cookies, rolled-oat molasses cookies, ginger snaps, molasses drop cookies, and soft molasses cookies. The following recipe for soft molasses cookies is one of six very closed related recipes – so close, in fact, to two others named Soft Molasses Cookies and three called Molasses Drop Cookies that an untrained eye might consider the recipes indistinguishable. Whereas my grandmother seemed to be on the lookout for the perfect oatcake, my mother searched for the perfect soft molasses cookie.

Soft Molasses Cookies

½ cup margarine
½ cup white sugar
¾ cup molasses
1 egg
2½ cup flour
1½ tsp ginger
1 tsp cinnamon
¼ tsp salt
2 tsp baking soda
¼ cup water

Cream margarine and sugar, blend in molasses and egg. Dissolve baking soda in water and add alternately with dry ingredients. Drop by tablespoon onto greased and floured cookie sheet. Bake 400, 10 min.

Winnie

My father recalls both that he grew up with molasses cookies and that he was often served them when on his church visits to rural farm households in Cape North. According to Dad, in Cape Breton a cup of tea was usually accompanied by chocolate cake, oatmeal cookies, or "ginger moosehunters, the big gingerbread cookies" (Henry Tye, Interview, 1999). Just as my mother transformed oatcakes into Cruncky Cookies, thus bringing her use of oatmeal into line with her own preference (and that of her family) for more highly refined and sweetened foods, she also fine-tuned her soft molasses cookies until she had just the desired taste and texture. Thus she simultaneously redefined and reproduced communities of eating that she had belonged to: both that of her childhood and of the rural Cape Breton community where she and my father lived when they were first married and where she learned to bake.

Although Dad valued the increasing sweetness of my mother's home baking, my brother grew up with it, so that it now represents for him how "good food" should taste. Today Mark links sweet nostalgic foods with being nurtured (see Locher et al. 2005, 281). He remembers how much he delighted in Mom's baking: the cinnamon rolls, made from the biscuit dough recipe given earlier, and the chocolate chip cookies that she made primarily for him and that gained neighbourhood celebrity.

Chocolate Chip Cookies

½ cup shortening
¾ cup brown sugar
1 egg

1 tsp vanilla
Cream shortening and sugar, add egg, vanilla ·

Add:

1 cup sifted flour
½ tsp salt
½ tsp baking soda
Add:

½ cup chopped nuts
Chocolate chips

Drop by spoonful on greased cookie sheet. Bake 375 for 10–15 minutes.

Mark recalls, "She always made me chocolate chip cookies and I really liked them and I know most of my friends really liked them too. They were quite famous, I guess. Everybody came over for chocolate chip cookies and they were always there ... It was never fail, there were always some there. That was very good. I loved her cinnamon rolls more than anything. I didn't realize it at the time but I really enjoyed them" (Mark Tye, Interview, 1999). Our next-door neighbour Helen Farrow confirmed Mark's memory of the chocolate chip cookies: "She always had them. I mean they were Mark's favourite ... When he'd come home from school, she'd really think that he was hungry. So, you know, she'd give him a chocolate chip cookie" (Farrow, Interview, 2003).

Unlike the recipes discussed above, my mother's directions for chocolate chip cookies were not passed down generationally or shared by friends. Since she did not make the cookies when I was growing up, I suspect she discovered the recipe in the late 1970s, after I had left home for university. Helen remembered Mom referring her to the back of a chocolate chip package for the recipe; indeed, her recipe is very close to the one for "Original Nestlé Toll House Chocolate Chip Cookies" currently found on Nestlé's chocolate chips. According to Nestlé, their cookies were created in 1930 by Ruth Wakefield, owner of the Toll House Inn near Whitman, Massachusetts, when she added bits of a semi-sweet chocolate bar into the batter of a batch of Butter Drop Do cookies. Although Nestlé claims the cookie's immediate and widespread popularity, Lovegren argues that the recipe was little known until Betty Crocker publicized it through her radio series "Famous Foods from Famous Eating Places" in 1939. By the 1940s, *The Joy of Cooking* contained a recipe for Chocolate Chip Drops, and Fannie Farmer had a similar recipe for Chocolate Crunch Cookies (Lovegren 2005, 146). Nestlé immediately capitalized on the success of the popular cookies, first adding the recipe to the wrapper of their chocolate bar (which, for a while, they sold with a chopper) and, after 1939, on packages of their semi-sweet chocolate morsels. Nestlé now promotes these as "the most popular cookie of all time" (www.verybestbaking.com/products/tollhouse/history.aspx). Like the other recipes for "good food," discussed above, the Toll House cookies had their roots in earlier baking traditions. Although, unlike biscuits and molasses cookies, they do not draw directly on Mom's experiences as a young girl in a rural community or on her Scottish ancestry, their base – Butter Drop Do cookies – does reach back to an earlier generation. As far as I know, neither my mother nor my grandmother made cookies by this name, but the recipe is close to that for dropped sugar cookies (with their many variants), published in the *Boston Cooking School Cook Book* (Farmer 1941, 666), which would have been very familiar. My mother (and grandmother) made versions of a dropped sugar cookie that may be related to an earlier Scotch Cake. Scotch Cakes with the texture of shortbread were rolled and cut out at Christmastime by both my mother and grandmother; at other times throughout the year they baked similar dropped cookies that were called Drop Cakes, or more often,

Droppies, by my grandmother. These white cookies usually had raisins or nuts added. My mother shared the following recipe with her mother and was one of her contributions to *Sweet Tested Recipes*, the church cookbook discussed more fully in the next chapter.

Nut Drops

⅓ cup shortening
½ cup brown sugar
1 egg
½ cup nut meats
1 cup raisins
1 cup dates (chopped)
¾ cup flour
⅛ tsp soda
¼ tsp baking powder

Bake in moderate oven 375 12–15 minutes.

In another version, my grandmother added common spices such as cinnamon and nutmeg. Without spice or fruit and nuts mixed in, the batter could be dropped onto a cookie sheet to form the base for Thimble Cookies. My mother got her recipe for Thimble Cookies during her first years of marriage in Cape North from her friend Eleanor Gwynn:

Thimble Cookies

1 c shortening
½ cup brown sugar
1 egg
2 tsp vanilla

¼ tsp salt
1¾ cup flour
½ tsp baking powder

Cream shortening and sugar and egg and beat well. Mix in flour, salt and vanilla. Form into balls. Place on greased cookie sheet and dent the top with thimble. Bake 5 mins in moderate oven, then dent again. Bake 15 mins longer. While cookies are still hot put jam or jelly in the depression.

In this way, like biscuits, oatcakes, and molasses cookies, chocolate chip cookies drew on, but reinvented, older models. With an eye to producing food we would enjoy and find tasty, Mom provided our family with that Barthes refers to as "flavorful survival[s] of an old, rural society" and brought "the memory of the soil into our very contemporary life" (Barthes 1997, 24). Barthes reminds us that this view of rural life is highly idealized, and for that reason food can be an expression of antimodernism that protests the condition of the present and mistakes a nostalgically imagined state for the past (see McWilliams 2007). I never felt either my mother or father yearning for a return to their past. Like many of their generation, they at least gave the impression of enthusiastically embracing modernity. They looked forward. Nevertheless, the food our family ate helped to root us in the working-class experiences and values of our parents' upbringing. As Rozin writes, "the application or production of appropriate and pleasing flavor is primary in our understanding of food and in our understanding of ourselves. It provides sensory labels that enable us to identify ourselves as members of a culture, a tribe, or a family" (2000, 137). With every bite, we were reminded that our rural, working-class roots ran deep.

If not in the actual recipes, then through their ingredients and preparation and the quantity in which they were produced, my mother participated in baking traditions that predated her and were widespread. Just as Handler and Linnekin understand tradition not as static but as continually reinvented and reinterpreted, so were these family and regional baking traditions in which my mother participated. The actual instructions for biscuits or molasses cookies may not have been handed down unchanged for generations, and may in fact have been dynamic modifications of other foods such as scones, cake bread, or oatcakes, but through the production of the foods, tastes, and techniques she shared with family and friends, my mother connected our family to what Rozin describes as a "culinary system" (2000, 134–5). We became part of the daily, weekly, and seasonal rhythms of Maritime life in all its past and present dimensions. Jam and pickle making, preparing for Christmas, baking that capitalized on seasonal produce such as rhubarb, berries, and apples – all of these domestic activities connected her diachronically and synchronically to other Maritime women. Even the daily and weekly production of baking represented a link with other women in the family, neighbourhood, and community. The baking patterns that Margaret Bennett observed in Quebec connect women: "Apart from Sunday, the day of rest, almost every day was baking day, especially in larger families which, in days past, were not unusual" (1998, 171).

The recipes of my mother and other women in the rural Maritimes were not only based on shared tastes; they were governed by shared principles. Chief among these was the understanding that home baking was economical. In fact, Mark now believes that our mother's motivation for baking as much as she did was primarily economic. To buy baked goods was unthinkably extravagant. When I was a child I often wondered where the tins that held her baking came from. They had been in use as long as I could remember, and I could not imagine an occasion so grand or special as to warrant the purchase of cookies. Like so many other things, from clothing to cleaning, that my mother provided for our family, baking was not something she could justify spending extra money on when she could do it more cheaply. Her recipes were inexpensively made, and most were created from a few readily available ingredients.

Other paradigms that shaped my mother's baking, such as the need for variety, also represented continuity. Her frugality was offset by a need to have several items available at any time: thus, economy and abundance coexisted in a delicate balance. As Margaret Bennett discovered in Quebec, "Baking day seldom means that only one item will be made. More usually a contrasting batch of scones, such as oatmeal, will be turned out, along with 'something for the cookie-jar'" (1998, 176–7). In this tradition, my mother and grandmother always baked several items at a time. It was important to have variety on hand, and they also felt that they must offer ample portions and never run out in front of company (see Shuman 1981, 78). Just as O'Sullivan and colleagues discovered that, among the older Albertan women they interviewed, "an abundance of food was deemed essential" (2008, 74), Maritime cooking traditions valued quantity. A woman must provide lots of food, and it was desirable to have food left over. A friend from Cape Breton once described to me how his mother would offer company second helpings even when she knew that there was no more food in the kitchen. She saw it as a mark of a good host to offer, because ideally she should never run out. She counted on their polite refusal. Her great confidence in the local codes of politeness was apparently never misplaced: to her son's knowledge, she never got caught.

This emphasis on quantity has deep roots. Although food historian Levenstein argues that, between 1896 and 1928, quality replaced quantity in the American diet (1988, 194), in earlier times quantity was a distinguishing characteristic. Levenstein writes that "[t]o nineteenth-century observers, the major differences between the American and British diets could usually be summed up in one word: abundance" (1988, 7). Bennett links an emphasis on quantity more specifically to Scottish hospitality in her description of the "impressive variety" of sweets women produced for social gatherings in Quebec. She notes, "Although shortbread is the only item in this category to be regarded as 'traditional', it is true to say, however, that serving a lavish spread on social occasions is considered characteristic of the Scotch hospitality" (Bennett 1998, 177). Levenstein observes that the concern over excess weight that developed in the United States, and in North America more generally, in the 1920s eventually led to more restrained attitudes toward high caloric food (1988, 166). However, for those who had lived through the Depression, even as young children, abundance represented security. Food should be there. In our family, it was. As my father, brother, and I remember, there were always several kinds of baking available.

My mother's mediation of abundance with economy was skilful. It was important to her to have lots of baking on hand, and yet equally important not to be wasteful in its production or consumption. One should have food left over, but that food eventually had to be eaten. The restraint of the Great Depression now long over, this principle has disappeared, sacrificed in favour of overconsumption, but it was the rule of my mother's kitchen. Although she always had a large selection of baking on hand, food was not thrown out. Knowing how much to make was the mark of a competent cook. Again, like the women interviewed by O'Sullivan and colleagues, who without exception emphasized the importance of having lots of food while at the same time reeling off a list of suggestions for using up leftovers, (2008, 76–6), Mom accurately estimated how much was "lots" rather than "too much."

Importantly, the recipes that were popular in our house reflected broader cultural trends; as Rozin points out, although traditional cuisines tend to be fundamentally conservative, they are rarely (if ever) static (2000, 140). As my father's comments above suggest, by the 1950s, when Mom married and began to bake for her family, aesthetics had shifted such that "good food" was lighter and sweeter than in the past. Just as

Helen Leach and Raelene Inglis show that Christmas cakes are sensitive to socio-economic trends and are reinvented depending on time and place (2003), over time coarse foods such as bannock, oatcakes, and "moose hunters" were reworked into lighter, sweeter fare: what my grandmother referred to as "sweet stuff." Levenstein traces this North American preference for increased sugar consumption to much earlier origins:

> By the mid-nineteenth century, falling prices for cane and beet sugars encouraged soaring consumption of these sweeteners among all classes. British "puddings," originally the main course fare, now became progressively sweeter and more diverse, mutating into an incredible variety of hot, cold, baked and steamed puddings, pies, tarts, creams, molds, charlottes, bettys, fools, syllabubs, junkets, and ices. These recipes were avidly imitated in the United States. In 1879, when 175 genteel women of Virginia pooled their favorite recipes into a cookbook, over one-third of the book consisted of recipes for desserts, including separate chapters not only for cakes and pies but also for icing, gingerbread, pudding sauces, fritters and pancakes, ice cream and frozen custard, jellies, fruit desserts, preserves and fruit jellies, as well as thirty-six pages of pudding recipes, and another long chapter devoted to jelly, blanc-mange, Charlotte russe, baked custard, creams, and various other desserts (1988, 6).

He continues:

> Sweet or sweet and sour condiments were particularly popular as accompaniments for meats, and as sugar prices declined in the nineteenth century they soared in popularity. Cucumbers, onions, and other vegetables were preserved in sugar, salt, and vinegar. Tomatoes and mushrooms were boiled down with sugar, salt,

pepper, and vinegar to produce "catsup." The result was a cuisine which, even excluding desserts, relied more on sweetness than did any other major cuisine in the world (1988, 7).

As Levenstein notes, the consumption of white sugar soared: "The combination of relatively low prices and historically high status proved to be unbeatable, and after 1880 white granulated sugar swept all competition aside. Farmers abandoned molasses and home-made sorghum, workers gave up molasses and brown sugar, and between 1880 and 1915 per capita consumption of white granulated sugar doubled" (1988, 33). My mother's baking reflects earlier baking traditions that relied heavily on molasses and brown sugar, but it also shows a growing reliance on and preference for refined products such as white sugar and white flour, which produced lighter biscuits, and the use of packaged ingredients such as chocolate chips.

Sweetness continues to characterize North American cooking. Barthes notes that North Americans consume about twice as much sugar as the French (1997, 20), and recent studies confirm that this trend has only increased since the decades of my mother's baking. For example, in their 2009 longitudinal study of eighteen recipes published in *The Joy of Cooking*, Brian Wansink and Collin R. Payne (2009) conclude that the average caloric count of recipes rose sixty-three percent between the 1936 and 2006 editions. As a comparison of the current Nestlé directions for chocolate chip cookies with my mother's 1970s version shows, recipes are calling for a greater use of high-caloric ingredients. Mom used shortening and brown sugar only, whereas Nestlé's recipe now calls for butter and includes both white and brown sugar. Significantly, the Nestlé recipe requires twice the amount of most ingredients as the earlier recipe, indicating the other trend pointed to in Wansink and Payne's study: growing portion size. On average, 2006 recipes in *Joy of Cooking* have about one fewer serving (1.1) than in 1936. Although serving sizes

LAURENE IN HER KITCHEN,
CHARLOTTETOWN, 1964

started to expand after World War II and continued to grow through the 1950s and 1960s, the biggest jump has been seen since 1996 (33.2%) (Wansink and Payne 2009).

GOOD FOOD FROM GOOD INTENTIONS

My mother and her friends relied heavily on food to nurture their families and to create contentment in their homes. Consistent with literature documenting the experiences of elderly women in Britain, New Zealand, Sweden, Thailand, and the United States, my mother and women in her circles believed "homemade food to be the basis of good health and an important aspect of caring for their family" (see O'Sullivan, Hocking, and Wright-St. Clair 2008, 65). Drawing on the foods and food practices of their own childhood, they consistently tailored familial and regional traditions that framed their baking to suit their own family's tastes. In this, they conformed to well-known patterns described elsewhere (e.g., Sydner et al. 2007; O'Sullivan, Hocking, and Wright-St. Clair 2008). In her examination of British women's conceptualizations of "good food," Anne Murcott draws on Nickie Charles and Marion Kerr's study (1988) as well as her own earlier analysis (1983b) when she concludes that women often privilege their family's tastes above all other considerations when producing food. She writes that "women are typically obliged to cater less to their own and more to their husbands' (and children's) tastes – an obligation that can conflict with the desire to provide food judged to be healthgiving." Thus, the women in Murcott's study report "a tension between food that is good for health and good for enjoyment" (1993a, 306). Faced with this conflict, they tended to value food that tasted good to their families over food that was "healthy" (Murcott 1993a, 308). Murcott suggests that part of the reason women privilege taste is their view that thinking about food's nutritional attributes belongs to a sphere beyond their personal day-to-day experience (1993a, 311). Food is not "good" if no one will eat it. Although Mäkelä reports that the tendency to prioritize men's preferences is "definitely weakening" (2000, 13), it was a central dynamic for us, and many other families, during the 1950s, 1960s, and 1970s.

CATERING TO TASTES

My mother is sick. I am only beginning to see how sick she is because she has hidden it so well. I know instinctively the cancer is back. In full force. Her energy, always boundless, is nearly gone; she isn't able to arrange the furniture or to unpack all the boxes in the house where she and my father have just moved. Yet she has a request: "I want you to make chow this weekend. Your father likes it." Over the weekend my husband, Peter, and I comply, buying a peck of green tomatoes and five pounds of onions. My mother sits nearby as we chop the onions into small pieces on the back step. The fumes are not as strong outside. We let the mixture sit in salt overnight and then boil it with sugar, vinegar, and pickling spices the next morning, bottling it just before we end what will be our last visit with my mother. My mother dies later that week, as far as I know never having tasted the chow she felt compelled to have us make for my father. It is her parting gift to him: he should have familiar meals even though she will no longer share them with him. But like the lovers' gifts in O'Henry's "The Gift of the Magi," my mother's chow is of no use to my father. After she dies, he does not prepare the evening meal of meat and potatoes he has eaten all of his life. It would take time and planning, neither of which he is willing to invest in something as mundane as eating. He lives on hot dogs he learns to cook in the microwave and on sandwiches made from sliced ham. In the spring the bottles of chow are untouched on the shelves of the basement cold room, covered with a thin layer of dust.

Chow

1 peck = 8 quarts

Cut up 1 peck of tomatoes small with 1 cup salt. Let stand overnight. Drain off and wash, drain off wash water. Put on stove with 2 quarts vinegar. When hot add 12 cups of white sugar, peel 5 pounds onions cut small and add to tomatoes ¼ package pickling spice in gauze bag. Cook until done (2 hours).

Gram Gillespie.

I see now, as I did not when I was growing up, that my mother's feeding of our family was a powerful expression of family dynamics. Patricia Allen and Carolyn Sachs summarize the findings of many studies when they state that "[w]omen's involvement with food constructs who they are in the world – as individuals, family members, and workers – in deep, complex, and often contradictory ways" (2007, 1). Moreover, the fact that control of food production and consumption is tied to issues of power and position is well documented (e.g., see Murcott 1983b; DeVault 1991; Julier and Lindenfield 2005, 4; Wilk 2006). My mother's gendered performance of foodwork made family roles, especially her own, tangible. It illuminated family structures.

In her classic exploration of feeding the family, Marjorie DeVault explores the organizing "logic" of women's foodwork; she writes that it is "a way of caring for others well that is central to the social contribution they make through their work" (1991, 87). DeVault emphasizes the complex ways women themselves are drawn into participation in prevailing relations of inequality (1991, 11): "As these women grew up, they learned, both from their own mothers and from more general ideas about what mothers *should* be, to participate in the social relations that organize the family work of feeding" (1991, 96). Beagan and colleagues suggest several ways in which women have justified this inequity, including their partner's higher income, ease and efficiency, and their responsibility for managing emotional issues in the family, all of which "may constrain their willingness or ability to perceive inequities" (2008, 656). Certainly, popular culture in the 1950s played a part in reinforcing the notion that food preparation was central to women's role in binding family ties. From Ma Perkins on the radio soap opera handing out wisdom over mixing bowls, to *Father Knows Best* and *Jackie Gleason and the Honeymooners,* where many scenes took place in the kitchen (Levenstein 1993, 103), the message was that feeding a family is women's work.

DeVault elaborates on the centrality of caring work to constructions of femininity: "It is not just that women do more of the work of feeding, but also that feeding work has become one of the primary ways that women 'do' gender" (1991, 118).[11] Similarly, Anne Murcott's 1983 study of thirty-seven households in South Wales argues that the cooked dinner symbolizes the home, a husband's relation to it, his wife's place in it, and their relationship to one another – and that, since women do the cooking, they do it as a service to their husbands, deferring to his tastes and fitting in with his timetable (Murcott 1983a, 179; see also Counihan 2004, 90, Allen and Sachs 2007, 9, and Sydner et al. 2007). Although all members of the family influence food choices, typically the husband's influence takes precedence. For example, in describing her research carried out in South Wales, Murcott writes, "It is striking how fluently women would talk not just of their own likes and dislikes but of their husband's preferences as well ... Part and parcel of intimacy is knowledge of others' personal idiosyncrasies" (1993a, 313). Marjorie DeVault's study of thirty households in the city and suburbs of Chicago, Illinois in 1982–83 also indicates that husbands' needs dominate (1991, 86). In fact, DeVault claims that the male presence at mealtimes is enough to increase standards of food (1991, 146).

My father's younger sister Peg recalls structuring her homemaking around her husband's preferences and work schedule. She tells me that she has few recipes from her own mother but estimates that she may have hundreds from her husband's side of the family. Learning to make the kind of food that her husband Bob enjoyed was part of her early efforts to become, as she describes it, "a very very good wife." During the many years of their marriage when Bob worked away from home during the week, Peg developed a routine that culminated with Friday's preparations for his arrival for the weekend. These included the baking of several items: "Every Friday morning I made at least three things, probably cinnamon rolls, biscuits, [and] Bob loved his chocolate cake ...

so I usually made a chocolate cake or a white cake with orange frosting for it or something like that and cookies" (Miller, Interview, 1999).

Peg's experiences reflect the complexities involved in how women negotiate what food to prepare for their husbands and families as well as how and when. DeVault writes:

> The work itself is defined in terms of service to others, and husbands' demands are given special force through cultural assumptions about appropriate relations between husbands and wives. What a husband insists on typically becomes a requirement of the work, and a woman who arranges the routine to satisfy her own preferences as well as his may simply be making her work more difficult. The fact that so many women frame these accommodations as 'choices' means that they are less likely to make choices more obviously in their behalf when the interests of family members conflict. In such situations, women seem to assume that they have made enough choices, and often come to define deference as equity (1991, 160–1).

Thus, even when a husband does not insist, his enjoyment or approval of a particular food or routine may be incentive enough for a woman to reproduce it. By taking into account her husband's preferences, a woman accommodates him at the same time as she appears to exercise her own choice (see Murcott 1983b, 87). Again, feeding one's family well, which includes feeding them what they, and especially the husband, want to eat, is part of what the woman defines as being a good wife and mother. In fact, Murcott notes that knowledge of her husband's food preferences reflects the very intimacy of their relationship (1993a, 313).

Much of my mother's work of feeding our family is organized around my father. We eat between 5:00 and 5:30 because Dad likes to eat when he gets home. It allows him an hour or so to work around the house, cutting the lawn or building his latest project, before leaving to attend an evening church meeting or sinking into the pile of paperwork he brings home every night from the office. We eat a rotation of economical cuts of meat or fish followed by something sweet for our main meal. Unless my father is away. Then we eat more casually, or more likely we go out. My mother loves to eat meals out, always at an inexpensive restaurant, where most times she orders a hamburger. Once my mother says that when she is on her own for supper she simply makes herself an egg. I am shocked by this revelation. We never eat eggs for supper.

She is keenly aware of my father's likes and dislikes, although she speaks only rarely of them. I am surprised on the day she rejects a recipe she sees in a magazine with the casual dismissal, "Your father doesn't like sour cream." I didn't know this. It has not occurred to me that my father dislikes certain foods. I have never seen him refuse anything. I thought he liked everything. My mother orchestrates meals around his tastes so well that he never has to refuse.

My mother's ability to feed my father well meant catering to his tastes and organizing our household around his schedule. It measured her success as a wife.

Mom subscribed to the Canadian women's magazine, *Chatelaine*,[12] for most of her adult life. It was full of articles and advertisements that reinforced the primacy of a wife's responsibility to feed and thus care for her husband. Directed at a readership of young married women, articles grouped under sections such as Fashion and Beauty, Housekeeping, Home Planning, Gardening, For You to Make, and Young Parents offered instruction on many aspects of domestic labour, including recipes to make for one's husband and children. Among the many examples from 1954, the year my mother married, is an occupationally themed series of ads placed by George Weston Limited, producers of biscuits, bread, cakes, and candies. The Weston ads extol the economic contributions of a woman to her country through the support of her family, and most notably her husband. At a time when Canadian women were challenging their return to the domestic sphere after their more public wartime contributions, these ads address women's tentative place in the labour market while affirming that their truest calling is to support their husbands in their work and to make them happy. Women are reassured that their domestic contributions are more than enough. Take three examples. In April 1954, *Chatelaine* ran a Weston's ad based on the fishing industry titled, "The First Mate." Prominently placed on the back cover, it showed a woman in a sou'wester with the following text: "Devout companion, indefatigable worker, fitting partner in marriage – the Canadian fisherman's wife is truly a man's first mate ... a partner capable of taking command of her family's destiny ... Her invaluable aid contributes mightily to her husband's endeavours as he helps further Canada's fishing industry, from the Atlantic to the Pacific ... Whether helping her husband in his daily work or instilling in her family the pride of decency and love of home, she is truly a first mate – to her husband and to her country." Weston's advertisement for the June issue, titled "One done ... One to go," depicts a young women entering her door and begins, "Five o'clock – one job done and one to go. Behind her is another day ... ahead is her home and family. For she is the modern wife whose skill and effort in office or plant is helping to build two big projects ... The Canadian Future and the Canadian Home ..." The ad goes on to assure readers that this wife, recently married and still childless, spends evenings with her husband dreaming of a future life that "their present labours will make come true. The house they will own ... the garden they will tend... the children they will educate and watch grow ... Canada is a working country ... and women stand side by side with their men to see that work is done" (75). A final example, from the October issue, focuses on farming. Titled "Under Her Wing," it begins: "Worthy wife ... devoted mother ... partner in progress, ... colleague and companion – the farmer's wife is all these, and more ... Her active dawn to dusk co-operation provides the vital team work that her husband needs in his essential job of feeding his family and the nation" (37). These few examples hint at how pervasive in popular culture during my mother's early years of marriage was the theme of supporting one's husband in his undisputable role as head of household.

Although my father's schedule and tastes were the primary factors that influenced my mother's food management, they were not her only considerations. She identified and reproduced favourite foods for the rest of us as well. Although I am no longer able to ask her how she managed to satisfy our competing tastes, women interviewed by DeVault and Murcott, as well as my mother's own friends, offer clues. They reflect a complex knowledge of family members' preferences when speaking of their baking. For example, Anne Green, my mother's high-school friend, indicates how changing family tastes shaped the evolution of her Christmas baking:

> I always make four or five pies. But I put them in the freezer. And I cook them just before Christmas. I usually make a couple of mincemeat, a couple of apple and a cherry. That's [my son] Gerald's cherry ... At one time I used to make a light and a dark fruit cake and I'd make a cherry cake. I mean when [my husband] Ralph was living, he loved that stuff. But I don't have any children that like fruit cake. No. They don't like squares. I mean my daughters-in-laws do but my sons don't eat many squares (Green, Interview, 2004).

She notes that, the previous year, her Christmas gift to one of her daughters-in-law had been a box of home baking.

Like other women of her generation, my mother worked within the parameters of my father's preferences to produce food that satisfied the individual tastes of her children (see DeVault 1991; Murcott 1993a; O'Sullivan, Hocking, and Wright-St. Clair 2008). I have clear memories of Mom baking marble, cherry, and mocha cakes at my request. My sister Cathy may have been less vocal about her preferences, because now she can remember Mom making only one dish especially for her: a strawberry graham wafer dessert (Cathy Tye, Interview, 1999). Most frequently, Mom catered to my brother Mark, who had the narrowest tastes. As a very particular eater, Mark presented the greatest challenge to my mother's aspirations to socialize her children (e.g., see Shuman 1981, Mäkelä 2000, 11, Counihan 2004, 147) and to please her family through food. Even though Mark's refusal, or disinterest, in what Mom served him was not a wilful rejection of family values, it disturbed my mother. As Counihan writes, "Because eating was a form of acceptance and connection, refusing to eat communicated powerful messages of rejection or distress" (2004, 148). Helen Farrow, my mother's friend and next-door neighbour, substantiated my memory of Mom being worried that Mark would be hungry. Helen recalled, "she was always so concerned about Mark not eating" (Farrow, Interview, 2003). Like women who figure in other food studies (see Counihan 2004, 150), Mom struggled to indulge his preferences even though it meant extra work for her. My sister Cathy remembers that she eventually shaped most of her baking around Mark's preferences. Everything Cathy recalls Mom making – cinnamon rolls, ginger snaps, chocolate chip cookies, peanut butter squares with chocolate on top, and brownies – was primarily "for Mark." This is a phrase she repeats three times as she tries to conjure up memories of the baking that surrounded her growing up. In the end, the child with the narrowest tastes had the largest role in shaping our mother's baking and the family's food consumption. Although I do not remember any family conflict arising from Mom's efforts to cater to particular preferences, especially Mark's, Cathy's recollection reflects how contested and politically charged this terrain might become if not skilfully manoeuvred (see Long 2000, 155). It also underscores the findings of many studies that point to the complexities of women's foodwork: typically, women's primary responsibility for feeding their families cannot easily be translated into either total control or total subservience (see Charles and Kerr 1988, McIntosh and Zey 1989).

With effort, my mother combatted Mark's refusal to eat, eventually finding items that he enjoyed. A recipe for chocolate chip squares has "Mark likes this" scrawled in my mother's writing across the top. This annotation, like a child's gold star from a teacher, is a mark of success, undoubtedly earned after earlier failed attempts. When Mark came home empty, Mom filled him up with sugar in the form of cinnamon rolls, chocolate chip cookies, and chocolate chip squares.

Chocolate Chip Squares

1/3 cup shortening

1½ cup brown sugar

2 eggs

1 tsp vanilla

1 cup flour

1 tsp baking powder

½ tsp salt

½ cup chocolate chips and walnuts

9" pan. 350 for 30 min.

Helen Farrow

Because the food Mom baked for us had connections with an earlier time, a more rural lifestyle, and her own childhood, it had a homeyness that we all interpreted as lending healthy connotations, if not ingredients. In reality, as children, my brother, sister, and I relied largely on sugar to appease both our hunger and our mother's fear of our hunger. In the evening, biscuits with jam and a cookie sent us to bed full.

One of my earliest memories is sitting next to my mother on a church pew. I spend lots of time in church pews as a young child. We're in a church service and my father is at the front, talking. I'm sitting with my mother's brown leather draw-string purse beside me. It's filled with peanut butter cookies, which my mother doles out as the service drags on. I sit quietly eating peanut butter cookie after peanut butter cookie. My mother apparently is less worried about the effects of my all-sugar diet than the danger of me making noise and drawing attention to us. I eat another cookie.

It is not uncommon for mothers to turn to sugar to comfort children (e.g., see Charles and Kerr 1988, Locher et al. 2005, 284); as my childhood memory of being placated with peanut butter cookies attests, sugar can quiet a family. Despite what we know about the energy-boosting effects of sugar, it also keeps children still – at least for a while. It makes people feel happy. As my grandmother would have said, "sweet stuff fills you up."

THE PUBLIC EYE

Recipes for food her family enjoyed were an important part of my mother's tool kit as a wife and mother. Her ability to work with those tools was judged largely by others she knew who made up her occupational folk group of mothers and wives. Although folklorists have not yet paid enough attention to domestic labour as a site of occupational folklife, anthropologist David E. Sutton's research on the food preparation of Kalymnian women demonstrates that baking can be an important means of displaying skill and intelligence (2001, 25). Speaking in the terms of occupational folklife, my mother's recipes made up part of the informally learned "expressive culture of the workplace" that she shared with other wives and mothers she knew. Baking was used by the community members as a measure of a woman's "status and membership in the work group" (McCarl 1986). Women in my mother's circle of female friends, engaged in their own efforts to feed their families well, assessed each other's work as feeders and nurturers with a keen eye. Unlike Sutton's experience of Kalymnians "constantly watch[ing] and comment[ing] on their neighbors' cooking" (2001, 25), however, the women's conversations I overheard as a child were not dominated by talk of food. Rather, supporting Laura Shapiro's finding that "unless food is their profession, [women] tend to take most culinary chores for granted and rarely go on at length about them" (2001, 48), my mother and her friends did not show an undue amount of interest in baking. Women were expected to be accomplished bakers, and only the exceptional stood out and were worthy of comment – whether by virtue of excellence or of ineptitude. The women exchanged recipes and sometime shared the results of their work – a cookie or square with a cup of tea or coffee – with friends and neighbours, but their continuous reassessment of one another was largely silent. Subtexts contained in the tastes and accounts of each other's baking and meal preparation helped them to evaluate each other's skills and to assign each a place on the ever-changing community "tally sheet" (Szwed 1966, 435). Decades after their shared experience as young wives and mothers, Mom's long-time friend Sadie Latimer, also the wife of a United Church minister, indicates how skilfully both the type of food my mother prepared and the way she served it was linked to my father's tastes. When I suggest that my mother was "a basic cook," Sadie immediately jumps to her defence. She counters with her own memory of my father's preferences: "I think a part of that was your father too that he liked the basic things: meat and potatoes ... He certainly didn't go in for fancy cooking. He liked his meat and potatoes. He liked his tea with his dinner. You know and he liked to have dessert. And apple pie would probably be a favourite. Yes, that's right. I think she certainly catered to your father" (Latimer, Interview, 2000).

Even though Sadie has only occasionally seen my father since my mother died, she accurately conjures his taste preferences from meals they shared together decades ago and from her memories of watching my mother work to meet those preferences. Sadie's comments reflect not just my mother's abilities but her own close observance of my father's tastes, indicating how women's surveillance of men's eating preferences extended beyond their own families.

My mother was sensitive to the scrutiny, as a story she used to tell reveals. It was an account of a time when she shared some of her freshly made pineapple squares with the milkman's helper.

Pineapple Squares

Blend and press in pan:
1 cup flour
1 tsp baking powder
¼ tsp salt
2 tbsp shortening
2 tbsp sugar
1 egg

Bake above mixture 10 minutes in 350 oven.

Remove from oven and spread with:
1 20 oz can crushed pineapple, drained

Combine and spread over the pineapple:

1 egg beaten
1 cup white sugar
1 cup coconut
1 tbsp melted butter

Bake 350 oven for 20 minutes or until set

Mrs. Wylie Phinney

(*Sweet Tested Recipes* 28)

The story of the pineapple squares was set on a Saturday morning. For several years, the timing of Mom's Saturday baking session coincided with the milkman's weekly collection. Often it was the milkman's assistant, Bill, who would be sent in to collect the milk money. When he arrived, Mom would give him a couple of cookies or squares, one for him and one for Dave, the milkman outside or in the truck. As my mother told the story,

One Saturday I had just finished making some pineapple squares so I asked him if Bill would like one of these pineapple squares. "Oh yes," he said, "Great, two or three." If I ask him, sometimes he will say that he wants two or three or whatever but anyway I just give him two. And I presumed that one was for him and one was for Dave. So, anyway, he just took these two squares and out he went. Now, Bill also spends a great deal of his time at the rink and I was

up watching Mark play hockey this particular night and on the left
of where I was standing were parents of one of the boys that was
also playing and on the right was another parent. I was surrounded
by these people. And anyway, Bill comes around. He always stands
around me, if I'm at the rink. He'll put his arm around me and he
often asks Henry for money to go buy pop or something. [*Laughs*]
He was laughing and talking so I said to him, "How did you like
the pineapple square?" And he said, "Oh I liked it," but he said,
"Dave, oh Dave got awful, awful sick." And then he went on to
say how he had thrown up all over the place and how sick he was
all this day ... Well, my soul, this couple standing beside me, well
she laughed and then she looked at me and I felt so embarrassed,
thinking that these people thought that my cooking was so terrible
[*laughs*]. And Bill was making it worse with each sentence. So anyway, the next week I guess it was, I went into the cafeteria to buy
some milk for our office and Dave happened to be there and Bill.
So I went over to Dave and I said "Look I apologize, were you
sick from eating that square?" And he said, "What are you talking
about? What square?" So I proceeded to tell the story and he
laughed and he said, "Bill never even gave me a square." He said,
"He ate the two of them right in front of me and I could smell
them." And he said, "Did they ever smell good." And he said,
"In fact he's never given me anything to eat anytime you've ever
given him anything." So I thought, "Oh my soul." So each time
I see this Dave we joke about the pineapple square. And not only
that, I was pretty quick to tell those parents that this was just a
joke on the part of Bill and that Dave wasn't sick at all (Laurene
Tye, Interview, 1986).

The humour my mother found in this story speaks to the public
dimension of feeding one's family well. As noted above, my mother's

success at feeding her family, and thus her success as a mother and wife, while taken for granted by her own family, was judged by those around her. Åsa Elstad's work on Norwegian fisher-farmer families rings true here: "The woman's prestige rested first and foremost on the household's dependence on her work, the daily responsibility for keeping people and animals, and the production of food and clothes ... The women were not only dependent on the status of their husbands. The management of the household, especially of cooking, also decided what prestige the holding had in the parish" (1999, 23). Although Bill did not seriously damage my mother's reputation, he played with the knowledge that in this small town women were judged by their culinary skills. When he called into question the quality of my mother's baking, he challenged her standing as a good wife and mother.

During my childhood, children had an important role in shaping women's reputations as good cooks. Although the recipe for my mother's chocolate chip cookies probably came off the back of a chocolate chip package, or was adapted from it, for some reason it could not be duplicated easily by others. Helen Farrow commented:

> Well, I've used the same recipe and they never turned out for me like they turned out for her ... The only thing that she ever told me was that she put all brown sugar like that recipe that's on the package. She said, "The only difference," she said, "I put all brown sugar in them." Now, I make them with all brown sugar but they don't turn out like hers. Hers were flat ... Whatever she did with them. Because I can remember her just plopping them on the pan and they'd come out just exactly the way that everybody liked them (Farrow, Interview, 2003).

As a result, the cookies, as Mom made them, became very popular among my brother's friends – even though, because I had grown up with an earlier recipe, I had no idea until I conducted by interviews with Mark and Helen that my mother's later version had earned such a reputation among a younger cohort of children. These cookies marked a symbiotic relationship between my mother and the children. Through the cookies, my mother extended her nurturing to my brother's friends who came to visit. Mark recalls: "I always think of those chocolate chip cookies and [my friend] Stephen. They were the best things in the whole world to him. He'd rather have one of those than anything in the whole world. He'd come down and I remember once Mom made a whole batch and sent them to his place. Even in university he thought about it" (Mark Tye, Interview, 1999). Chocolate chip cookies offered to visiting children were a material sign of my mother's acceptance of them. The cookies came to represent an important character trait that both my father and Sadie remember in my mother: acceptance of other people. Sadie comments,

> I very seldom remember your mother you know being critical of people and she could meet anybody. She had that knack. It didn't matter who they were from the lowest to the upper class, your mother would be the same with them. So then she always fit in with the crowd she was with because she, that was her. What you saw was what you got. And she was so friendly and outgoing. Not too many people have it.

She continues,

> I remember her telling me about this guy, the young guy that came to school and his hair was all dyed and frizzed up and she said, "You know, everybody criticizes those people but they don't fall out of bed and go to school. They get up and they have to work on their hair," she said. She made me look at it from a different angle,

that they had to put some effort into that. And she looked at that as effort and accepted it (Latimer, Interview, 2000).

The making and sharing of cookies for children was one expression of my mother's acceptance of others. At the same time, the children's enthusiasm for her cookies raised her status among mothers in the neighbourhood who, like Helen, the next-door neighbour, begrudgingly admitted their own inability to reproduce the quality of cookies she made from a simple commercially produced recipe. Finally, her notoriety among preteen children as a particularly good cook reflected well on my brother, whose pride in still audible in his voice when he recalls the cookies so many years later. Their popularity was a measure of his mother's nurturing.

INVISIBLE WORK

It's five o'clock and my father comes in the back door. He puts a paper bag with the remnants of his lunch on the counter beside the sink. He drops his attaché case in a corner behind the door. My father is home. The feeling in the air increases. It's as if everything is turned up a notch at the same time as the volume in the house is noticeably lower. No one speaks. My mother puts supper on the table within minutes of his arrival. The table is already set. My father sits down, now dressed in work clothes. Like every other night he eats quickly and quietly, sometimes without speaking to anyone. He holds his head in his hand as he eats supper, which is a familiar combination of meat and potatoes covered with chow. It is accompanied by biscuits and followed by a plate of cookies and squares. There may be a dessert, perhaps an apple pie. If my father does speak, it is of routine things: paint for the house, the yard work he will do, the time of his meeting at the church this evening. Nothing is revealed. He never comments on the food he eats.

His body language tells us he is too tired to care or too busy to notice. It doesn't matter.

Friends like Sadie Latimer and Helen Farrow appreciated how expertly my mother orchestrated the planning and preparation of food around my father's timetable and my brother's particular tastes, but this work went unrecognized within our family. Avakian writes, "Food preparation, like housework and what Micaela di Leonardo has called 'kin work,' is part of the invisible labour of women. Though absolutely central to our survival, it is what is taken for granted" (1977, 6). Ironically, given that Sadie can identify my father's preferences decades after she was introduced to them, they remain invisible to me. It is a mark of my mother's success: so well did she organize food around them, that Dad's tastes were never obvious. A second irony is that patriarchal middle-class gender constructions of my childhood that instructed my mother to feed her husband and children well in order to be a good woman, also taught us not to notice.[13] Our refusal, or maybe inability, to recognize Mom's work, meant that we did not acknowledge the food she prepared as a gift. Looking back, it is clear to me now that, although we saw it as trivial and inconsequential at the time, the food my mother served us and our responses mattered. Very much.

Only in retrospect does Mark have an appreciation of Mom's work and of the care she expressed through baking. As a child, he took it for granted, unaware either of the specific recipes she made for him or of the fact that his preferences shaped what the family ate. And, as he says, he didn't realize how much it meant to him. Perhaps unable to offer details about baking practices that were part of a domestic culture that he didn't fully belong to, my father now assesses my mother's work by her efficiency. She made cookies quickly: "[She'd] whip those batches up," he comments. As a retired administrator with his own reputation for organization and efficiency, my father appreciates these same capabilities in my mother, although because they were expressed in gendered, often domestic realms, I suspect that, like other meanings, my mother's capability as demonstrated in her baking is more evident to him in retrospect.

Interestingly, none of us in the family speak of Mom's baking as personally nurturing. As we reach back in memory to recall my mother's tastes, we also struggle to give her credit. Baking was part of the important yet largely invisible work that she performed as a wife and mother. In a cruelly ironic twist of patriarchy, the better the job my mother did in feeding the family, the more invisible her work became to us. We now have difficulty fully articulating its meanings. When asked to talk about Mom's baking a decade after she died, my father faced the dilemma of trying to honour the contribution he knows she made – not just to the children through the cookies that first come to mind – but to him. Much of my mother's baking was done so that there would be biscuits for my father to have with supper or to eat before bed. He liked pie for dessert. Squares and other items that were easily packed allowed him to have something sweet as he ate lunch at his desk. Only after pointing to her baking for children does my father reminisce about dishes that were meant more particularly for him: squares that were made to take to a social event, for company who might drop in, or for my father's lunch bag. He recalls:

And then squares. There'd be some square with chocolate on the top of it. I can remember that. Basic, standard. And there was mint or something or other, mint frosting on it, green. But there'd be squares, pans of squares. Not a big variety of them. There were two or three different kinds. One always had a chocolate covering on it. And it was … good … And another had some frosting on it that had some green in it. I don't know why I [remember this].

That appeared regularly because it was supposed to be attractive. And as I say the peanut butter and the chocolate cookies were regular. And then pies. The apple pies. She'd whip up a pie. There wouldn't be too many lemon. Apple was the staple. And cinnamon rolls. Biscuits (Henry Tye, Interview, 1999).

Dad wants to appreciate the food that was made especially for him, but in part he struggles against the masculine self-image he has perfected over his lifetime. He sees himself as above such mundane considerations. It's just food, after all.

Although my father's lack of attention to Mom's meal-planning undoubtedly relates to the gendered role constructions of his generation, I confess that I shared this disinterest. I also impatiently shrugged off Mom's questions about what to have for supper or what to bake on Saturday morning. I, too, told her it didn't matter. Now, I know that it did. Only in retrospect do I appreciate the effort my mother put into providing us with what she understood as "good food." My father now knows this too. "Do you remember the strawberry pie your mother used to make that was so runny, the juice went all over your plate?" he asks me after my mother died. Long-ago tastes like that of strawberry pie take on new meaning. They are elusive, like memories of the times they represent. "Other people don't make that," he assures me. I nod in agreement, reading his subtext: "Like her strawberry pie, your mother was special. Our family is special." After I know that my father misses the pie, I find that I miss it too. Every summer I bake a pie for us as soon as strawberry season arrives. Working without a recipe, I make a filling of strawberries, flour, and sugar and cook it in a pie shell. I do this without speaking of the pie's meanings. On the surface it's just fresh strawberry pie, because it's strawberry season, but for both my father and me the taste of that strawberry pie is a tangible connection to my mother and to the family we were when she was alive. It reminds me of Clara Sereni's claim, when speaking about her novel in recipes, *Keeping House*, that her interest in cooking and food was as a form of caring (Jeffries 2005, 5). My mother's baking, made more powerful by the recognition that it was an activity she did not enjoy, was an expression of her care.

My father has come to deeply value my mother's nurturing since her death; in fact, he has elevated it in his memory such that she has become the perfect wife and mother. "It's quite something," he reflects proudly, "how when we married your mother moved away from her family and her village to follow me to remote Cape Breton where she didn't know anyone. That was quite something when I think of it now. I took her away from her family." He marvels that she left the familiar to follow him into the unknown; but the food she prepared for us, the tastes that came to define our family, reveal that rather than being "taken away" from what she knew and valued, she took her past with her. Baking was one means by which she passed on lessons from her rural, working-class childhood, establishing them as cornerstones for another generation.

* * *

My mother's baking reflected how she understood and enacted her role as nurturer within our family. Like other women of her generation, her work in feeding her family well was an important expression of her care for us. So familiar were the tastes in my mother's kitchen cupboard, however, that only recently have I reflected on how she constructed that task. Much of the baking my mother did as a nurturer was connected to the food she ate as a child and, more generally, to regional baking traditions. In our house "good food" was homemade: it was familiar and it was rooted in the baking traditions of my mother's youth. Through a reinterpretation of familiar biscuits and molasses cookies, she passed on to her children cultural values, such as economy and self reliance, as well as personal values, such as the importance of accepting others. Food was sweet, and in a reflection of wider trends, it grew sweeter over time. The fact that there was always lots of baking on hand made its presence all the more reassuring. Variation was tailored to individual tastes. And, although much of the food my mother produced was structured around my father's tastes and schedules, it was also made with a careful eye to other family members' preferences, especially those of my younger brother, who was the most particular eater. In catering to specific tastes, she gave pleasure to our family and made coming home a more welcome event. At the same time, that tailoring to individual likes and dislikes shaped what the family ate and ultimately created our family tradition (see: Long 2000, 147, O'Sullivan, Hocking, and Wright-St. Clair 2008, 70).

The power of this everyday baking shows that it is not just at special occasions – Christmas or Sunday dinner – or even at structured meals, that family tradition is forged and family identity articulated. While the importance of festive meals is well documented (e.g., see Long 2000, Mäkelä 2000, O'Sullivan, Hocking, and Wright-St. Clair 2008, 72), as is the shared family meal (e.g., see DeVault 1991, Lupton 1996, Mäkelä 2000, Bentley 2002, Counihan 2004, 121), everyday food that may be eaten outside of structured meals is less appreciated. Yet our family's experience shows that it can provide a key metaphor of well-being (see Sutton 2001, 27). Although my father, sister, brother, and I never fully appreciated the careful orchestration or labour behind the containers full of fresh baking, and thus the nuanced ways in which my mother cared for all of us, when we opened that kitchen cupboard, when we tasted those biscuits, cinnamon rolls, or chocolate chip cookies, we knew we were home. They welcomed us like old friends, reminding us in their tastes of who we are.

CHURCH LUNCHES AND LADIES' TEAS

Pineapple Cheese Dessert

½ cup graham cracker crumbs
2 tbsp butter
Leave 2 tbsp crumbs for top
Whip until fluffy
1 8 oz package cream cheese
½ cup icing sugar
Stir in 1 20 oz can crushed pineapple drained. 1 pkg Dream Whip. Mix with milk. Fold in last. Chill well.

Sadie

At the same time as she rushes to prepare supper, my mother takes a large mixing bowl down from the cupboard. In it she pours some melted margarine and stirs in crushed graham wafers. She is making a dessert for her women's church group. "I'm on lunch tonight," she explains. I am not sure I have tried Pineapple Cheese Dessert, but it is familiar to me. I have seen my mother make many fancy desserts like this: a fluffy filling on top of a graham wafer base. Its cloudlike texture is different from the everyday food our family eats, and its ingredients are exotic: crushed pineapple and Dream Whip. If I haven't already recognized the dessert's special status as an adult food for polite occasions, the graham wafer base clearly marks it. As I watch Mom fold pineapple into the whipped topping, I hope there will be some left over.

My mother spent many of her supper hours preparing food to take out to evening meetings. As she baked, she talked about the events of the day or of the past. She would laugh when she told me that my first sentence was "*Daddy chuuch*." Apparently, by the time I was a little more than a year old I would use this phrase to account for my father's continual absence, no matter where he might be. "*Daddy chuuch*," I would say with confidence whenever anyone asked. My mother was amused by my insistence, especially when my father was standing beside me, but generally I was not far off the mark. He often was at church, attending an endless schedule of committee meetings, related to both administration and programming. His volunteer commitments outside the church took him to more meetings: Home and School in Parrsboro; the Protestant Orphanage and Addictions Services in Charlottetown; and Minor Hockey in Amherst. After we moved to Amherst and his position as a church administrator necessitated travel to churches throughout Atlantic Canada, his community work lessened. When he was in town, however, church obligations still filled his time. As we ate our evening meal, my mother would routinely ask, "Henry, what time are you going out?" The assumption was that my father would not be home.

In truth, the lives of both my parents were structured by church and community events. My mother was often out as well. When I was growing up, my weeknights were usually spent with babysitters until I was old enough to take on the responsibility of caring for my younger sister and brother. Occasionally, Mom went with friends to a social event: a play, for example, or her bridge club. But, like my father, she found that most of her evenings and many of her weekends were taken up with community and church work: meetings to establish education for Deaf children in Charlottetown or to create a Headstart kindergarten program for economically disadvantaged preschoolers in Amherst. Most often, however, she was at "*chuuch*" or, more accurately, was doing church work. In every place we lived she sat on church committees, sometimes leading youth groups and always actively supporting the United Church Women's group, known as the UCW.

Many of these meetings, as well as most community and church events, required that she bring food. In light of this, it is not surprising that her recipes – Jam Filled Squares, Banana Squares, Strawberry Jell-O Squares, and Pineapple Brownies – speak loudly of what it meant to her to be a church woman in general and a minister's wife in particular. Like my childish "*Daddy chuuch,*" these recipes reflect the centrality of the church to our family's life at the same time as they point to the gendered work that my parents performed there. They show how important church gatherings were to my mother's production of food, both in terms of the food events she supported and for her acquisition of recipes. In the following pages I examine recipes that she learned and made from *Tested Sweet Recipes,* a fund-raising cookbook created by members of a women's church group in the late 1950s. These recipes, which formed the basis of her lifetime production of social food, help me consider how my mother's baking for church and community events articulated an idealized vision of a particular period and of women's place in it. Although church gatherings had benefits for women, some of which I explore in the next chapter, first I consider them as sites of disciplinary power and of women's labour.

FEEDING THE UNITED CHURCH

The United Church of Canada, the church my parents supported and my father's employer, was created in 1925 through the union of what were then the main Protestant denominations: Presbyterians, Methodists, and Congregationalists.[1] From its inception, the United Church embraced an ecumenical and socially liberal ideology. Scripture was not interpreted literally. The commitment of the United Church to social justice and inclusion have led some, including my father, to refer to it as "the New Democratic Party at prayer."

The United Church is the largest Protestant denomination in Canada. Although the 2001 census reported that approximately 2.8 million Canadians, or 9.6 per cent of the population, identify their religion as the United Church, during the decades when my mother was active as much as 25 per cent of the population had a United Church affiliation. Shirley Davy writes about the popularity of the United Church particularly, and of organized religion more generally, in the postwar years: "Between 1945 and 1966, the United Church built 1,500 churches and church halls, and 600 manses. Unlike the period of cynicism and disillusionment that followed World War One, the years after World War Two saw a renewed interest in the old Canadian values and in traditional doctrine. Parents who had shown little interest in the church prior to the war were sending their children to Sunday School and finding their own way back into church life" (1983, 48–9).

Davy credits this commitment to organized religion to a desire for normalcy that characterized the period and resulted in an atmosphere of social conformism (1983, 49). As my father remembers it, the majority of Protestant families in the communities where he has lived had an affiliation with the United Church. Beyond that, he recalls that in the 1950s and 1960s almost every family had some religious association, so that even if women my mother knew were not directly involved in United Church activities, they were connected, even peripherally, to other churches.

Women made many of their contributions through the United Church Women, or UCW, a group created in 1962 through the amalgamation of the Woman's Missionary Society and the Woman's Association. Paralleling the church's organizational structure, at least when my mother was active, the UCW was made up of "units," small groups of women who met monthly either in the church parlour or in each other's homes. When all of a congregation's units came together, it was referred to as a meeting of the general UCW, or more typically just as "General." I remember my mother occasionally attending regional or provincial meetings, but most of the work of the UCW was done at the congregational level.

An important way that UCW members furthered the life and work of the church was through their provisioning of food. As in-house caterers, they carried out work that included both social and fundraising events, ranging from receptions after Sunday service to church suppers and afternoon teas. Many of my mother's recipes, like the loaves and fishes of the biblical parable, could be cut into seemingly countless pieces and made to "go round." My memories are close to those of Daniel Sack, who begins his book on food and American Protestantism with the statement: "When I was young, church meant food" (2000, 1). Sack goes on to recall several food events, from after-church coffee hours to fundraising suppers, prompting his claim that "[i]t is hard to imagine popular American Protestantism without food" (2000, 3). Sack argues that this connection with food is an historical one: Protestant churches were built and sustained around food (2000, 2)

Just as my mother's production of food for a family was a significant way in which she "did" gender, the amount and kind of food she made for church events was another mark of her successful womanhood. It was important both to contribute and to be asked to contribute. When

LADIES IN THE CHURCH KITCHEN, PARRSBORO,
c. 1960

I talked to my mother's best friend, Anne Green, about women's church work, she told me of an elderly woman in her Presbyterian congregation who was insulted when she was no longer solicited for food: "I've got two or three older ladies [on my list to call for donations of food] and I think you come to an age that I shouldn't be calling them. I was embarrassed to be calling them. And did one woman complain. She said, 'Nobody is calling me.' She said, 'I can always get cans of things'" (Green, Interview, 2004).

Anne explained that the offended woman was referring to the canned meat or fish needed for sandwich fillings. Even if she could no longer bake for or serve at church functions, it was important to her that she

BAKED GOODS READY FOR SERVING AT AN ANNIVERSARY PARTY,
EUREKA, c. 1978

still contribute to the church women's food production. DeVault argues that it is not women's personalities or skills that suit them for the role of homemaker, but rather that they are continually recruited, whatever their psychological predispositions, into participation in social relations that produce their subordination (1991, 13). This point applies to women's feeding of the community as well as the family: with no woman "off the hook," my mother and others of her generation produced enormous amounts of food for a whole host of church occasions. In fact, the church's insatiable demand for food is a point that all my mother's friends raised when I talked to them about their baking. Anne commented, "Every time you turn around there's a funeral reception or there's something ... We have soup and dessert luncheons (Green, Interview, 2004). Mom's friend Helen Farrow joked about her experience in the United Church: "The church is really good for eating [laughs]. I hear them talking all the time, 'My goodness we can't do anything in this church without eating' " (Farrow, Interview, 2003).

I am a guest at my mother's UCW unit meeting. Valentine's Day is approaching, and as a folklorist I am on the evening's program. The plan is that after a short business meeting I will talk for about twenty minutes on the origins of Valentine's Day to the dozen or so women who make up this unit. As I look around I see that, with one or two exceptions, the members are elderly. In fact, I know that this is why my mother has chosen this unit. She has told me that they needed a younger person to help with their work – and besides, she says, she enjoys the older women. As I wait for the business meeting to conclude, I am struck by how quickly the women volunteer for the various requests that are made: We need two members to serve lunch after church next Sunday; we need two pans of squares for General; who can supply lunch for our next unit meeting? The women respond immediately: "I will do it," says one elderly women, offering to serve at the church luncheon; "I'll look after that," says another in response to the request for squares. I am not used to this. In the academic committees I belong to, things proceed differently. One must wait for a requisite period of silence to pass, often followed by a direct request to one of the participants: "Do you think that you could do this for us?" To my amazement, these women do not list the many reasons why they cannot help out, as my colleagues and I do. Before one of us agrees to take on anything new, we normally play a competitive round of "I am busier than you," a game where we go around the room, each of us listing the many obligations that weigh us down in a bid to top the others and thereby buy our way out of the current task, or at least lessen our sense of obligation to take it on. We publicly reaffirm how busy, and therefore how important, we are. The person who eventually, and often reluctantly, agrees, emerges as both the loser and the winner: burdened with a new responsibility but also having gained moral capital within the group. The UCW women do not engage in this competitive mode of decision-making; they quickly and apparently eagerly offer their help. I feel no sense that the chosen volunteer is not the winner; nor is any evasiveness or feeling of guilt publicly displayed by the others. This level of willingness to come forward is new to me. For a long time afterward I remember the women's quickness to volunteer, and puzzle over it. Are these women of an earlier generation even more susceptible to the social pressures than the younger ones I work with? Or are they more generous spirits?

Characteristically, church women volunteered. Well beyond my mother's UCW unit, church women readily offered to make and serve food for church events; this was part of how they supported their churches and their communities. Helen Ward told me that the women she knew never minded volunteering. She traced the decline of her own church to the moment when the women could no longer bake:

> We always had a Strawberry Festival. And we always had suppers in our church. That was even before we had the basement [hall] and that was when the hall was on the side. And everybody baked for it and never thought anything about it, you know. But then in the last few years we couldn't even have a supper. There aren't enough people in the community to bake or to do the work. They were all getting older and not able to do the things. But we always baked for the church (Ward, Interview, 2004).

Catered receptions, suppers, luncheons, dessert parties, teas, and garden parties make up a fund-raising complex that literally kept churches going for generations; many, like the Wesley United Church in Helen

Ward's account, have been forced to close their doors when women are unable to orchestrate these events. Perhaps for this reason, after her marriage to Presbyterian minister Ewan Macdonald in 1911, author L. M. Montgomery became critical of churches that depended too heavily on this kind of female-led fundraising. In a journal entry for 23 July 1924 she laments the state of one of her husband's churches: "Zephyr had its garden party tonight. I spent the evening washing dishes for the gorging crowds, inwardly resentful of the fact that I must waste my time thus, when I had so much work to do of my own. A church that cannot pay its way without an annual garden party is a farce" (1992, 196).

Despite Montgomery's reservations, congregations throughout Canada depended on their women members. In her examination of the UCW, Shirley Davy emphasizes the group's importance to the sustainability of churches: "The money contributed by women's groups to their congregations is generally thought of as 'secondary' income. There is ample evidence, however, to show that several of our churches were built, and are sustained, by women" (1983, 30). Davy refers to a church in British Columbia that was financially dependent on the UCW for fifteen years, and to another in Manitoba that took out a $10,000 loan during the Depression and made annual payments of $750 to pay off the large debt on the church building. As she describes, "churchwomen across Canada write that the funds they've raised have been *essential* to congregational life; paying the minister's salary; building, buying, renovating, furnishing and insuring the church and manse; purchasing pews, hymn books, Sunday School materials; paying off debts; and paying for emergency repairs made necessary by such natural calamities as fire, flood, hail and wind" (Davy 1983, 30). From old minute books, Davy cites examples ranging from supporting the minster's salary to paying the church's oil bill and making an overdue mortgage payment (1983, 30). Her view is shared by my father, who comments that, in his own experience, "The UCW kept churches going" (Henry Tye, Interview, 1999).

Shirley Davy stresses the remarkable accomplishment that this level of financial support represents, given that women had no capital of their own. Instead, they raised money through ingenuity and the expert use of their domestic skills, which included hosting food-related events. My mother's recipes show, however, that in terms of foodwork women of her generation built and sustained churches through the production of a particular kind of food and the orchestration of specific food events; as Vincent Miller, drawing on Bourdieu, reminds us, distinction is both a system and an activity (2004, 150).

TESTED SWEET RECIPES

Searching for something new to bake for my son Callum, I pick up a well-worn community cookbook that has my grandmother's name scrawled inside the cover. As I flip through the pages I am struck by the faint scent of her kitchen. It is a slight volume, only forty-four pages of recipes for breads, cookies, squares, cakes, and desserts. The cookbook's technology dates it; the recipes were typed on a typewriter rather than a word processor and then duplicated on a Gestetner or mimeograph machine rather than a photocopier. Its cardboard cover has a hand drawing of a gingerbread man in a chef's hat with the title, *Tested Sweet Recipes* across the top and the words "The Friendly Group of Trinity United Church, Parrsboro, N.S." underneath.

Clearly, my mother was part of the women's church group known as The Friendly Group that produced the collection. She contributed several recipes: Date Nut Drops, White Cookies, Egg Tarts, Banana Cup Cakes, Caramel Squares, Coconut Squares, Fudge Icing, Cherry Cake, Lemon Sponge Pie, and One-Half Hour Pudding. As I flip through the recipes, I notice that they look vaguely familiar. Many – including some of Mom's own – are annotated in her handwriting with the comments "Good" or "Real good," to indicate to her mother which recipes were the best bets. Stains and Xs reveal that my grandmother followed Mom's advice and tried many of the recipes. I decide to do the same. I begin by making Raisin Cake, followed by my mother's One-Half Hour Pudding. As I work my way through the collection I am startled to recognize these as the tastes of my early childhood, although I had long forgotten most of them. Later, when I find my mother's own copy of *Tested Sweet Recipes*, it is clear to me that it was used heavily. This is where she learned to bake, I realize. This was her training ground.

Patricia Storace writes, "Every cookbook, more or less consciously, is a work of social history" (1986, 62). Increasingly, scholars have recognized that cookbooks reveal important cultural scripts (e.g., see Gabaccia 1998, Wheaton 1998, Neuhaus 1999, Theophano 2001, Zafar 2002, Robyn Smith 2008). In part because, until recently, only women capitalized on the fund-raising niche of the community cookbook (Bower 1997a, 137), even modest publications such as *Tested Sweet Recipes* represent rich sources for information about earlier women's lives (see Kirshenblatt-Gimblett 1987, Black 2006). Anne Bower urges that "[w]ith careful, contextualized reading we can glean from these texts much about how their women compilers saw themselves and projected their values" (1997, 137).[2] My father echoes Bower: *Tested Sweet Recipes* conveys meanings to him through both the type of food church women made and the manner in which they served it. He describes each recipe in the collection as "a reflection of each women's values" (Henry Tye, Interview, 1999).

Bower warns that, despite their usefulness, community cookbooks are not always accessible, for the stories they tell are often incomplete. She describes them as "communal partial autobiographies" (Bower 1997b, 30) in that they represent "a subtle gap-ridden kind of artifact, that asks its reader (at least the reader who seeks more than recipes) to

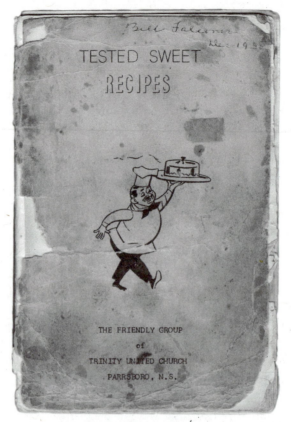

TESTED SWEET RECIPES

fill those gaps with social and culinary history, knowledge of other texts (such as commercial cookbooks), and even personal knowledge" (1997a, 140). My father helps to supply this needed context for me as he fleshes out my knowledge of the contributors. In the light of this supplementary knowledge, including my father's memories and the recollections of my mother's friends, *Tested Sweet Recipes* offers insight into the community of church women that my mother belonged to, offering clues to a range of experiences and attitudes that touch on class, modernity, gender constructions, and religious belief.

My father claims to remember the production of *Tested Sweet Recipes* well, which he estimates to have been in 1958 or 1959: "It was made during our time, when we were in Parrsboro. I typed all the typing in that with two fingers and ran it off on my Gestetner. This was out of our Gestetner and stapled together. We produced it and they sold it" (Henry Tye, Interview, 1999). He describes the cookbook as one of several projects that would bring together women of this congregation. As my father recalls, women gathered regularly for meetings of the Ladies Aid or the Woman's Missionary Society (later the UCW), but they also got together to plan church events, maybe a play or fashion show. The cookbook was an extension of these women's gatherings: "In those times all of the functions at the church concluded with refreshments or lunch. And so sweets were all brought by the women who attended those meetings and that's where these recipes would be brought, sampled, used, tested, and then vouched for and put in this book" (Henry Tye, Interview, 1999).

As the title, *Tested Sweet Recipes,* implies, sugar was as essential to the church women's baking as it was to the baking Mom did for our family, albeit in a different form. The cookbook comprises 146 recipes divided into the five categories of breads, cookies, squares, cakes, and desserts. In general, they call for more labour and expensive ingredients than the oatcakes my mother grew up with or the molasses cookies she served at home. They depend on refined products such as white flour and white sugar and use lots of eggs. The cakes, cookies, and loaves produced are not usually dark in colour but are light in both texture and appearance. Cookies are not quickly dropped on a baking sheet but are carefully cut out in neat shapes. They convey the message that food should be tidy and contained. There is no room for messiness here.

In his foundational work on sugar, Sidney Mintz (1985) links the rise in Western consumption of sugar with issues of social class; he stressed that to understand the social messages inherent in sugar one must consider both the form sugar takes and how it is used. Unlike the food produced for our family, which made use of molasses and brown sugar, recipes in *Tested Sweet Recipes* almost exclusively call for white sugar. In fact, "1 cup sugar" is the most common ingredient listed. White sugar appears in every recipe, either alone or in combination with brown sugar, molasses, or icing sugar. Less frequently, jam or a sweetened industrial food such as condensed milk or marshmallows is required. As in the following recipe for "Porcupines," white sugar is often referred to simply as "sugar" and is usually among the first ingredients listed. As noted in the last chapter, this is consistent with a worldwide trend that saw white sugar increasingly replace other forms, such as brown sugar and molasses, such that by the twentieth century modern cooks were relying almost solely on this form of sweetener (Levenstein 1988, 33).

Porcupines

2 eggs (well beaten)
1 cup white sugar
1 cup dates
½ cup walnuts
½ cup coconut
1 tsp vanilla
½ tsp salt

Enough flour to make stiff to roll in small balls, then roll in coconut. Bake in moderate oven until lightly browned (about 20 minutes).

Mrs. J.J. Chambers

(*Tested Sweet Recipes* 28)

For my mother and other church women, the food's meaning came from its sugar base in combination with the use of exotic and/or modern ingredients. Here the "exotic" was constructed through the addition of eight specific ingredients[3] that alone, or in combination, are present in over two thirds of the recipes: citrus (26 per cent), walnuts (25 per cent), raisins or dates (16 and 11.5 per cent, respectively), coconut and chocolate (each 15 per cent), cherries (10 per cent), and pineapple (9 per cent).

Orange and Raisin Squares

½ cup shortening
1 cup white sugar
2 eggs
1 cup raisins
1 whole orange
¾ cup sour milk
½ tsp milk
1¾ cup flour
1 tsp soda or 1 tsp baking powder

Put the raisins and orange through chopper, mix in usual method. Bake in moderate oven.

Mrs. Ralph Wasson

(*Tested Sweet Recipes* 29)

As in this recipe for Orange and Raisin Squares, ingredients were special but available, expensive but still affordable. Importantly, these tastes were strange enough to signal status but familiar enough not to be threatening. For example, citrus is called for in a variety of forms – fresh orange or lemon, lemon extract, or mixed peel or citron – in approximately a quarter of the recipes. Although citrus does not, of course, grow in Nova Scotia, it was a familiar imported product by the 1950s. Perhaps because it combines well with spices already common to Nova Scotian baking of this generation – ginger, cinnamon, and cloves – it became a popular add-in. Walnuts, raisins, dates, and coconut were also relied on heavily. Walnuts were used almost exclusively when nuts are called for in *Tested Sweet Recipes,* and often referred to by the generic term "nuts." Almonds decorate the tops of two fruits cakes, and almond extract is called for in six recipes, but no other nuts (such as pecans) appear. Walnuts would have been another familiar ingredient to Nova Scotian church women in the 1950s, having been a part of English cookery since at least the seventeenth century (Davidson 2002, 999) and brought by early settlers to the United States and Canada. At the time *Tested Sweet Recipes* was compiled, walnuts would have added contrast to a loaf or cake in both taste and texture without incurring great expense; they were an "add-in" that could be made to stretch. Walnuts are picked at various stages of development, depending on their use, but all the recipes in *Tested Sweet Recipes* call for ripe walnuts that had been shelled and sold in packages of half-kernels or broken pieces. If the pieces were too coarse, women would have cut them into smaller bits with a knife or a hand chopper.

Recipes such as Raisin Cake were also familiar to my mother and the other church women who grew up with the heavy use of raisins in baking.

Raisin Cake (My mother's note in margin: Good)

1½ cups raisins
¾ cup sugar
¼ cup butter

1 tsp soda (scant)
1 tsp cinnamon
1½ cups sifted flour
½ cup raisin water
1 egg well beaten
1 tsp nutmeg
¼ tsp salt

Simmer raisins for 20 minutes in enough water to leave ½ cup juice. Cream butter and sugar, add egg and raisin water, flour sifted with soda and spices. Add raisins dredged with flour. Bake at 350 1 hour. Ice with almond butter.

Mrs. Willis Canham

(*Tested Sweet Recipes* 35)

Dates and coconut were also well known. From the 1870s the Intercolonial Railway linked Maritime communities to American producers, and companies such as the United Fruit Company and Dole were major importers of walnuts, raisins, and dates. Coconut, and after 1895 shredded coconut, became a popular baking ingredient. Less frequently used, but also belonging to this category, were cherries and pineapple. Cherries were usually dried or candied, but they could also be fresh when in season or, sometimes, canned. Women relied on pineapple, most often in canned form, to add freshness and moistness to their baking, It was also candied in the case of fruit cakes. Like the other add-ins, pineapple would be considered special but not unfamiliar or prohibitively expensive. It was fancy but not strange.

The use of exotic and newly available ingredients in *Tested Sweet Recipes* marks the beginning of a period of rapid development and increased availability of convenience and industrial foods. I return to my mother's use of some of these convenience foods in the next chapter, but suffice it to say that they were beginning to make their presence felt in the late 1950s. For example, contributors to *Tested Sweet Recipes* made use of chocolate in the form of unsweetened squares or cocoa, as in this recipe for Brownies.

Brownies

¼ cup shortening
1 cup white sugar
1 egg
½ cup boiling water
1 tsp vanilla
1 cup sifted flour
1 tsp baking powder
1 tsp salt
4 tbsp cocoa

Cream shortening and sugar, add egg, dissolve cocoa in boiling water. Mix in usual method. Bake in moderate oven.

Mrs. Wylie Phinney

(*Tested Sweet Recipes* 25)

My mother, like her mother before her, relied on chocolate produced by Baker's Chocolate, an American company established in 1780 in Massachusetts. By the 1920s, Baker's Chocolate was available in a number of flavours, including blocks of unsweetened baking chocolate, a staple of my grandmother's.[4] *Tested Sweet Recipes* is clearly positioned at a transitional moment in the production of convenience foods, in that

THE UNITED CHURCH WOMEN SAY GOODBYE TO THEIR MINISTER AND HIS
WIFE AT A CHURCH TEA, CHARLOTTETOWN, c. 1967. LAURENE, THE GUEST
OF HONOUR, IS WEARING A CORSAGE.

only one recipe calls for chocolate chips. Again, as I will discuss in more
detail in the next chapter, chocolate chips became a mainstay of Mom's
later baking, especially that aimed at children. Although some recipes
call for Dream Whip, Jell-O, graham wafer crumbs and/or marshmallows, in the 1950s mixes or other convenience foods were not yet a
widely accepted part of home baking. These recipes are one indication of
how, as historian Margaret Conrad states, during the 1950s "the whole
fabric of Atlantic Canadian society was being rapidly altered" (1993,
384). *Tested Sweet Recipes* speaks to women's position at the intersection of the "two Atlantic Canadas," which Conrad describes in the
following terms: "one largely rural and isolated ... the other essentially

urban and fully integrated into mainstream North American culture" (1993, 382). It also reveals women's willingness to embrace modernity, and their desire to be part of a rising urban middle class. Working on Pierre Bourdieu's premise that "taste classifies and it classifies the classi- fier" (1984, 6), the women turned to recipes, such as raisin loaf, that drew on regional baking traditions but called for refined ingredients. A reflection of how the women wanted to see themselves and how they wished others to see them, such recipes were part of their presentation of an ideal self, or what Erving Goffman defined in his foundational work, *The Presentation of Self in Everyday Life,* as their "front," by which he means "that part of the individual's performance which regularly func- tions in a general and fixed fashion to define the situation for those who observe the performance" (1959, 22). The making and serving of this particular kind of baking was important to the women's performance of their middle-class femininity. In fact, their collective efforts might well constitute what Goffman termed a performance team, whereby a set of individuals cooperate in staging a performance (1959, 79).

According to Anne Bower, community cookbooks often reflect class concerns. In one charity cookbook she analysed, Bower reads tensions and anxieties about the authors' middle-class status: "The subtext of this 1909 recipe collection emerges from the selection and arrangement of recipes and foodstuffs, the vocabulary and tone of the recipes' lan- guage, the use of terms without explanation or definition, the decorative graphics, and the way recipe contributors are acknowledged. Even the advertisements at the back of the book participate in the textual projec- tion of a special middle class community" (1997a, 140).

Although the authors of Bower's text were Jewish women working to maintain hard-won middle-class Americanized status in the face of increased immigrant populations, charity cookbooks do represent a pub- lic forum for women to project an idealized image of home and self (see Ireland 1981). Just as in Bower's example, the twenty-one authors of

Tested Sweet Recipes emphasize their middle-class membership in several ways that contextualize the recipes they contribute. In identifying their contributions, the women highlight their marital status. The women sign their recipes using their husbands' names (all but one are married), so that my mother appears as Mrs. J. H. Tye. This form of identification immediately underscores the women's own social successes (they have achieved the social goal of marriage) and their authority (they have established skills as homemakers). They are wives, and these recipes come from their domestic experience. The names also speak loudly of social ranking, however, for women in the community outside the church group, the local audience for which this modest book was intended, would immediately recognize the husbands as the town's economic and social leaders. Significantly, as my father looks over the names of the contributors, he identifies the woman in all but three cases by her husband's occupation. His listing suggests that the families come from a cross-section of Parrsboro society and reflect both the town's history of shipbuilding, lumbering, and agriculture as well as its emergence as a modest mercantile centre. There are three farmers, two insurance salesmen, two bank managers, a beneficiary of "old money" made through lumbering and shipbuilding, a grocery store owner, a mechanic and garage owner, an electrician, an employee of the electric company, a lawyer, a sailor, a postmaster, a fisheries officer, a jack of all trades, and a politician who was also a furniture store owner and undertaker.

Dad's comments suggest the difficulty of identifying status solely on the basis of occupation, however, for at least some of the men were engaged in occupational pluralism; the most interesting combination being the politician who also operated a furniture store and a funeral parlour. But he also mentions a farm family whose income was supplemented by the husband's wages as a railway employee. Furthermore, in his role as minister, my father sometimes glimpsed his parishioners' private worlds, so that his brief introductions so many years later reveal complexities of people's lives that affected their respectability. His memories reflect something of the town's stratification: old money counted for more than new, and the few professionals were highly regarded. They also indicate something of the "tally sheet" mentioned in the last chapter that members in a small community maintain for each of their members (Szwed 1966, 435). One's position is never completely and solidly fixed; rather, it is constantly shifting. A family's reputation in the community would thus not be based solely on income, but would take into account character traits of both the woman and her husband. For example, Dad explains that one of the most successfully employed men was an alcoholic and that "no one knew how difficult it was for him," and as I look at his wife's recipe, I think "and for her." As he talks of another of the town pillars, who carried on a long-time extramarital affair, my father indicates how community members' assessments of each other would have been a careful balance of what they knew of an individual's private circumstances and that person's public persona. Personality and how one dealt with one's lot in life would also influence one's rating on the tally sheet. Dad refers both to women who he thinks flaunted their wealth and position and to those who did not. He also speaks of one woman at the lower end of the economic scale who, as he puts it, "managed to rise above" her husband's reputation as an unreliable worker.

Finally, the women staked out their middle-class position through the sale and display of thirty-seven ads. Many of the businesses were owned by, or employed, their husbands. Others, without apparent family connections, demonstrated the support of local shops and services: beauty parlours and barber shops, restaurants, and clothing stores. The slim volume is powerfully endorsed by the small town's commercial sector, lending credibility to the women's effort through association. The subtext is that the shared narratives of *Tested Sweet Recipes* belong to the town. Through their use of refined ingredients, their identification with the town's middle class, and their desire to speak for all residents of Parrsboro, the compilers of *Tested Sweet Recipes* support Jack Goody's observation that with the increasing dominance of the middle class, concern with status was "greatly aided by the use of printed books," especially "manuals of domestic behaviour including the ubiquitous cookbook" (1982, 152).

CLAIMING PLACE: MIDDLE-CLASS LADIES AND THE CULT OF DAINTINESS

Strawberry Jell-O Squares

2½ cup graham wafers [crushed]
½ cup butter

Bake 15 minutes at 350.

Top of stove:

1 tub strawberries (little juice)
½ cup white sugar
1 pkg Strawberry Jell-O

Boil together for 2 minutes. Stir well. Cool. When mixture is cool add 1 pkg Dream Whip (whipped stiff). Place all on graham wafer base. Store in fridge until ready to serve.

In the idealized middle-class vision articulated in *Tested Sweet Recipes*, and in my mother's recipe collection as a whole, women and men occupied distinct social roles. Based on a long cultural association of women with sweet foods or tastes (Mintz 1985, 150), and on working-class conventions that afforded men more than their equal share of the family's meat supply, such that women often made up for it with an increased consumption of sugar (see Reeves 1999), by the twentieth century sweet food was considered appropriate for women. It is an association that translated into the popularization of "dainty food": delicate and/or rich recipes filled with whipped cream and other calorie-laden ingredients that were deemed suitable for women (Inness 2001c, 54). Sherrie Inness argues that the cult of daintiness that became popular in the early 1900s had its beginnings in the new home economics movement, and that women involved in domestic science sought to conceal food: "In other words, the domestic scientists wished to transform food into something more ethereal – something suitable for women to consume … During a time of social upheaval, when Progressive Era middle-class women were demanding something more out of life than an eternal spot in front of the stove, dainty cooking assured people that women were still ladies" (2001c, 56).

My mother and her fellow church women joined others across North America during the 1950s and 1960s as they expressed their femininity through the production and consumption of dainty food,[5] which Inness describes as "[f]oods that were ornamental and ladylike – tea sandwiches, small decorated cakes, and gelatin desserts." She continues, "'Daintiness' suggested a whole feminine ethos about how women should look and act. It was also a way for women to distinguish themselves from men – who, at least according to the media, possessed an uneasy relationship to daintiness at best" (Inness 2001c, 55). Inness's characterization of the gendered nature of dainty food draws on the work of food historian Harvey A. Levenstein, who argues that the cult of daintiness worked to define women as distinct from men:

Women … were expected to like 'dainty' foods. These were normally prepared for women's luncheons and other functions where

hearty-eating men were not present ... Women's food ... reflected
the persistence of the nineteenth-century double standard and the
Victorian ideal of womanhood. It was dainty in taste as well as
quantity, for to have lusty tastes in foods seemed to betray a weak-
ness for other pleasures of the flesh as well. It was also expected to
display a certain degree of complexity – the "frills" that men dis-
dained or did not notice and women, with their higher aesthetic
sense, appreciated (1993, 35).[6]

Serving and consuming dainty food became an accepted statement of
middle-class femininity. As Inness claims, "The ability to provide a wide
selection of dainty and delectable dishes also served as a marker of a
family's class background, as a sign of middle-class tastes, since only
well-off people can afford to think about the taste and appearance of
foods" (2001c, 59). Daintiness costs money to achieve, and Michael
Symons attributes its popularity to the fact that it helped businesses
increase consumption: "Not surprisingly, the great promoters of daintiness ... were the modern food companies ... They could persuade
shoppers to ask for highly advertised embellishments like chocolate, desiccated coconut, custard powder and jelly. They could convince women
to accept a new role as consumers." (1982, 139, quoted in Inness 2001c,
57).[7] Sherrie Inness echoes this view, drawing on Thorstein Veblen's
foundational *The Theory of the Leisure Class* (1899), which described
how women's possessions gave status and prestige to their husbands
(2001c, 57).[8]

Daintiness did not find expression in my mother's baking through
recipes for oatmeal cookies, for as Sherrie Inness writes, "the dainty food
fad also sought to remove food from its plebeian beginnings and transform it into something more suitable for ladies" (Inness 2001c, 56).
Instead, daintiness was constructed by my mother and other church
women through dishes such as Strawberry Jell-O Squares. Through their
use of refined white sugar and refined white flour, with add-ins such as

walnuts and pineapple, marshmallows, and graham wafers, my mother and her friends expressed an acceptance of modernity that positioned them as middle-class consumers.[9]

Undoubtedly, the recipes in *Tested Sweet Recipes* were aimed at producing refined dishes even if, as Stephen Mennell points out, it is often much easier to recognize refinement in cookery than to define it (1985, 114).[10] They conform to the principles Bourdieu lays out when he writes, "The antithesis between quantity and quality, substance and form, corresponds to the opposition – linked to different distances from necessity – between the taste of necessity, which favors the most 'filling' and most economical foods, and the taste of liberty – or luxury – which shifts the emphasis to the manner (of presenting, serving, eating etc) and tends to use stylized forms to deny function" (1984, 6). However, the recipes do not set the bar so high as to be out of reach. *Tested Sweet Recipes*, and my mother's recipe collection in its entirety, presents a rather modest version of classed daintiness. "Exotic" foods such as citrus, walnuts, and dates, in addition to industrial foods such as graham wafers, were considered fancy but not overly extravagant. These ingredients were well within the reach of middle-class women of my mother's generation, especially given the small quantities required. *Tested Sweet Recipes* assured its readers that it was possible to be a lady, and then pointed the way. Judging from my mother's written comments in her copy of the cookbook, it is clear that she took the promise seriously. Her annotations support Jessamyn Neuhaus's view, based on the examples from the 1950s that she examined, that cookbooks not only represent what authors and corporations believed women should cook, but also offer clues as to how women interpreted cultural prescriptions and what they actually cooked (1999, 536).

Tested Sweet Recipes shows the importance of mentoring by experienced church women. Although nearly half the contributors submitted 1 to 5 recipes, the rest writing somewhere between 6 to 10, three women were responsible for 40 of the 146 recipes. Even though, when my father looks over the top contributors' names more than forty years later, he does so through a male lens, he describes two of the three as "older" than my mother and, in fact, one of these two as "considerably older."[11] His memories suggest that several older women shaped *Tested Sweet Recipes* through their knowledge of both how to make the dishes and what to include.[12] They would have introduced younger women, like my mother, to what Robert S. McCarl might term a "canon of work technique," that "body of informal knowledge used to get the job done" (1986, 72). At the same time as Mom acquired a canon of work technique as a young wife and mother in order to nurture her family in the way she aspired, she mastered a parallel canon that allowed her to function in public contexts. As McCarl notes, one of the features of a canon of work technique is that it "establishe[s] a hierarchy of skilled workers based on their individual abilities and exhibition of that knowledge" (1986, 72). Baking and other food preparation helped to create this hierarchy; through the making and sharing of food, women learned how church ladies should volunteer their time and talents and what form those efforts should take. The standards for these performances were exacting, as illustrated in two food events that provided important stages for the church women's gendered performances: the lunches that normally concluded all church meetings, and ladies' teas.

LUNCHES

Meetings ran the church. My parents got together with other church members to coordinate programming, plan fundraising, and address property issues. Men's groups, women's groups, and youth groups were part of larger local and regional networks that met regularly. And there were always special projects. As the church calendar moved from one season to the next, special days were marked: the men's winter ham supper; the Easter sunrise service; the women's Thanksgiving tea and sale; and the youth group's candlelight Christmas church service. In Parrsboro the church roof needed replacing. That undertaking paled next to a project in Charlottetown, where the congregation built a church hall. After the bank refused to extend a loan, members financed the building through the sale of bonds. It all took a lot of organization and many meetings. Dad recalls some of my parents' church work in Parrsboro:

> The church was the centre of social life and there was something at the church every night. There would be functions and they always had refreshments that the UCW put on. For instance, the Ladies Aid would meet once a month and the Woman's Missionary Society would meet once a month so there's two afternoons … And then they put on projects, like they always had a fashion show every spring so this would spread over a month so the planning committee would be together, go around to people's houses and … of course there was always the cup of tea in talking about these things (Henry Tye, Interview, 1999).

Hello Dollies

½ cup melted butter
1 cup graham cracker crumbs
1 cup coconut
1 small pkg chocolate chips
½ cup nuts
1 can Eagle Brand milk

Mix crackers and butter, pour milk over all. Bake 350 for 30 to 40 min.

The lunch that concluded meetings was by definition light fare, something to "tide you over" rather than a meal to fill you up. Generally, it consisted of one or two small courses: bread, biscuits or sandwiches followed by sweeter cookies, loaves, squares such as "Hello Dollies" or, sometimes, cake. Although the first course might be omitted, the second was a must. As it was designed to accompany tea, or sometimes coffee, lunch was most often food that could be eaten in one's hand: biscuits pre-sliced and spread with jam, or sandwiches made from store-bought bread with crusts removed and cut into quarters. Squares or slices of fancy loaves were common. These items could be consumed standing up or sitting down and, importantly, they could be served and then cleaned up easily so as not to significantly interrupt or prolong the meeting.

To some extent, the lunch that was served depended on the location, size, and nature of the meeting it was part of. It was also governed by community norms. As my father recalls, lunch in rural Cape Breton frequently consisted of oatcakes followed by cookies such as ginger snaps or molasses cookies (Henry Tye, Interview, 1999). These are the types of foods that Helen Ward also remembers being served for lunch at church and community meetings and functions in rural Pictou County in the 1920s and 1930s. Sandwiches and possibly oatcakes or tea biscuits were followed by sweets: "Date squares [or] it could be oatmeal cookies. One of the favourites that I make is Bachelor Buttons: rolled cookies put together with icing" (Ward, Interview, 2004). These recollections echo L. M. Montgomery's many descriptions of lunches that she prepared or was served in Prince Edward Island and Ontario. Montgomery's journal entry for 6 January 1925, detailing preparations for hosting the ladies' church group, could have been written by my mother or many of her friends several decades later: "Exceedingly busy, getting ready for Guild executive which meets here tomorrow night. I swept and baked cake, cookies and date loaf" (Montgomery 1992, 216).

As a Presbyterian minister's wife, Montgomery sometimes felt the strain of food preparations, as when she wrote on 11 August 1925 of a quilting bee: "I spent the forenoon making sandwiches and putting quilts in the frames in the church. This afternoon we had the quilting and served tea. It was a rather hard day and it can't be said I enjoyed any part of it" (1992, 243).

Of all the church's food occasions, lunch was the most informal. However, even seemingly impromptu lunches were governed by expectations and a set of standards. Lunches should consist of foods from the highest register of everyday food and, if they were collectively prepared, could be divided up according to each woman's speciality. For example, in outlining what usually made up lunch in Eureka, Helen Ward paused to recognize individual women's expertise: "Catherine, I think she makes the nicest oatcakes around here. I don't know where she got her recipe but she does make beautiful oatcakes" (Ward, Interview, 2004).

Just as with home hosting, public lunches were expected to exhibit quantity and variety. Ideally, even a modest lunch offered a choice of more than one food, and a pre-planned lunch for a large meeting was sometimes expansive. As a newly married minster's wife in 1949, Joan Colborne attended a World Day of Prayer meeting in a rural Prince Edward Island that was jointly sponsored by women of the United Church and Baptist Church:

> The Baptist ladies were hostesses and they served tea and *quantities* of food after the prayer meeting. The amount of food that people eat here on the island is simply prodigious. Do you know that the Ladies Aid here decided that too much food was being served so they limited the amount to *five* different kinds of food, and the person at whose home the meeting is being held has to provide it all. I am hesitating to invite the group to the manse until I learn to make five different kinds of things fairly well and certainly. Then

the Springfield West Women's Institute met on Tuesday night, of which group I am now a member. They have not limited the food there yet, we had seven different kinds (Colborne 2003, 48).

When Colborne hosted the Ladies Aid at her home approximately a month later, she wrote to her parents about the pressure she felt as a new homemaker to produce the required five foods that comprised "lunch" in this part of Prince Edward Island:

> Then on Thursday night I entertained the Ladies Aid. As that was my first real entertainment job it was quite a strain. I had to have the house looking fairly decent, and then according to the rules, I had to have five different things to eat. So we planned, sandwiches, Ritz biscuits with cream cheese and a slice of olive, brownies, macaroons and spice cake (2003, 63).

Colborne's experience of lunch supports Margaret Conrad's observation, cited earlier, that during the 1950s the Atlantic region was on a rapid journey toward modernity. Greater availability of ingredients in Maritime small towns and cities in the post-war years translated into more varied lunches, often made up of richer foods of finer texture that allowed more scope for the demonstration of expertise. They more clearly and confidently embraced the ideals of daintiness. My father remembers first encountering this more elaborate lunch after he moved to Parrsboro in the late 1950s. It was this lunch that became the source of and motivation for producing many of my mother's early recipes: "The meetings inevitably concluded with lunch and discussion of what was for lunch because that person would be baking their speciality or something and your mother would come with a recipe and then she'd say, 'I think you'll like this. And Saturday I'm going to make it.' So she was trying a wide variety of things" (Henry Tye, Interview 1999).

Learning early on in her married life how to produce a good lunch served my mother well, for these food events did not significantly change over her lifetime. Her friend Anne described lunches currently served at her church in Pictou County that are not substantially different than those my mother experienced in Parrsboro over forty years ago. Anne remarked that sandwiches are accompanied by "loaves and we'll make tea and coffee. We try to have cheese, maybe, cut up cheese and pickles. There's a lady that makes scones" (Green, Interview, 2004). Helen Farrow's comments also support the idea that lunches have stayed the same over the years; however, she does note that foods such as muffins or loaves have replaced those with an even higher sugar content:

> There's not as much along the sweet line, like say for General [meetings of the UCW] now, they either have sandwiches or maybe muffins or they would have sweet bread. But they would only have one thing. It wouldn't be the great big lunches that they used to have but they do have a lot of lunches at church, like you know quite often after church, you know right after church, they'll have something. They'll have a quick luncheon or something like that for some special little occasion (Farrow, Interview, 2003).

Health concerns over the last few decades may have modified lunches, such that muffins sometimes replace or accompany squares or cookies as an alternative, but the basic structure of lunch and its dependency on sugar has not been seriously challenged.

LADIES' TEAS

The foods, as well as the organizing principles of specialization and variety, that governed lunches reached their peak when the church women organized other food events such as wedding or funeral receptions, major fund-raisers such as church suppers, or ladies' teas.[13] Jean Colborne's letters through 1949 and 1950 demonstrate that lunches were part of a larger network of food events that included weddings, showers, and other church or community functions. For example, Colborne describes a wedding reception where fifty people sat down to "a huge supper of chicken and ham and salads and dessert, and at our table alone there were ten different kinds of cakes" (2003, 93). Likewise, Anne Green describes an elaborate selection of foods and speaks appreciatively of individual women's specialities in talking about the soup and dessert luncheons her church group currently hosts: "We have soup and dessert luncheons … this is a money raiser. And we have all kinds of desserts. We have maybe two kinds of soup. Well, I have a list of people to phone and what to get from them. And I usually make a rhubarb torte … And people wait for that rhubarb torte. You wouldn't believe. By the end of it, it's gone" (Green, Interview, 2004).

The most formal of all church food events was the tea. At teas, the principles of variety and quality reached a pinnacle at the same time as they were coupled with higher standards for presentation than lunches, fund-raising luncheons or suppers, which could run the gamut from casual, stand-up, self-service meals to sit-down dinners at waited tables. That said, the food served may not have differed markedly from that featured at the other food events just described. For example, one 1940s etiquette book my mother owned stipulates that the food at an informal or casual tea "should be quite simple – dainty sandwiches and cakes served with tea, coffee, or chocolate" (Eichler 1940, 215). At a formal tea, "[t]he food served should not be so substantial that it interferes with dinner. A typical menu might consist of a light salad, hot rolls or muffins, tea or coffee, and cookies. Neither dessert or rich cakes should be served at a tea" (Eichler 1940, 216).

However, what separated the ladies' tea from other events was not so much its food as its formality. Teas offered women the opportunity to focus on elements such as presentation and etiquette. Paper plates or

TRAINING YOUNG WOMEN IN THE ART OF POURING TEA: YOUTH
LEADER MARGE FRIZZELL, CHARLOTTETOWN, c. 1965

Styrofoam cups might have been acceptable for an after-church lunch, but the formality of a ladies' tea required white tablecloths and china cups.

I am ten years old and I am serving at my first church tea. I move tentatively toward a table where four women are seated, waiting to be served. The teacup teeters precariously in my hand. I make the delivery successfully, more through good luck than good management. As I return, a middle-aged woman and long-time Girl Guide leader takes me aside. "Diane, *this* is the right way to carry a cup of tea," she says as she takes the tea from my hand and shows me how to grasp the saucer with one hand and the handle of the cup with the other. "This is the way it is done," she repeats confidently.

Just as there was only one right way to carry a cup of tea in Amherst in the mid-1970s, I know that church women had many rules for the right way of doing every task. I learned this listening to my mother's stories when she returned from a church supper or tea. Then she talked of those women who were particularly difficult to work with: they were critical and exact, making their points without humour. For them, producing a tea or supper properly was serious business. In their presence the church kitchen could become a site of tension and conflict as personalities clashed and issues of control surfaced. I also know from her stories, however, that the church kitchen had another side. It could also be a place of camaraderie where everyone worked for a concentrated period toward a common purpose. In such circumstances a mishap or offhand comment could become a longstanding joke or saying. This is the stuff of legend:

An elderly woman in Amherst tells me about Lide, whose reputation as a local character was due in part to her inability to work with other church women. She recalls, "No one could work with Lide you know. She was always on the outs with somebody." Lide's curt, "Not too much help please," not only had the immediate desired result of driving other church women out of the kitchen, it had the lasting effect of securing her place in community folklore. Outside of Lide's hearing, and under the guise of humour, others capitalized on her marginality when they used Lide's phrase, "Not too much help please" (Hunter, Interview, 1986).

This reminds me of another story, one that my mother used to tell about the demanding standards of a group of older church women she met in Parrsboro. Her narrative was not set in the kitchen but in a church hall around a quilt frame. Newly arrived to the church, my mother joined members of a women's group who were making a fund-raising quilt. She was welcomed warmly, as was everyone who came out that day to help. As the afternoon wore on, however, my mother was shocked to see that, unbeknownst to inexperienced or aged quilters in the group, their stitches were removed by the others after they left. These contributions were deemed unsuitable by experienced seamstresses, who demanded that there be eight to ten stitches to the inch. This important moment of learning for my mother stayed with her. Beneath a surface of civility and pleasant conversation, women judged each other and their abilities critically. To be fully accepted, one had to contribute in very specified ways and according to exacting criteria.

That teas continue to demand a higher degree of etiquette than other church food events is reflected in Anne Green's description of the two annual teas she helps to organize. As she contrasts the way that teas in their former incarnation "used to be" with the women's recent compromises, her comments speak to the ongoing struggles of organizers to balance heightened expectations for the "proper" way of doing things with practical concerns:

There's tables set up with a table cloth. And usually the Christian Ladies, it's a younger group of women, they decorate our hall for our teas ... [In the last few years] we have done away with the silver service. We have it displayed now because they've been donated. We have a table that's all set up with a nice tablecloth and this is the way it used to be. And there would be one at each end and there would be somebody replenishing the hot water and the tea and the coffee which was a job. There'd be somebody replenishing the cups and saucers and it was a lot. And then you stood in line to get the tea and coffee. By the time you got it back to the table it wasn't hot. That's what we felt. So we did away with that. Some hard feelings along the way ... We still do our fancy cups and saucers. Oh yes we do and make sure they're matched. And you should know what trouble that is. Because people don't see them the same [laughs]. Anyway, we put them on the table to start with. Like they're set, the table is set. And there's a lady that goes around with the tea and somebody else goes around with the coffee and it's hot whenever you get it (Green, Interview, 2004).

Even though the women of Anne's group resort to less formal service in the name of practicality, they retain visual cues, such as the display of the silver tea service, that both signal the tea as a formal occasion and assure themselves and their customers that they do know how such occasions should be properly performed.

As a folklorist, I now understand church ladies' insistence on precision as a marker of their belonging to a specific folk group. Women read each other's willingness to master the skills of the group as a signal of commitment to shared values. Drawing on a long history of the use of etiquette by elite groups as a social marker to distinguish themselves from lower socioeconomic groups (see Bourdieu 1984) and from the uncivilized forces of nature (see Mennell 1985), the church women turn to shared codes of etiquette and presentation in an attempt to align themselves with higher social groups. As Stephen Mennell writes, "Tastes in food, like tastes in music, literature or the visual arts, are socially shaped, and the major forces which have shaped them are religions, classes and nations. In European history, religion has been a relatively weak influence on food, class overwhelmingly the strongest. People have always used food in their attempts to climb the social ladder themselves, and to push other people down the ladder" (1985, 17). Bourdieu writes, more specifically, that "[t]he denial of lower, coarse, vulgar, venal, servile – in a word, natural – enjoyment, which constitutes the sacred sphere of culture, implies an affirmation of the superiority of those who can be satisfied with the sublimated, refined, disinterested, gratuitous, distinguished pleasures forever closed to the profane. That is why art and cultural consumption are predisposed, consciously and deliberately or not, to fulfil a social function of legitimating social differences" (1984, 7). Through the organization of formal food events such as ladies' teas, the women relied not only on food, but on its presentation and service, to reassert their position within a community power structure. Within the group, command of sewing or baking, as well as knowledge of etiquette and an appreciation for the proper way to do things, helped to establish hierarchy and to identify leaders.

FOOD AND FAITH

Banana Nut Cake

2½ cups sifted cake flour
2 tsp baking powder
¼ tsp baking soda
¾ tsp salt
½ cup shortening
1 cup white sugar
2 eggs
½ cup chopped nuts
1 tsp vanilla
2 tbsp milk
1 cup mashed bananas

Sift together flour, baking powder, soda and salt, work shortening with spoon, gradually add sugar, add eggs, unbeaten, add nuts stir in vanilla, add flour mixture alternately in thirds with bananas and milk, beating after each addition. Turn into greased floured cake pan. Bake 350 for about 55 minutes.

Mrs. Bruce Fullerton

(*Tested Sweet Recipes* 34)

Other subtexts in *Tested Sweet Recipes* speak of the women's sense of
religious duty. Inside the front cover is "The Kitchen Prayer," by Klara
Munkres,[14] which stands for a Foreword and positions the recipes that
follow as a form of religious service.

> Lord of all pots and pans and things;
> Since I've no time to be
> A saint by doing lovely things,
> Or watching late with thee,
> Or dreaming in the dawn light,
> Or storming Heavens gates,
> Make me a Saint by getting meals,
> And washing up the plates.
>
> Although I must have Martha's hands,
> I have a Mary mind;
> And when I black the boots and shoes,
> Thy sandals, Lord, I find.
> I think of how they trod the earth,
> Each time I scrub the floor;
> Accept this meditation, Lord,
> I haven't time for more.
>
> Warm all the kitchen with thy love,
> And light it with thy peace,
> Forgive me all my worrying,
> And make my grumbling cease.

Thou who didst love to give man food,
In room or by the sea,
Accept this service that I do –
I do it unto thee.

This poem, and a second one called "The Housewife," by Catherine Cate Coblentz,[15] which marks the end of the recipes and the beginning of fourteen pages of ads, establish women's domestic and caring work as an extension of their religious faith and locate the cookbook within this context.

Religious poems or prayers are commonly located within the covers of church cookbooks, as Anne Bower observes: "In both the nineteenth and twentieth centuries the cookbook is used to define women's role as moral centre of the home and/or demonstrate the ways that food rituals can reinforce religious teachings. This is one of the most consistent and enduring plots in community cookbooks" (1997b, 43). The message links to the work of social reformists such as Frances Willard, founder of the Women's Christian Temperance Movement, who identified the mission of the ideal woman as "to make the whole world homelike." Willard and other social reformers were supported by the home economics movement. As Shapiro writes, "the sense of mission that fueled the domestic-science movement and gave it much of its most rousing public vocabulary reflected a safe and sturdy identity traditional among American women activists. Women had long been the guardians of religion in American life ... Every woman was empowered to think of herself as a missionary, assigned to her own household, and one of the few respectable outlets for an independent woman with more energy that her house could contain was real missionary work, on the frontier or in foreign countries" (Shapiro 1986, 121–2).

Women were seen to have a valuable role to play in social reform. In particular, middle-class women had a responsibility to address social ills through the application of their domestic skills. Shapiro claims:

[T]he surest "antidote" to social and economic distinctions was the prominent example of a middle class. The ideal home life that was promoted by domestic scientists was defined not by wealth or even occupation but by correct habits and sensibilities … Cleanliness, order, decorum; a visible refinement; a cultivated intelligence – these features of what domestic scientists called "right living" comprised a standard of domesticity they hoped to instill everywhere in American society, although they were aware that some populations would require a more thorough overhaul than others. With scientific cookery as the chief means – as well as much of the goal – they hoped to regulate the messy sprawl of American society and to filter out the most unsettling aspects of its diversity (Shapiro 1986, 136).

I do not know to what extent my mother and her friends saw themselves as reformists or how highly they valued their voluntary church work and service to the community. Neither do I know whether they recognized any link between the food they produced and their moral beliefs. I am certain that in concocting Lemon Squares or Macaroons they were not purposefully conforming to any formal dietary religious laws.[16] However, the consistency of their baking with respect to common ingredients, form, quantity, and combination did qualify it as a genre unto itself. For example, my brother Mark refers to the pans of Strawberry Jell-O Squares or Coconut Squares that left our home for church functions as "United Church recipes." He recognized this as a particular type of baking when he encountered it as a young adult. Immediately after our mother's death in 1989, Mark moved to Charlottetown for a year to live with our father. There he was frequently invited out for dinner by sympathetic women of the congregation. The meals often ended with sweets or a dessert that Mark immediately recognized as ones he had seen Mom make years earlier: "When I was around with Dad, we'd go to eat and the sweets would almost all be the same" (Mark Tye, Interview, 1999). As a child, Mark would have had access only to the scraps or leftovers after the desserts were sliced; they were made primarily for adult consumption. Now his changed status as an adult, a newly bereaved son, and a visitor with the minister, made him an appropriate recipient of the baking. Mark not only read the sweets he was served as acceptance into an adult circle: they were "United Church recipes." For my mother and her friends, the connection between their morality and cooking may well have been implicit, but it was recognizable enough, as my brother realized, to identify the women as a group. Significantly, this kind of distinguishable identification is the quality underlying religious dietary laws (see Kass 1994, 196). Although none of the squares, cakes, and fancy dainty desserts were exclusively United Church, or even Protestant, dishes, they still served as everyday, concrete reminders for church women like my mother of a classed and gendered construction of order as it was created in their lives and of a religious faith that they enacted within their church and community.

This is consistent with Daniel Sack's findings concerning the role of food in American Protestantism. For example, Sack suggests that women in the 1950s followed prescriptions when performing church food events that meant that middle-class hostessing took on new dimensions when it was carried out on behalf of a church. Sack quotes from a publication aimed specifically at church women, *Christian Etiquette* (Parrott 1953), that "offers suggestions for good manners at a church social" (2000, 69). The book recommends that a church dinner should be sophisticated: "It is the finishing touches which make or fail to make a church dinner whether it be a pot luck or banquet. Provide center-pieces for the tables. Use candles. Pick pretty teen-age girls for waitresses and have them wear identical aprons. Provide dinner music on records if musicians are not available" (Parrott 1953, 70–7, cited in Sack 2000, 70). Sack points out that, while these events were similar to other parties, when hosted by church ladies they were to be Christian, or at the very least not worldly (Sack 2000, 70). Although these occasions undoubtedly served many purposes for the individual women who organized and attended them, their outward form reflected their official function: contexts for Christian fellowship, and events designed to support and extend the work of the church. Like the church women Sacks describes, my mother and her friends turned to recipes for squares and to codes of etiquette for tea parties that were familiar expressions of middle-class womanhood across North America and reinterpreted them for religious purposes.

CHURCH WORK

For church women, food was not only a means of articulating a particular vision of the world; it was also a lot of work.[17] Those who married ministers faced the heaviest demands. In Maritime Canada in the 1950s and 1960s the role of minister's wife was the materialization of church women's ideals. Women married to clergy lived under constant scrutiny; their appearance, their children's behaviour, their social skills, and their domestic abilities were all potential sources of judgment. In facing the impossible challenge of fulfilling an ideal, they had little privacy. Members of the congregation might drop by the manse at any time, and so while the occasion of lunches and teas signalled other church women's performances, my mother lived most of her life on display. After our move to Amherst in 1967, Mom continued to host visiting ministers and church people from out of town who were attending meetings with my father.

Ministers' wives of my mother's generation were expected to show leadership through the production of food. Not only were they supposed to contribute well-made food to the full range of food events in each of the churches their husbands served, they were expected to entertain members of the congregation as well as visiting clergy. L. M. Montgomery's journal entries chronicle the incessant demands made upon her for prepared food. For example, on 28 June 1914, she writes of serving dinner at her home for several minsters who were being ordained and then helping to prepare supper in the church basement afterward. In the same entry, she also reports going to another food event, the Sunday School picnic, where she ate several sandwiches, a piece of lemon pie, and a piece of gooseberry pie (Montgomery 1987, 148). Eleven years later there are no signs that the demands have diminished as Montgomery outlines her week in terms of her hosting and food production: a succession of visitors arrived on Monday and Tuesday followed by a lawn social in Georgetown on Wednesday. On Thursday, 2 August 1926, she writes: "I cooked all day and visited in the evening. Friday I made jelly roll, cherry pies, tarts, cookies and a date loaf for a Sunday School picnic ... Saturday I rose at 6, made sandwiches and lemonade, then went to Stanley Park for a long, bored day"(Montgomery 1992, 300). A final example taken from 30 October 1926 sums up yet another week shaped by food demands:

> So tired again. Same old story. Thursday and Friday I baked and brewed all day, making cake, jellies, salads, mock chicken etc. for the supper. Thursday night we went to tea in Union with a dull stupid family who gave us half cooked sausages for supper. Most of the Union families are nice cultured people who set excellent tables, but this is one of the few poor ones. Last night our fowl supper came off and was a big success, as such things go ... Mrs. Sam McClure brought a turkey which she kept secreted and after the concert all we performers ate it. Things like this are really pleasant when one is not too tired to enjoy them (Montgomery 1992, 311–2).

Although Montgomery's experiences as a minister's wife predate my mother's by a generation, not much had changed by the time my parents

A VISITING MINISTER IS SERVED TEA: REV. KEN FINLAY,
AMHERST, c. 1978

married. Sadie Latimer sums up her life as a young minister's wife in the 1950s: "A minister's wife was expected to do a lot of entertaining" (Latimer, Interview, 2000). In specific reference to my mother, she emphasizes, "Your mother would do a lot of entertaining … [and she] would have had to bring food to meetings and affairs of the church … she was certainly involved in everything that went on in the church. She was a great support to your father in his church work" (Latimer, Interview, 2000). Next-door neighbour Helen Farrow confirmed that my mother's heavy hostessing duties contributed to her having more baking in the house than other women in the neighbourhood. Although when we lived in Amherst my father no longer had a congregation, he still frequently hosted ministers who were attending meetings as both a gesture of sociability and a cost-saving measure. My mother's ever-present supply of baking, like the Coffee Squares below, the recipe for which was obtained from a women she knew through the church, prepared her for the often unexpected guests that my father brought home (Farrow, Interview, 2003).

Coffee Squares

---

2 cups white sugar

2 eggs

1 cup cooking oil

1 cup warm coffee

2 tsp vanilla

3 cups flour

1 tsp soda

1 tsp salt

Pour on top of this the following:

1 cup chocolate chips

1 cup walnuts

Bake 350

Kay Wood, September 1978

Culinary demands could be particularly daunting for young minister's wives. Newly married in 1949, Jean Colborne was not only trepidatious about the required five foods for hosting the women's group, she was intimidated by a fundraising turkey supper to which each woman was expected to contribute six pies. In the end, having not yet made one pie on her own, she found the prospect of this so daunting that she fled home to her parents (Colborne 2003, 126). Unfortunately, the next couple of decades did not bring much progress. In the late 1970s, a study conducted among minister's wives reported that the women faced continued demands. Their greatest complaint was the unrealistic expectations they faced from congregation members. One clergy wife bemoaned: "We are expected to give so much. It's hard to give joyfully anymore" (Mace and Mace 1982, cited in Oden 1988).

Of course, not all ministers' wives conformed. Some publicly protested what they felt to be unreasonable expectations. For example, in 1935 Jean Stevinson contributed a column to a series in *Chatelaine* magazine titled "The World's Worst Job." Here she pointed out some of the drawbacks to being a minister's wife, objecting particularly to the attitude that a minister's wife was church property. More often, women voiced their objections privately. For example, in her journals L. M. Montgomery often lamented the unrelenting demands on her time and energy and complained of intense fatigue. This notwithstanding, both her journal entries and her recipes indicate that she fulfilled the social expectations for a minister's wife. In fact, she took great pride in her domestic skills and excelled at them. My own mother echoed Stevinson's attitude when my father was preparing to leave his administrative job and return to the pulpit. She had revelled in her paid employment and was not prepared to return to an unpaid support role. She swore never again to take on a full-time unpaid position for the church.

I remember this statement of refusal, however, because it was singular. My mother always prepared lunches and served at ladies' teas or church suppers without comment. Undoubtedly, she must have sometimes felt burdened by the expectations she faced as a church woman and, perhaps especially, as a minister's wife. Yet she never showed it. My mother shared what Elaine and Kelly Crawford describe as Montgomery's "highly developed sense of propriety and the dedication she brought to her duties as a minister's wife[, which] meant that she was unfailingly prepared for Session meetings, Sunday School picnics, and visits to or from members of the congregation with the appropriate salads, cakes, jellies, biscuits or cookies" (Crawford and Crawford 1996, 3). As

Mom's friend Sadie remembers, my mother "wanted to do things and she wanted to them well. And as I say, she was a good minister's wife. She was a worker" (Latimer, Interview, 2000).

Lemon Squares

1 can sweetened condensed milk
juice of 2 lemons
1 box graham wafers
salt

Line pan with graham wafers placed close together, then empty milk in bowl, stir, add juice of lemons and salt. Stir again, cover wafers with about half of this liquid, add another layer of wafers, then another layer of liquid. Cover top with another layer of graham wafers. Chill for two hours. Frost with butter icing.

Mrs. Ken Atkinson

(*Tested Sweet Recipes* 20)

The work my mother performed in making dishes such as Lemon Squares depended on an underlying female ethic of care – or what Cora V. Baldock refers to as "the myth of altruism as a female preserve" (1983, 290). Baldock argues that in the tradition of Western liberal thought altruism is part of the private sphere which, given women's associations, contributes to the view that women are "the embodiment of the altruistic spirit, of the caring and helping mentality needed for the charitable activities of the voluntary sector" (1983, 290–1). In their study of women's voluntary service, Milroy and Wismer were struck by how forcefully the hegemonic power of the public over the private sphere came through again and again in their data (1994, 7). Consistent with these findings, the food produced by my mother and her friends, and in fact the whole complex of voluntary work they accomplished, legitimized conventional gendered power relations both ideologically and economically (Little 1997, 203). Located in what feminist researchers have termed "the third dimension of rural work" (Milroy and Wismer 1994, 1; Little 1997, 197), women's community labour cannot be adequately understood through the traditional divisions of public and private (see Little 1997, 197, Abrahams 1996). Rather, it is intricately connected to women's work responsibilities both in the home and in the labour market. As Milroy and Wismer write, "although it is not paid work, it is also not 'voluntary' in the sense that it is not discretionary. Like domestic work, it is cyclical, never-ending and essential. Its spacial location is neither home nor work place, primarily, but community" (1994, 72). As seen in Joan Colborne's experiences of being a new minister's wife, in the 1950s church women were both assumed to have particular skills and were expected to use them to fill church needs;[18] this was a yardstick by which femininity was constructed and measured. It was unthinkable to Colborne that she not contribute her share of food or that she admit her inability to easily meet the expectation. Her coded resistance took the form of flight.[19] Women's mastery of domestic labour is also taken for granted in *Tested Sweet Recipes*, whose brief instructions often assume that women already know how to bake. *Tested Sweet Recipes* offers to help women hone their skills and build up their repertoire of desirable recipes, but it rests on the premise that readers know the basics – which is exactly how my mother used the collection as a new wife. It became an important resource that helped to ensure that, unlike Colborne, she did not have to evade social expectations. In part because of this community cookbook, she was able to meet the community standards for contributing to and hosting church food events.

In the end, community cookbooks such as *Tested Sweet Recipes* present a double-edged sword. In his discussion of English and French cooking traditions, Stephen Mennell points out that, historically, "expenditure in consumption of many kinds was a necessary expression of the seigneurial ethos of rank ... It was a compelling necessity and was not freely chosen" (1985, 113). Recontextualized within my mother's circle of middle-class church friends, the pressure continued. They felt that they had little choice but to contribute to the ever-present demands for refined food, and their work in doing so went largely unacknowledged.

Women's food production, entertaining, organizing, and other activities in the complex of volunteer work are extensions of the domestic and emotional work that women characteristically do (see Fishman 1978); this interpretation is supported by the more general findings of researchers of women's volunteerism. Jennifer Hook (2004) classes women's volunteerism along with informal support and domestic work under the category of unpaid labour, which, as she points out, tends to go unrecognized, and Arlene Kaplan Daniels (1987) argues that when men perform such socially integrative activities they are more highly rewarded than women when they do them; in fact, these responsibilities are not regarded as "real work" when performed by women.[20] Rather, they are considered to be the enactment of naturally feminine qualities (Daniels 1987, 408–10). Thus, my mother's production of lemon squares and coconut loaf was part of a larger complex of women's very gendered volunteer work that benefits men in yet another way: that is, by publicly legitimizing gender divisions. As Little writes, "Gender relations and the balance of power between men and women clearly underpin, in a very important way, women's commitment to voluntary work. Male approval for the amount and type of voluntary work women did appeared to be a very necessary basis for that involvement. Again, this ties in with beliefs about the nature of rural society but it also fundamentally linked to stereotypical ideas on gender role and the appropriateness of women's place in the community" (1997, 202).

Food brought women together and allowed them to contribute in concrete and very meaningful ways to their communities; however, volunteerism of the type my mother and her friends took part in was also a source of powerlessness for women. As Wendy Kaminer argues of women's volunteer activity more generally, it "both liberated women and kept them in their place" (1984, 1). Church women's production of food legitimated their position as unpaid domestic workers, who were often pressured to perform important, but invisible, work that church and community members – women included – did not recognize as work.

Moore and colleagues observe that the status given to women in the context of community work, the skills that they acquire in the course of their volunteering, and the perception of the worth of that work all relate to their wider relationship with paid employment and with the domestic space (cited in Little 1997, 202). In fact, writing in the early 1970s, Doris B. Gold linked women's volunteerism, which she estimated as contributing a value of 14.2 billion dollars to the United States economy in 1965, to their marginality in the labour market (1971, 385). In the context of Maritime Canada, church women's work has paralleled the American situation Gold describes. Their volunteer service confirmed an existing division of labour. As Margaret Conrad writes,

Women in Atlantic Canada in the 1950s, as elsewhere in North America, were largely defined by their unpaid reproductive and service roles. Most of the women who comprised over 20 per cent of the paid labour force were single, divorced, or widowed. A federal law barring the employment of married women in the civil service was repealed only in 1955, and provincial jurisdictions were slow to follow the federal lead. In 1956 Nova Scotia passed legislation requiring equal pay for equal work, but no attempt seems to have been made to enforce the law; and, in any event, because men and women were segregated in the work-place, comparisons were difficult. Nor were women encouraged to raise their employment aspirations. Strict quotas were placed on the number of women accepted into many of the professional programs in the region's universities, and women were barred by law and custom from the boardrooms, clubs and taverns where power was often mediated. While women could legally vote and hold public office, they were marginalized in auxiliaries to major political parties and restricted in such civic duties as jury service. Young women coming of age in the 1950s were encouraged to take up one of the traditional female professions of teaching, social work, nursing, and clerical work, or train on the job to be a stewardess or bank teller. Their primary objective, reiterated by books, movies, television, and time-honoured social conventions, was to find a husband (Conrad 1993, 386–8).

Even as late as the 1970s, not much had changed in terms of women's participation in the paid labour force. Although they then made up 8.5 per cent of the labour force, as Della Stanley notes, "Numbers alone did not ensure women greater respect or equality in the workplace. Women were still relegated to lower-paid jobs in the often non-unionized clerical, sales, and service sectors" (1993, 453). Given the relationship of women's volunteerism to their paid work, Little comments that "[f]or many women involvement in voluntary work is an important source of power" (1997, 202), but "[a]t the same time, women's participation in voluntary work was in some senses a function and reflection of their own powerlessness and of the hegemonic power of paid work over unpaid … [S]ome women felt a sense of obligation concerning involvement in unpaid work in the village; they were powerless to resist the social pressure to contribute" (1997, 202).

Some studies, such as that by Doris B. Gold, suggest that a lack of suitable employment opportunities for women was key to their volunteer involvements. Community work was an alternative to the paid work that they would have gladly taken if it were possible; other women indicated that their volunteer work would prohibit them from taking up paid work, and, finally, some women complained of the pressure they felt to do volunteer work if they did not hold full-time jobs (Little 1997, 201). All this applied to my mother. She highly valued paid labour and, after her first years of marriage in Cape Breton, worked part-time and later full-time in the labour force, albeit at jobs such as kindergarten teacher, teacher's assistant, or school secretary, which were fitted in around her other jobs: her family and community work. And, as the preceding discussion indicates, my mother and middle-class women of her generation who were not usually full-time wage earners were pressured to do lots of community work (Little 1997, 201). Yet its unpaid status in a cash economy undermined the importance of this work. As Daniels writes, "The fact that the work of volunteers is not paid tells them the work is not important" (1987, 405).[21]

As with her paid employment, my mother juggled the demands of church work to accommodate family responsibilities.[22] Most of the time it did not present serious conflicts; when it did, she made arrangements for babysitters or, less frequently, my father to provide a meal.

My father loves to tell about one of first times he was left alone with me for supper. Although I am only months old, he feeds me a cold hot dog. Later, my mother is horrified by his story but throughout my childhood he continues to creatively sabotage my mother's attempt to leave things for him to serve. On one memorable occasion he practically, but not very successfully, combines all the leftovers in the fridge and heats them in one pot. The exact ingredients now elude me but the memory of canned spaghetti and canned beans remains. He boasts of how skilfully he reduced his clean-up to the one pot, but I remember his conglomeration being greeted with disgust by my sister and me.

My father supported my mother's church work. He fed and cared for his children when my mother needed to be away for church work and he willingly offered the technical support of running the Gestetner that produced *Tested Sweet Recipes*, for example. But he never carried out the child care or domestic duties so well as to be taken for anything but a stand-in for my mother, whose job it truly was to manage the household. The kind of support my father showed was likely typical of men of his generation.[23] By enabling their wives to perform gendered volunteer work, the men did not need to do it themselves. Conveniently, as Little (1997) notes, it got them off the hook. Further, the women's work supported the men's projects, financially, physically, and emotionally. The women's production of food brought groups together for events such as church suppers and meetings, thus promoting sociability among members.[24]

The countless pans of squares my mother produced had importance beyond their value in signalling a pleasant end to a church meeting or even their financial contribution to a fund-raising supper. Mom and her friends knew that food helps bring people together. Sharing a cup of tea and a sweet made congregations more cohesive and helped build communities,[25] for as researchers indicate, this kind of women's community work constitutes "maintenance work – part of the 'social glue' which holds a community together" (Milroy and Wismer 1994, 72). Just as Milroy and Wismer discovered that the everyday acts of women living in Kitchener-Waterloo over the course of a century constituted the work of community-building, (1994) the food production of my mother and church women contributed to bringing people closer together and making communities stronger. Writing on food and Protestantism, Daniel Sack emphasizes the meanings the church congregation invests in the act of eating rather than the nature of the food itself. He writes, "While the actual food is important, it is eating that gives food meaning. Around the Communion table, bread and wine become a connection to God. In the social hall, coffee becomes community. In the soup kitchen, rice and beans become hospitality" (Sack 2000, 2). Thus, Sack argues that it is not what is eaten at a church's social hour, or even the sharing of it that is as religious. Rather, it is the creation of community. In doing what they saw needed doing, my mother and other church women helped create better places to live. And, as Milroy and Wismer suggest, their efforts have much to teach us about the work of building communities (1994, 11).

* * *

Church women's voluntary service had some underlying benefits. Some women expressed their creativity and took enjoyment in the work, priding themselves on their ability to produce flaky pastry and light biscuits. As the next chapter shows, church groups brought women together and created important opportunities for friendship and enjoyment. Notwithstanding the value of church work, it was considered obligatory by my mother and other church women, whether or not they consciously felt this burden. Baking helped them fulfill their social obligations. Thrust into small-town life in the late 1950s, my mother was faced with having to quickly learn a new repertoire of baked goods that was considered to be more refined than the foods she grew up with. In order to contribute in the way that was expected of her, she took advantage of her interactions with church women to gather recipes, but it is also obvious from the signs of wear that she relied heavily on recipes in *Tested Sweet Recipes*. This community cookbook became the foundation of my mother's baking for church and community functions, and she continued to regularly produce many of its recipes for the rest of her life. In addition to instructing my mother on how to make tasty squares and loaves, the subtext of *Tested Sweet Recipes* offered her directions on how to be a church lady and a good minister's wife. My mother's making and serving of the particular version of dainty food it contained marked her acceptance of those ideals. Her baking of social food – squares and loaves that could be easily divided and that were based on valued ingredients, refined, exotic and modern – articulated a classed and gendered vision of modernity and of women's place in church and community life. Because public and private regions blurred in the public life of a minister's wife, this new way of baking became familiar in our home when my father's colleagues and members of the church congregation visited. The overlapping of my mother's workplace and home meant that this more refined way of baking merged with, and to some extent eventually replaced, the coarser rural foods Mom used to nurture her family. How food supported women's friendships, and sometimes expressed female resistance, will be the subject of the next chapter.

BAKING FOR A THIRD PLACE

For what modest claim it is, my mother's skill in the kitchen far exceeded that of her mother and both of her daughters. It was enough to win her friends' praise, as when Sadie assured me that she was never offered a poor meal at our house, even when her visits were unexpected (Latimer, Interview, 2000). But is it possible to read this success in other ways? Janet Theophano contends that although women may have conformed to the images and ideals they and others constructed, they also found them useful points of departure for reflection (2001, 139). Meredith Abarca makes a similar point when she writes, "The language of cooking, with its gendered discourse, also opposes the dominant culture" (2001, 122). Referring to Laura Esquivel's *Como aqua para chocolate (Like Water for Chocolate)*, Abarca claims, "In this film, the act of preparing, cooking, and serving food is a multifaceted, gendered discourse of health, pregnancy, sensuality, sexuality, retaliation, and liberation ... The simultaneous co-existence of such discourses coming out of the kitchen has a subversive function" (2001, 122). Building on the notion that women's preparation, cooking, and serving of food can contain expressions of resistance, I explore my mother's baking for the complexities that lay behind a competent exterior, or what John Dorst (1989) might call "cracks in the veneer."

Recent scholarship has revealed the transgressive, and sometimes subversive, nature of women's traditional culture, in forms ranging from song (Langlois, in Radner 1993; Bourke, in Radner 1993; Greenhill 1997), to jokes (Thomas 1997), narrative (Gordon, in Radner 1993), material culture (Pershing, in Radner 1993) and custom (Greenhill 2005). My own work has examined a variety of ways in which Nova Scotian women past and present have protested the conditions of their lives through folksong (1995), personal experience narrative (1989), legend (2002), belief (1996), and custom (Tye and Powers 1998). This growing body of feminist folkloristics highlights women's complex use of traditional culture. One example is Elaine Lawless's examination of women's personal narratives of domestic violence, which exposes women's problematic relationship to patriarchal master discourses (2001). Lawless demonstrates the impossibility of understanding the women's stories in isolation, outside the context of larger social discourses that both shape and confine them. Drawing on Labov and Waletzky's notion of "tellability," she explores the failure of narrative to capture a woman's experience. She refers to this as "unspeakability." Lawless also points to the inability of narrative to always bring about change in a woman's life; contrary to popular perceptions of the importance of breaking silence, telling one's story does not necessarily make things better. To be heard and acted on, the women's stories must be constructed and shared in particular ways. Lawless's analysis demonstrates that telling one's story is not always a simple or straightforward act.

In part, Lawless draws on Joan Radner and Susan Lanser's earlier and important work on feminist coding, which pointed out the disguised nature of many women's critiques. Radner and Lanser explain that "[c]oding occurs in the context of complex audiences in which some members may be competent and willing to decode the message, but others are not" (Radner and Lanser, in Radner 1993, 3). They specify that feminist coding involves the communication of "messages critical of some aspect of women's subordination" (1993, 3) and that "[t]he essential ambiguity of coded acts protects women from potentially dangerous responses from those who might find their statements disturbing" (Radner, Preface, in Radner 1993, viii).[1] Importantly, Radner and Lanser do not require that a woman *intend* to convey a feminist message in order for it to be one. Because they locate meaning in the communicative context, they shift the site of intention from the author to the receiving community: "As we are using *intentionality*, then, we mean assumptions inferable from the performance-in-context, which includes what we know of the performer and her circumstances but does not rely on the performer's own words for its guarantee" (Radner and Lanser, in Radner 1993, 7). Applied to my mother, this means that determining whether she consciously used baking as a vehicle of resistance is not important; her intention – or lack of it – does not take away from the power of the baking's messages.

BAKING AS FEMINIST CODING

Coded critique can find expression in domestic acts such as cooking and baking, as Susan S. Lanser shows in her exploration of the hidden meanings in women's claims that they can't cook. She reads women's statements that they cannot cook as their refusal to cook, a refusal that frees them from domestic responsibility. Similarly, Wendy Welch (1997) identifies underlying feminist messages in women's use of coffee to secure a social space for themselves. My mother's coded use of baking was along these lines. Hers was a more subtle resistance than that of the minister's wives mentioned in the last chapter: Jean Stevinson, whose *Chatelaine* article challenged what she felt were medieval demands placed on a minster's wife, and Joan Colborne, who escaped to her parents when she doubted her ability to meet others' high expectations. Mom conformed to cultural demands that she produce certain kinds of baking at the same time as she subtly challenged them and the patriarchal ideology they embodied.

As explored in the last chapter, three quarters of my mother's recipes (a substantial 76 per cent) fall under the categories of squares or loaves (which includes recipes labelled as cakes, loaves, and breads). These are "social" foods that could be cut up or sliced into many pieces. Although sometimes they were made only to be shared within the family, they were of a recognizably higher register than cookies or biscuits. These were kept on hand to be offered to company, or were designed to be shared by a group. The many recipes that sprung from meetings of my mother's United Church Women's group facilitated interaction and sustained women's gatherings. Their arrival signalled the end of business. Recipes for Fudge Squares and Pineapple Squares bear the names of women whom my mother knew through many different associations: her church and other volunteer work, her paid work, and her interactions with neighbours. Susan J. Leonardi comments that, "[l]ike a story, a recipe needs a recommendation, a context, a point, a reason to be" (1989, 340, cited in Jefferies 2005, 11). Bolstered by Watergate Cake or Lemon Squares, women talked. Helen Farrow immediately identified several reasons why "lunch" after church meetings is worth the bother: "It does get to be a lot of work but I don't know, there's something to be said about it though because you do enjoy that social part of it. And you get to know people better, the people that you're working with and so on. That's your chance to get to know them really, isn't it? And you relax before you go home" (Farrow, Interview, 2003).

As discussed in the last chapter, the sugar-laden recipes served at church and other meetings reflect a certain kind of sociability based on underlying power relations that speak loudly of Western exploitation as well as emerging class and gendered identities. Orange and Raisin Squares and Date Chews were the medium through which women in my mother's circles expressed their middle-class presence and the power of the white middle-class institutions, such as the church, that brought them together. However, there is also a precedent for women within organizations such as church groups to work for social and political change. Just as there is a long history of women using fundraising cookbooks to promote their causes, their social gatherings have had hidden agendas. Although church functions such as social teas were, undisputedly, powerful disciplinary sites for women, they sometimes also offered rare opportunities for sociability, personal growth, and even social change. They provided women with culturally approved social outlets and allowed them time away from family responsibilities. Leadership skills honed in a church women's group could be directed to more radical social causes, as the history of suffrage in Canada attests (see Bacchi 1993). Women first campaigned for the vote, using Protestant and temperance associations as their springboard. Jessica Sewell argues that suffragists purposely used these groups as part of their effort to emphasize their domesticity and maternal femininity. In the formation of these groups, they showed that they still retained their domestic skills even as they argued for their rights as full members of the public.

In particular, Sewell notes how suffragists in California used tea in the construction of this safe, domestic image. When it first arrived in about 1630 in France and then in England approximately twenty years later, tea was primarily a drink for aristocrats. Eventually its use was widespread and Thomas Lipton, a tea merchant in Glasgow around 1850, came to dominate the American tea market (Bacchi 1993, 9–10). As time went on, tea developed a gendered association; it became a woman's drink (Christensen 2001, 6), and to represent themselves as feminine and domestic, suffragists made use of existing meanings of tea in multiple ways, in tea parties, tearooms, and by selling tea (Sewell

RELAXING AFTER A CHURCH SUPPER, CHARLOTTETOWN, c. 1965

2008). Although I cannot know all the purposes for which my mother and her friends gathered over tea after a meeting, I suspect at least some of the talk was critical. I base this in part on clear memories of Mom returning from church or social events with the remnants of a batch of squares; as I polished off the leftovers, she would share with me her critiques of people and events, and occasionally of church decision-making and policy.

On the most basic level, Banana Bread and Pineapple Squares were subversive in that they helped to carve out precious social time for women. These sweets helped to structure and to extend the length of the visits my mother had with female friends and acquaintances, for as she once said, "It is easier to talk to someone with a tea cup in your hand."

Helen Farrow emphasized, "Oh yes, and your mother always had something to give you in your hand. It didn't make any difference if she was working or not, she always had something, a muffin or something. Where you'd catch me lots of times without it, you wouldn't her" (Farrow, Interview, 2004). In these contexts, the sharing of baked goods increased the women's pleasure, bringing together two indulgences: sweets, and time away from one's domestic role. Women of my mother's generation were expected to nurture their families with a filled cookie jar and, at the same time, to maintain a slim figure. Baking intended for their enjoyment and not their family's provisioning became a subversive treat. Time for themselves and with one another was another indulgence. Paul Christensen writes about seldom seeing his mother when she was not working; he expected her to be busy. He writes that tea offered his mother solitary respite from her work (Christensen 2001, 2): "But tea was the thing she had claimed as her island, her one sandbar in the sea of housework" (2001, 5). Christensen's experience resonates with my own. When at home my mother rarely sat and was never idle. Generally, she did not take time to do anything just because she enjoyed it; her activities had purpose. A cup of tea or coffee with a neighbour or friend who dropped in was respite.

In Amherst in the 1970s and 1980s, Mom belonged to a group of women who met one or two mornings a week from 10:00 to 11:00 for tea or coffee. About ten years before my mother moved to the neighbourhood, three stay-at-home mothers initiated the practice of gathering together for morning coffee when their children were preschoolers. By the time my mother joined in, around 1970, the group had expanded to ten to fifteen neighbourhood women. When I talked to Helen Farrow in 2003, the group had been meeting for approximately forty years. At that point, Helen still relied on members for new recipes, and she indicated that her own hosting of "coffee" was one of the only occasions she baked now that her children were adults living on their own.

SOCIALIZING AFTER A MEETING OF THE UNITED
CHURCH WOMEN, AMHERST c. 1980

That the coffee group has lasted for over four decades speaks of its importance to participants. In many ways, these informal meetings constitute the women's creation of a "third place," which Ray Oldenburg describes as "a generic designation for a great variety of public places that host the regular, voluntary, informal, and happily anticipated gatherings of individuals beyond the realms of home and work" (1997, 16). Although Oldenburg is thinking of informal public spaces such as barber shops and general stores, the coffee group is consistent with his understanding of the impetus to establish third places; it represented the women's own remedy for loneliness and isolation (1997, 20). Further, it offered members the functions Oldenburg associates with third places; it became neutral ground where the women could gather for relaxed enjoyment and where conversation was the main activity. "Coffee" brought women in the neighbourhood together and provided them with a sorting area where they could can find out whose company they enjoyed and whom they might want as a closer friend.

At this point I can only guess at what morning coffee meant to my mother and her friends, but I expect that for at least some of these women at some points in their lives, it was highly valued. That my mother maintained her connection with the group even after she entered the workforce and was no longer available during weekday mornings is an indication of its importance to her. Often on a day off from work, she would host coffee. Oldenburg writes of women's historic exclusion from what has been the male-dominant tradition of the third space (1997, 232). Accordingly, he underscores women's need to create their own third space, for life in the suburbs is often very lonely for women (Oldenburg 1997, 237): "Teas, tennis and telephoning compensate the modern wife's exile from community but not adequately" (1997, 236). Given the isolation of homemaking and the dissatisfaction that most women experience with housework (Friedan 1974 see Oakley 1974, 182) and what Adrienne Rich calls "the ultimate lack of seriousness with which women were regarded in that world" (1976, 27), morning coffee would have been a welcome point of commonality and support that offered a means of coping with the stresses of motherhood. Although I was rarely around on those weekday mornings when the women met at our house, when I was there I was struck by their laughter. For an hour, as they drank their coffee and ate coffee cake or muffins, my mother and her friends laughed. Some of the women, like our neighbour Dot Bent, were natural performers. Dot always saw the humorous side of things and had a knack for telling a funny story. Others in the group formed her audience. What I overheard sounded like fun.

Growing up, I considered these coffee group gatherings as inconsequential. They fell under my radar, along with that of many others in the neighbourhood. Held as they were at a time when husbands and children were away at work or school, they slipped our notice. In retrospect, I suspect their longevity attests to their feminist coding. Under the guise of trivialization, these gatherings were just "coffee" and not to be taken seriously; however, as Radner and Lanser argue, feminist coding disguises critical messages. Oldenburg, too, notes the tendency for third places to be "political fora of great importance" (1997, xxiv). Finally, drawing on Janice Radway's classic work on romance-novel readers 1984), it is possible to read the coffee group as subversive solely because, under its umbrella, the women carved out time for themselves. In itself this is a significant act of resistance within a culture that did not award women personal time or space. The sweets the women ate with their coffee were one way they expanded or made more pleasurable their contacts with one another. Sharing tea or coffee helped them negotiate role demands. As Davis discovered in her work on quilters and diarists, "Quiltmaking and journal writing could perform a ... mediation in women's lives, that between the role expectation that they be stoic, self sacrificing, and hard-working and their desire for some measure of personal indulgence" (1997, 217). These forms, like baking, allowed women to conform to expected behaviour at the same time as they assuaged the role conflicts they experienced (Davis 1997, 221). Viewed in this light, my mother's recipe collection offers insight into women's attempts to create a space for themselves when there were few opportunities to come together away from a male gaze.

COMMUNITIES OF CHOOSING

Never-Fail Pastry
---

5 cups flour
1 lb lard or shortening
1 tbsp sugar
1 tbsp salt

Blend well. Put one egg in measuring cup and beat with fork. Add enough cold water to fill cup. Add flour to mixture and blend slightly. Use little flour when rolling out (will keep two weeks in fridge).

Helen F.

Helen, Dot, Sadie, Winnie ... their names comfort me. They were important and reassuring to me as a child. I am not surprised that I can bring them to mind instantly, even though I haven't thought of many of these women for years. And now they come into my mind laughing. Suddenly I can hear their laughter again; that warm laughter that was part of my childhood world. Most of Mom's recipes come from these women. It makes me think of Janet Theophano's words: "If nothing else, the compilation of recipes or the editing of printed texts offered women a site in which they could 'write' their own books, their own lives and histories. Through these texts, women developed lineage and community affiliations and identified themselves as members of a community of women" (2001, 141). Recipes placed my mother in a network, or several intersecting networks, of women. They aligned her with women she wanted to be connected with: not just accomplished cooks, but women with similar interests, values and social positions. These networks sometimes made connections with women elsewhere, as indicated by my father's memory that the recipe for Chiffon Cake had "made the rounds" in Cape North in the 1950s.

Chiffon Cake

First Bowl:
2¼ cups cake flour
1½ cups sugar
3 tsp baking powder
1 tsp salt

Mix well and add
½ cup oil
5 unbeaten egg yolk
¾ cup cold water
Grated rind of 2 oranges

Beat with spoon until smooth. In large bowl put 1 cup egg whites and ½ tsp cream tartar. Beat until very stiff peaks. Do not underbeat. Pour egg yolk mixture gradually over beaten egg whites, gently folding until blended. Don't stir. Pour into ungreased pan 10 x 4″. Bake 350 for about 50 minutes.

With their production of Chiffon Cake, women in Cape North defined themselves locally at the same time as they joined millions of other middle-class women throughout North America who made the cake after *Better Homes and Gardens* introduced it in the May 1948 issue.[2] Chiffon cake provided my mother and her friends with a new, modern vehicle for the performance of femininity. Given its popularity, women not only had to know how to make a cake well, they needed to know how to make this particular cake, and my mother's recipes helped her fit in. I read my mother's recipes as an extension of her gatherings with other women: meetings of her church group, bridge club, and coffee group. Relying on baking and coffee or tea, they transformed aspects of their obligatory meetings into a social, or third, space where they nurtured one another and, more importantly, where they nurtured themselves. In her collection I find not only traces of the networks of women that she was a part of, but also reminders of how within larger groups of church or neighbourhood there were networks of choice. She *chose* these women.

By consciously including herself in a community of successful and like-minded women, my mother publicly identified with the middle-class qualities they shared. Just as Gantt talks about how making a cake and bringing it to a community event can be assertion of cultural control (2001, 82), placing oneself within a community one views positively is an affirmation of self. My mother's recipes attest to the ways that women looked after one another as they gathered together for a cup of coffee or tea over pans of squares or "gooshy" desserts. They record important connections to social worlds – worlds that blurred time in drawing together female friends and positive memories from various temporal stages of her life. In a life full of social expectation and obligation, my mother's recipes speak of worlds of her choosing.

COOKING AND CREATIVITY

I can't conjure up a single memory that encapsulates the totality of who my mother was so I try to remember the things that made her happy. Perhaps this is where I can find the clues. I recall that my mother laughed a lot. She liked people. People liked her. It now strikes me as significant that everything I can think of that she enjoyed took her outside of the house; she liked to go out. She loved her bridge club; she liked to shop. Even the food that seemed to give her the most pleasure was eaten in a restaurant. She loved to eat out. She liked Crispy Crunch chocolate bars and Coca Cola.

Mom never seemed to place much value on the recipes she collected and used. They were treated casually. Looking back, I cannot recall her ever indicating to me that there was a "right" way to make something, like light pastry or fluffy biscuits. The fact that her collection contains several recipes for each reflects her willingness to try new recipes for even the most foundational dishes in her repertoire. Although the kitchen was my mother's space (see Abarca 2006, 20), it was not her haven. She did not show the love of cooking that my friend Valerie Mansour's mother did, for instance. Alexandra came alive in her kitchen. With animated instructions, she shared very particular directions for how to do everything. In her kitchen there was one right way to do things, and her standards were high. When she showed me the correct way to make stuffed grape leaves, she stressed the importance of sitting down: "Sit down when you roll grape leaves. Take a load off your feet whenever you can," she advised. She often instructed Val in the kitchen and would mentor me as well if I showed any interest in what she was cooking. It all stood in stark contrast to my own mother, who did not invite help. It was easier for her to do it herself. Although Mom would have relented if pressured, she was not interested in guiding her children in the kitchen. I remember her providing recipes at my request after I left home, and that she mailed many recipes to her own mother, but she never initiated the sharing of a recipe with my sister, brother, or me. As a result, when I became interested in such things in my twenties, I turned to my friends as often as to my mother. For example, even though Mom produced pies on a weekly basis, I recall consulting a friend to learn how to make pie crust. Afterward, she added the pastry recipe I brought home to her collection.

My mother's apparent disinterest in food, despite the hours she invested in procuring, preparing, and serving it, again presented a contrasted with Val's mother, who found deeply meaningful expression in her family's foodways. Although Mom would sometimes report a positive reception to something she made – "The women in the church group really liked this. You should try it" – she never revealed that she cared very deeply about the food she made. On the other hand, Val's family highly valued the Lebanese dishes Alexandra made as a symbol of their cultural identity. I remember the excitement in that household over the annual arrival of Lebanese groceries from Montreal just before Christmas; after she graduated from high school, Val put together two collections of her mother's recipes. For these members of a very small Lebanese community in Amherst, food was a primary expression of their family identity and ethnicity. In our home, on the other hand, food was rarely spoken of and we never gave my mother the kind of recognition and appreciation for her cooking that Alexandra earned from her family.

Birthday Cake

1 cup butter or margarine

2 cup sugar

3 eggs

3½ cup flour (3¼ cup if not cake flour)

1⅓ cup milk

1 tsp baking powder & salt

1 tsp lemon extract

Cream butter and sugar. Add eggs one at a time beating 5 minutes after

each. Add flour, baking powder and salt alternately with milk. Flavor with
lemon. Bake 1½ hours in moderate oven.

Winnie '68

Blend writes that "reproducing a recipe, like retelling a story, requires
that they [women writers] maneuver between personal and collective
texts, between an autobiographical 'I' and various forms of a political/
cultural 'we'" (2001, 147–8). Baking can provide moments of solitude
and reflection, creativity, and peace; it can be a positive moment in
women's lives. My mother may have preferred baking to some of her
other domestic work; however, she did not find a great deal of creativity
there. I suspect that her experience was more the paradox that Erika
Endrijonas describes from the 1950s, when "cooking ... was viewed as
an outlet for creativity; however, this creativity was encouraged in very
structured, controlled ways. Additionally, while women were expected
to express their creative energies through their cooking, this creativity
was subordinate to the need to be of service to the family" (Endrijonas
2001, 159).

As folklorists have explored in other contexts, a major source of
creativity in everyday life comes from the manipulation of forms of popular culture (e.g., see Narváez and Laba c.1988). Daniel Miller (1998)
has alerted us to the ways in which even shopping for items can be an
expressive experience. The ingenuity my mother and her friends demonstrated in combining convenience foods connects them to larger traditions of female adaptive reuse, from rugmaking to quilting, that reflect
both resourcefulness and an appreciation for latent possibilities in
materials at hand. As Gerald Pocius's work on the use of space in Calvert,
Newfoundland, demonstrates, adopting and adapting new products can
be part of a complex creative process. For example, Pocius argues that
even when residents of Calvert take up new forms of housing, they will

live in them in old ways, according to traditional patterns of spatial use. Just like the people Pocius interviewed, my mother's and her friends' kitchen creations, such as Watergate Cake, combined the old and new in sometimes unexpected ways.

Watergate Cake

No need to grease pan.
Put:
1 package cake mix – Duncan Hines
¾ cup Crisco oil
1 package Jell-O instant pistachio pudding
3 eggs
1 cup ginger ale
½ cup walnuts
1 tsp almond flavoring
Bake 350 for 45 min.

Topping – prepare while cake is cooking:
1 package Jell-O instant pudding pistachio
1¼ cup milk
Beat together
1 large container Cool Whip

Beat three ingredients together. Set until ready before putting on cake.
Cake has to be cold.

The adaptation of commercial ingredients also figured in the creation of my mother's most overtly creative enterprise: children's birthday cakes. Following directions cut out from a woman's magazine, she carved cake into a number of shaped pieces and then assembled these

CATHY POISED TO BLOW OUT THE CANDLES AT HER THIRD
BIRTHDAY PARTY, CHARLOTTETOWN, 1965. DIANE IS SEATED
TO HER RIGHT.

MARK CELEBRATING
HIS SIXTH BIRTHDAY
WITH A SPIDERMAN
CAKE, AMHERST, 1976

with brightly tinted icing to produce a duck, train, or space ship. Cookies, or more often candies, became decorations. These cakes were not professional accomplishments; nor were they intended to be. The icing that held the various pieces together was applied liberally with a butter knife rather than through a cake decorator's icing bag with rosebud-shaped tip. As children, we considered the cakes special. They were the most elaborate food we encountered throughout the year, rivalled only by a similarly constructed bunny cake made each Easter and decorated sugar cookies at Christmas, and we often had a hand in their construction. We appreciated the birthday cakes as much for the candles on top and the money hidden inside as we did for their novel shape and decorations.[3] They were not admired by either children or adults as any kind of artwork; as with most things, we children valued the journey rather than the destination. For us, the construction process, the challenge of blowing out candles and the hunt for hidden treasure in the form of coins wrapped in waxed paper, were the attractions. In our house, even the most special food did not offer a contemplative experience. Although this was in part due to a larger cultural silence surrounding food and food preparation that had its roots in my parents' Scottish heritage and mainstream Protestantism, I also see it, in part, as an expression of my mother's refusal to be defined by her domestic role. Just like the "moral" of the stories Abu-Lughod collected from Bedouin women, my mother's recipes indicate how "things are and are not what they seem" (Abu-Lughod 1993, 19).

CODED RESISTANCE

"She'd be done by noon and you wouldn't even think she'd be doing anything" (Mark Tye, Interview, 1999).

In retrospect, it strikes everyone I ask about my mother's baking how little time she seemed to spend doing it. Mark recalls her weekly Saturday morning baking as blur of activity: "She'd be done by noon and you wouldn't even think she'd be doing anything" (Mark Tye, Interview, 1999). My father remembers, "I've seen her after supper whip up the stuff, she's rolling something and the square pan is out there and she's putting the stuff in there and she's rolling the crust for a pie ... and it would all happen in an hour" (Henry Tye, Interview, 1999). These descriptions are not atypical of women's work; for example, Edward T. Hall (1983) characterized women's conceptualization and use of time as polychronic, given their constant multi-tasking. My mother was a fast worker, but her recipes facilitated her ability to make several at once within the span of an hour. None were complicated or required more than a few "standard" inexpensive ingredients she always had on hand: flour, sugar, eggs, margarine, baking soda and baking powder, and processed foods like chocolate chips, marshmallows, peanut butter, and graham wafers. The huge majority of her collection (99 percent) are recipes clustered under three categories: cookies, squares, and loaves (including breads and cakes). Recipes, or their categorical structure, became very familiar, so that just in the way oral performers acquire a frame on which different narratives or songs can be hung (see Lord 1965, Buchan 1972), my mother internalized a series of methods so that eventually she could produce cookie variants – peanut butter cookies or chocolate chip – with considerable speed.

Hers were not delicate recipes. In fact, they were resilient and able to accommodate a high degree of what Lisa M. Heldke describes as "fiddling around." Out of her own personal experience, Heldke writes:

> I can make equally wonderful chocolate chip cookies either by dumping all the ingredients in a bowl at the same time and stirring them together, or by first mixing butter and sugar together, and

then adding eggs one at a time. Chocolate chip cookie dough is extremely resilient; when I mix the ingredients for it, almost anything *can* go and they'll still turn out. If I attempted the same sort of radical variation in technique when I was making puff pastry, I'd probably produce all sorts of interesting food products, but only some of them would resemble puff pastry (1992, 260).

Pineapple Squares

Graham Base
Then
½ cup butter
2 eggs
2½ c icing sugar
vanilla

Add
½ pint whipped cream (Dream Whip)
crushed pineapple
2 T sugar
Put in fridge

Simplicity and ease defined my mother's recipes. Her recipe for Pineapple Squares, scrawled on a bridge score pad in my mother's hurried handwriting, came from her friend and neighbour, Dot. The recipe's scant instructions – with amounts omitted and directions for how to construct a graham wafer crust skipped over – not only bear witness to the fact that both my mother and her friend were experienced cooks, but also to the familiarity of this kind of dessert to the women. By the 1980s, when my mother acquired this recipe, she would have needed only a quick outline for a graham-wafer dessert, for she had already made

many. These desserts were quickly and easily concocted; most did not require cooking and relied on industrial foods. As Laura Shapiro observes
of women writing in to a newspaper column from the 1950s, simple
recipes were highly valued. She observes that when women "submitted
their favorite recipes to the special section in 1959, the word they used
most often to explain why they treasured a particular recipe was 'easy.'"
(2001, 51). Supporting Neuhaus's finding that "[r]ecipes from the postwar years emphasized ease in preparation, and relied heavily on brand-
name products and prepackaged foods" (1999, 533), my mother's recipe
collection contains several variations of "easy" desserts that incorporated graham wafer crumbs as well as convenience foods such as Dream
Whip, Jell-O, and canned fruit.

As Pineapple Squares and its close relatives attest, my mother and
her friends most enthusiastically embraced the graham wafer, which they
crushed and mixed with sugar and melted butter or margarine as a
dessert base. Like Watergate Cake above, these desserts represent a
repurposing of ingredients not originally envisioned by their creators.
Although the packaged graham crumbs now available indicate the manufacturers' recognition and exploitation of women's use of graham
crackers as a dessert base, the contemporary product is far removed
from its original. Invented in 1829 by Sylvester Graham, a Presbyterian
minister, avid vegetarian, and temperance advocate, the crackers were
Graham's answer to cholera as well as to the many other physical and
social problems that he linked to improper diet. Graham recognized that
"refining" food depleted it of much of its nutritional value (Sokolow
1983, 117), and he particularly targeted commercially available milk
and bakery bread made from refined flour. Instead, Graham advocated
eating bread made from ground wheat flour with a high fibre content;
this became known as "graham flour," after its proponent.

Ironically, the graham crackers my mother and her friends used in
their desserts were not only much sweeter than the original, but contained mostly white rather than graham flour. After 1898, Nabisco

produced graham crackers as a popular snack food with greater amounts of sugar, honey, and other sweeteners than in the original recipe and with cinnamon added to enhance the flavour. Sometime after 1938, when the *Watkins Cook Book* published one of the first recipes for graham cracker pastry (Lovegren 2005, 152), Nabisco and other major cereal companies promoted crushing graham crackers as the base for rich, sweet desserts that would have horrified Sylvester Graham.

Dishes like Pineapple Squares relied on another convenience food, whipped topping, which was often mixed with canned or frozen fruit. Significantly, in this recipe, Mom notes her intention to use Dream Whip rather than fresh whipped cream. Dream Whip Topping Mix (1957) and Cool Whip Whipped Topping (1966), both products of Kraft Foods, would have been always kept on hand in our kitchen, and I rarely remember my mother purchasing fresh whipping cream. As with the other convenience products she adopted, Cool Whip was featured in many General Food recipes, providing what Wyman describes as "the mortar in a whole array of quickie gourmet dessert recipes all the rage in the late 1960s and early 1970s, including mousse (Cool Whip whipped into instant pudding); chiffon pie (Cool Whip whipped into unset Jell-O); and trifle (Cool Whip layered with pound cake, Jell-O pudding, and Bird's Eye frozen strawberries ...)" (2004, 64). Wyman concludes, "Rare is the community or church cookbook even today that does not call for Cool Whip in at least one recipe (and usually many more)" (2004, 64).

Lemon Dessert

---

1 pkg lemon Jell-O with 1½ c boiling water. Let set until of egg white consistency (or thicker). Then beat well. Add ½ c. lemon juice and 1 c sugar. Fold this into 1 can beaten evaporated milk (make sure the milk is very cold before you beat it and beat it very stiff). Line a pan with crushed butter wafer crumbs. Add filling and top with more crumbs. Sadie

Almost as ubiquitous as graham crumbs and prepared whipped topping in these "quickie gourmet desserts" was Jell-O. Although Pineapple
Squares did not require Jell-O, other recipes in Mom's collection, like
Lemon Dessert, did. As Wyman (2001) notes, Jell-O was a very common ingredient in this kind of dessert and perhaps more than any other
ingredient it was readapted in salads and desserts. The first patent for a
gelatin dessert dates to 1845, but according to the Kraft Foods website,
it was 1897 when American carpenter and cough medicine manufacturer
Pearle B. Wait developed a fruit-flavoured version of the gelatin, and his
wife, May Davis Wait, named it Jell-O. Only then did home cooks begin
to abandon the time-consuming process of clarifying sheets of prepared
gelatin by boiling with egg whites and shells and dripped through a jelly
bag before they could be turned into moulds (www.kraftfoods.com/
jello). The product's popularity skyrocketed with the sale of the rights
to Jell-O in 1899 to Orator Francis Woodward. Woodward launched the
advertising campaign "America's most favorite Dessert" in 1902 that
featured ads for Jell-O gelatin in women's magazines, like *Ladies Home
Journal*. Woodward recognized both the product's versatility and the
fact that women needed help learning to incorporate Jell-O into their
baking (Wyman 2004, 114) so that in 1904 he introduced the first in a
series of Jell-O gelatin recipe books that contributed further to the product's popularity. The establishment of a plant in Bridgeburg, Ontario,
the next year further opened the Canadian market, and by the 1950s my
mother and her friends were enthusiastically creating desserts out of an
expanded line of flavours comprised of the original four flavours of
strawberry, raspberry, orange and lemon as well as cherry, peach, apple,
grape, black cherry, and black raspberry. There was also a line of instant
puddings that in 1976 added pistachio, a flavour my mother used in her
later baking.

My mother's embrace of the graham-cracker-base dessert was part
of a much larger movement. She and her friends joined middle-class

women throughout North America in the 1960s and 1970s who enthusiastically adopted a range of creamy desserts. As Lovegren writes: "Desserts were concoctions of whipped cream (or Cool Whip or Dream Whip), or sour cream, or cream cheese, or ice cream, with sticky cornstarch glazes, or ultra sweet butterscotch or chocolate sauces on top" (2005, 300). These desserts were so popular that a version of the strawberry dessert my mother made for her church group and the other women's gatherings mentioned in the last chapter was ranked by *Better Homes and Gardens* in 1975 as one of their fifteen "all-time favorite" recipes from their test kitchens.[4]

Relying on convenience products such as graham wafers, whipped topping, and Jell-O, my mother produced updated, and less laborious, versions of earlier dishes like chiffon pie. Lovegren dates the first mention of chiffon pie to the 1922 edition of *Good Housekeeping's Book of Menus, Recipes and Household Discoveries,* where it appeared under the name of coffee soufflé. The recipe combined gelatin with uncooked, beaten egg whites, as Lovegren notes, reinventing the older gelatin sponges or snows that were popular in the 1940s by placing them in a crust; in turn, they helped to usher in the era of the crumb pie shell and crushed graham cracker base (Lovegren 2005, 149). In time, whipped chilled evaporated milk took the place of the egg whites (Lovegren 2005, 153) but, as noted earlier, by the 1960s and 1970s, when my mother and her friends produced so many of these desserts, the time and effort they demanded was reduced even further with the substitution of prepared whipped topping.

As Sherrie Inness points out, in a modern kitchen of the 1950s or 1960s, food was expected to be as contemporary as the appliances: "Convenience foods of all kinds, including the TV dinner, were an integral part of this image of modernity and progress. They came into their own in the 1950s, and the media celebrated them as a way to turn cooking into a quick and pleasant task. Cookbooks assured women that packaged convenience foods simplified cooking and left cooks more time for other tasks" (2001c, 157–8). So successful were the marketers that Jessamyn Neuhaus identifies reliance on brand-name products and pre-packaged foods, and emphasis on ease of preparation, as characteristic of recipes from the postwar years (1999, 533).

While manufacturers pushed their new products, there were limitations. Women were supposed to use convenience foods to lighten their load by incorporating them as easy ingredients, but not to escape from the task of meal preparation altogether by substituting them for home baking or cooking. Women were expected to "be creative" with processed foods (Neuhaus 1999, 533). This recipe in my mother's collection, unappetizingly called "Dump Cake," is an example of how women sometimes pushed the boundaries of "home-made."

Dump Cake

1 can cherry pie filling in bottom of pan
1 can crushed pineapple not drained on top
Then sprinkle yellow cake mix over all
Add nuts and coconut

Bake 350 for 25–35 minutes

Should cut into squares

My mother incorporated other convenience foods into her baking, ranging from packaged chocolate chips to powdered milk and Velveeta cheese. Her recipes support Endrijonas's description of the 1950s, the decade of my mother's first years of marriage and the period when she was learning to bake, as a time both of acceleration of the "de-skilling" of daily cooking that had begun in World War II (2001, 158) and the "heyday" of prepared foods that ultimately led to a new definition of what constituted "home-cooked meals" as homemakers found a new balance between convenience, taste, and duty (2001, 159). According to Lovegren, the trend continued for another decade: she describes the 1960s as "the high point of instant food, quick food, space age food" (Lovegren 2005, 217). As the example of Dump Cake indicates, my mother's recipes embraced modernity through their use of convenience foods that include cake mixes and canned fruit and pie fillings. Jell-O, prepared dessert toppings like Dream Whip or Cool Whip, and graham wafers became staples.

Newton writes that, even by the turn of the century, Jell-O was on its way to becoming a million-dollar business and a means for woman to show creativity in the kitchen, nurturance of the family, and a clever if innocent sophistication (1992, 252). Sales for Jell-O peaked in the late 1960s (Wyman 2004, 115); Ireland describes Jell-O as "ubiquitous" in that virtually every American – and I would say every North American – has had some experience with Jell-O (1981, 108). According to Newton, the original target consumer for Jell-O was the American housewife, "who was assured that this product would please her family (be both tasty and 'fun'), make her somehow a better wife and mother, and allow her to exercise kitchen creativity" (1992, 252). Newton continues: "[C]ertainly Jell-O's invention is tied with wholesomeness, purity, and domesticity" (1992, 252). One woman Newton interviewed for her 1992 article on Jell-O described her earlier creation of moulded Jell-O as "the most sophisticated thing you could do. There wasn't anything as elegant. It was the center of the table" (1992, 252). While sales continue to be bolstered by a new range of Jell-O ready-made products, as Newton notes, "the image of the food product has changed from being the ultimate in the American housewife's repertoire of tasty and elegant salads and desserts to an embarrassment, a symbol of gauche unsophistication often tied, not to the trendy coasts, but to the rural –

the hick-Mid-West" (1992, 255). There has been a cultural shift, but in my mother's day Jell-O was promoted as the base for "Busy Day Desserts." It was a modern product that ads promised would ensure it was never too late for real homemade desserts (www.kraftfoods.com). Home cooking could be realized with minimal effort. Jell-O brought together modernity and mothering at the same time as it promised women a creative outlet and escape from laborious tasks.

Some writers have argued that these kinds of products democratized dessert and salad-making (e.g., LeBesco 2001, 134) in that food that requires a great deal of time and labour to create or elaborate utensils to produce and serve carries with it the prestige of elevated purchasing power. By the 1950s, Jell-O opened up fancy gelatin desserts that had been associated with status, wealth and at times manual dexterity and industriousness (see Wyman 2004, 114), to members of the middle and working classes. Neuhaus refers to Jell-O as "meta-food" and identifies it as a trend from the 1950s to make food from other food, such as graham wafers, canned cherry pie filling, or ginger ale (1999, 534). Jell-O and Dream Whip on crushed graham wafer crackers filled the bill. Made of several layers, it was considered fancy but was not labour intensive to produce. It belongs to the type of food that, as Neuhaus writes, "aimed to elevate the status of cooking and gave the *impression* of time and trouble taken" (1999, 535). Sherrie Inness notes that Jell-O also helped democratize the fad of daintiness that influenced women in the 1950s (2001c, 63). Delicate yet affordable, Jell-O provided a convenient vehicle for the expression of both status and femininity.

At the same time as Jell-O and other convenience products offered women an opportunity to imitate more labour-intensive cooking, it also allowed them to break free from those earlier traditions (see LeBesco 2001). Convenience foods, combined with simple, formulaic instructions, allowed my mother to produce "home-made" dishes quickly and without much planning. Although, as Sherrie Inness emphasizes, the marketing of convenience foods encouraged women to leave the kitchen to pursue other interests only after they had fulfilled their household responsibilities (2006, 20), time away from domestic tasks like baking did mean time for other things.

HIDDEN TRANSCRIPTS

I sit not so patiently through yet another Women's Studies meeting. We are at a crossroads; an underfunded, under-supported interdisciplinary program in a university organized around disciplines and departments. Those of us who have supported the program for years on top of all our other responsibilities are tired. I am very tired. The meeting proceeds as we go over familiar frustrations: the seeming impossibility of making necessary structural changes in the face of university administrators who don't seem to get it and who are reluctant to commit additional resources. "What are our options?" we ask again. "How can we make change happen?" Some people around the table think it is time to the go to the media. "Embarrass the administration," a colleague recommends, "then they'll listen." I cringe. I doubt that public embarrassment will win us the administration's support. "Let's request a meeting and try to explain our position," I suggest. Several others now shift uneasily, just as I did, at the idea of going public. They read this suggestion as conservative. They may be right, but I often leave these meetings feeling misunderstood because I do not agree that I am more conservative than the others in this group. It strikes me again that those of us in the room embrace a variety of strategies for change, I feel that our chances of making a difference are much more likely if we can find ways to work within the system. Whenever I think about this issue, I decide that my commitment to working within the system has deep roots. My parents worked on social justice issues as part of larger structures, such as organized religion. I wonder now about my mother. What were her ideas of how to bring about change?

In Mom's recipes I recognize examples of what James C. Scott terms a "critique of power spoken behind the back of the dominant" or "hidden transcript" (1990, xii). Although it is impossible to assess whether the women's groups to which my mother belonged were purposely subversive, I believe that, like the Bedouin women Abu-Lughod worked with, they engaged daily in minor defiances as they resisted existing systems of power at they same time as they supported them (Abu-Lughod 1990). I have come to see my mother's constant baking as a form of distraction, a type of implicit feminist coding as defined by Radner and Lanser (1993). Authors have pointed to various forms of distraction that women turn to, from lullabies (Langlois, in Radner 1993) to funeral laments (Bourke, in Radner 1993). Davis writes that even diarists rely on distraction to express themselves: "Most diarists were not so self-revealing. In fact, they seemed to use their writing and sewing as distractions, coping with traumas in their lives by avoiding the direct expression of their intense feelings" (1997, 225). As a form of distraction, baking helped my mother deflect attention from her life beyond the domestic sphere, and in doing so allowed her to do and be other things. Baking that was "always there," as my brother put it, satisfied family demands for something sweet. Sweets were just one of many ways women of my mother's generation made family members feel good. As discussed earlier, my brother coming home to chocolate chip cookies was so affirming that it has had lasting repercussions.

Cookies became an important currency in a house where there was little time for conversation. In contrast to many middle-class parents today, whose enthusiastic hands-on parenting style threatens to stifle their children's independence, my mother and father belonged to a more distant generation of parents who were less involved in their children's social lives. In our house, children from preschool age on were expected to take responsibility for finding their own social contacts and for amusing themselves. Home was not a place of talk, and we rarely sat down with the sole purpose of speaking to one another. Rather, my parents generally talked with their children while they worked. As a young child, I would sit on the basement step and talk to my father as he varnished a board for a construction project. Or I would chat with my mother while she carefully cut out a dress pattern. Our family meals were not occasions for conversation; they were got through quickly, almost as if with the aim of refuelling for what would follow. My mother looked forward to having supper over early and the kitchen cleaned up so she could move on to other things. "Eating late makes the evening too short," she would argue in defence of our early supper hour. My parents had other things to do. In light of all this work, fresh cinnamon rolls could assure a child that he or she mattered. They provided tangible evidence that children were listened to, respected, and certainly worth investing time in. At the same time, quickly produced homemade baking distracted attention from the time my mother and other women created for themselves. With the cupboards well stocked, no one in our family questioned Mom's decision to seek pleasure for herself outside of the house, whether that was spent shopping or socializing.

Cultural critics have linked postwar cookery to a domestic ideology that sought to limit a woman's life to the domestic sphere (see Neuhaus 1999, 543). It was an ideology that demanded acquiescence. As the brief overview of *Chatelaine* ads from the 1950s in the last chapter shows, women of my mother's generation were bombarded by images of the competent housewife in her kitchen; it was an ubiquitous image in the popular culture of the 1950s. Levenstein points out that from women's magazines to popular radio programs like "Ma Perkins" and early television programs like "Father Knows Best," the powerful, overriding message was that cooking was central to women's successful performance of gender (see Levenstein 1993, 103). Women were shown exercising a complete monopoly over family food preparation, and popular culture presented fathers' culinary responsibilities as consisting of carving joints on festive occasions or perhaps drying the occasional dish. Like June Cleaver in "Father Knows Best," most often popular culture examples were positive but the directive could be expressed negatively and directly. For example, in 1950, *Vogue* magazine described women who did not cook well as "nervous, unstable types" who would probably end up on a psychiatrist's couch (see Seid 1989, 103). Some researchers have pointed to indications that this gender discourse was not as simple as it may first seem. As Neuhaus writes, "One of the most significant ways that postwar cookbooks indicated the cultural debate around the nature of women's role in society was to give credence to the belief that cooking meals every day for one's family could be a tedious task" (1999, 543). In acknowledging that women might not always find the work of feeding their families rewarding, postwar cookbooks articulated an anxiety that white middle-class women might not be completely fulfilled in their roles of wife and mother (Neuhaus 1999, 540). Neuhaus points to the repetitive insistence that women take responsibility for and find fulfillment in cooking for their families as an indication that women were challenging these expectations. She contends:

> The women who baked, basted, glazed, and decorated throughout postwar cookbooks were figments of the postwar American imagination. They were expressions of desires and fears in a nation strained by the war and baffled by the unstoppable social changes that shaped the 1950s. These women were as fictional as Betty

Crocker and constructed for a very similar purpose: to soothe and to reassure. The recipes and rhetoric of postwar cookbooks, by their continuous repetition, tell social historians a story of strained and tested gender norms.

When a cookbook author advised her readers that they would find deep fulfillment in daily cooking duties, other possibilities were, paradoxically, raised (Neuhaus 1999, 546).

Neuhaus argues that the repeated assertion of authority actually worked to destabilize it (1999, 546) and that the constant repetition of gender norms revealed deep underlying fears and uncertainties about those norms (1999, 546). She concludes:

When authority does not conceal itself, but is repeated in text, a space where resistance or subversion may be enacted is created. By stating assumptions about women's lives, cookbooks left room for those 'assumptions' to be questioned. Cookbooks, in their efforts to seal up the growing cracks in gender ideology, actually left traces and clues about just where the cracks had begun to show. The dominant discourse that positioned cooking and food preparation as a natural, deeply fulfilling activity for all women spoke to the possibility that perhaps it was not (Neuhaus 1999, 547).

The emergence of a domestic humour literature, led by authors such as Peg Bracken with an open expression of their dislike for homemaking and cooking, was one indication of women's refusal to accept the rigid role definitions of this domestic ideology (Neuhaus 1999, 544) and prefigured issues that would surface more openly with the rise of the women's liberation movement (Walker 1985, in Neuhaus 1999, 545). Read in this way, my mother's use of food to extend women's gatherings, as well as her reliance on convenience foods and her embrace of easily made recipes, was an expression of resistance to the dominant gender ideologies that promised total fulfillment in the kitchen. After all, as my father proclaimed, "[your mother's] life was not invested in cooking" (Henry Tye, Interview, 1999).

TASTING THE PAST

My mother's recipes are in jeopardy. After her death, her little recipe box remained closed until I discovered it a few years ago. It was as if her Chocolate Chip Cookies, Date Squares, and Shortbread had died with her. It is not surprising, of course, that her recipes are no longer made. Like so many others across North America, my family and I are quick to purchase prepared food rather than make it from scratch at home. These days our sweets are more likely to come from a supermarket bakery than from our own kitchens. However, some of the factors that have led us away from home baking suggest that lack of time and increased availability of store-bought goods do not tell the whole story. In our case, at least, answers are both more individual and more complicated. To consider what motivates my family to look to food as the embodiment of memory, or alternatively to find meaning elsewhere, is to raise larger questions about how food allows us to remember and what it allows us to forget. As an articulation of family dynamics, my family's uses of past tastes signal our individual understandings of what it means to be part of a family. Affected by our subject positions, differing relationships to

HENRY, MARK, CATHY, AND DIANE, CHARLOTTETOWN, 2005

those past tastes show the influence of many factors, including age, gender, and disability. They speak loudly of our personal experiences of belonging to, as well as a sense of isolation from, the family we are part of.

REMEMBERING

When we do follow Mom's recipes, it is largely to remember her and the family we were when she was alive. It is a present reminder of her nurturing and of the sense of family identity she passed on to us. Locher and colleagues write: "The nostalgic longing and consumption of particular food items sustain one's sense of cultural, familial, and self-identity. When we are physically disconnected from a community, a family, or

DIANE AND MARK DECORATING CHRISTMAS COOKIES,
AMHERST, c. 1975

any primary group that defines who we are, our sense of self may become fractured. In these instances, consuming food items intimately linked with one's past may repair such fractures by maintaining a continuity of the self in unfamiliar surroundings" (2005, 280).

For me, the selective reproduction of my mother's baking is part of the nostalgic longing and search for continuity between the past and present that these authors describe. I do not turn to her recipes when I make food for public consumption; for these occasions, they are as useless to me as my grandmother's recipes were to my mother after she married. The potluck dinners I attend with colleagues and friends demand healthier contributions than Mom's butter- and sugar-laden baking. Nor do I look to my mother's recipe box when I entertain friends. At those times, I emphasize the main course rather than dessert and opt for Asian or Middle Eastern influenced dishes.[1] It is only when I prepare food for my family that I consider concocting a dessert with a graham wafer base or making Peanut Butter Balls. Then these dishes become gifts. The strawberry dessert is so sweet that the children in the family won't eat it, but I serve it to my sister when we get together because it was her childhood favourite. When my brother reminds me of how much he loves the taste of chocolate and peanut butter, I produce a version of the Chocolate Bon-Bons that Mom used to make for him.

Chocolate Bon-Bons

---

1 cup peanut butter
1 cup icing sugar
4 tbsp butter
½ cup chopped nuts
½ cup coconut
1 cup Rice Krispies

Mix and form into a ball. Dip in one 6 oz package chocolate chips melted over hot water, add 2 tbsp parawax. Put on wax paper and chill.

In the way that Daniel Miller (1998) characterizes shopping as an act of love, these dishes communicate my feelings for my sister and brother at the same time as they bring our mother into the present, making her a part of our time together. The food we share is a physical reminder that she lives in us and continues to be a part of the family.

Making tasty food – some of which was once my mother's food – has become part of how my family sees me and how I see myself. This piece of my gender performance as daughter, sister, wife, and mother is part of my mother's legacy. Reproducing her baking reinforces my position as the family's eldest female, and it is a partial claim of her authority and a display of competency that everyone in the family recognizes. Making appropriate food the way it "should" taste is an achievement that my family – father, brother, sister, and five nieces, as well as my partner and my son – all appreciate.

By producing food that is familiar to the older members of the family, I introduce it to the next generation. David Sutton talks about the importance of food events in providing possibilities for future "prospective" memories (Sutton 2001, 31). This responsibility has fallen to me, although I am no longer clear how it came to be negotiated. Have I taken it on, or was it given to me? In her introduction to Clara Sereni's novel in recipes, *Keeping House,* Giovanna Miceli Jeffries claims that "[f]ood that accompanies the ordinary and extraordinary occasions of life is the glue of memory" (2005, 13). I know that I feel a sense of obligation to supply that glue.

Above all, making my mother's food is an act of self-nurturing. Tasting a cookie, I am a child again watching my mother bake, or eating a meal that my grandmother prepared. Just as taste defined home while I was growing up, now it takes me home. For me that homeland is not only geographically but temporally removed. Peanut butter cookies transport me through time.[2] These tastes, along with other everyday and special foods my mother produced, have become part of what Tad Tuleja (1997) calls my "usable past." Every fall Mom joined women across the Maritimes in making pickles and preserves. When I cut up cucumbers for the same mustard pickles each September, they now tie me as much to another time as to another place. Pickles bring me back to long-ago autumns when I sat on the back step with my mother, and sometimes my grandmother, helping prepare their pickles. Sutton points out that Proust does not single out taste in his famous description of the madeleine; rather, a certain taste and smell hold the promise of a return to the memorable whole (2001, 88). This is true for me. It is the smell of vinegar cooking on the stove that helps recall all earlier autumns. This is what ties me to my great grandmother, whom I know only by a few family stories, her photo, a glass plate she once owned, and the taste of her pickles.

Mustard Pickles

7 lg cucumbers
Peel, cut in small pieces, set aside for 2 hrs. with ½ cup salt.

Heat:
3 cup vinegar

Add:
2½ cups white sugar
½ cup flour
3 tbsp mustard
1 tsp ginger
¾ tsp turmeric
Add ½ cup water.

Mix into a paste, add to hot vinegar and pour over drained pickles.
Cook on low heat for ½ hour or so.

Now that I live in Newfoundland, these recipes and tastes have taken on increased importance. Comfort foods here are different from the Maritime baking that grew out of agricultural roots. I sometimes long for the oatcakes and biscuits of my youth, which reflect the Scottish ancestry I share with many other Maritimers and symbolize a way of looking at life and a particular way of being. My feeling of connectedness comes from the sense of an imagined community that, as Sutton describes it, is "implied in the act of eating food 'from home' while in exile, in the embodied knowledge that others are eating the same food" (2001, 84). This is the case for me.

In talking with my father and brother, I discover that they also find meaning in our family's past tastes, albeit in ways that are different from mine. Consistent with the low priority that my father gives to food, he invests neither significant time nor money in its preparation and consumption. He eats easily prepared meals, a piece of fruit, or a bowl of oatmeal. He depends on invitations out for full-course meals. He does, however, share my enjoyment in the sense of community or *communitas* that comes from seasonal food activities, and he continues two of the many of these that my mother carried out each year. In July, Dad lines the shelves of his basement cold room with bottles of homemade strawberry jam. This is something he used to help Mom with, and since her death he has carried it on. Like everything he does, this enterprise is one of quantity. Even though he lives alone, he preserves at least a flat of strawberries, producing dozens of bottles of jam. Some years he organizes the whole family to gather at his house for a communal effort. My sister, brother, and I, along with all the grandchildren, hull berries. In an assembly-line production, we prepare berries and then boil and bottle the jam. My father enjoys having everyone work together to produce the family's winter supply of jam. Some years he makes other kinds, usually raspberry or blueberry. Many autumns he also takes on the more arduous task of making apple jelly. But strawberry jam is his staple. He never misses a summer, and all year round he eats the jam on his morning toast.

My father's second seasonal food activity takes place in the fall. At Halloween he purchases a pumpkin, which he carves into a jack-o'-lantern. Later, he boils up the pumpkin and makes it into pies. He follows a recipe in *Tested Sweet Recipes* that my mother used for the filling and then bakes it in a ready-made frozen pastry shell.

Pumpkin Pie

1 cup sugar	½ tsp ginger
1½ tsp cinnamon	½ tsp salt
½ tsp cloves	2 eggs (beaten)
½ tsp allspice	1½ cups canned pumpkin
½ tsp nutmeg	1 lg can evaporated milk

Blend sugar, spices and salt in bowl. Add eggs, pumpkin and milk. Pour into unbaked pie shell. Bake 425 for 15 minutes. Then reduce heat to 350 and continue baking 40 minutes. Cool.

Mrs. James Farrell

(*Tested Sweet Recipes* 40)

After my mother died, my father experienced the passing of time differently. Seasons were not distinctively marked as they had been when my mother's food preparations signalled the passing year. Fried mackerel, stewed rhubarb, and rhubarb pie no longer announced the arrival of spring. A variety of fresh foods and the making of jams did not punctuate the summer. Fall went unmarked by preserving and pickle making. Late fall and winter did not bring baking and other preparations for Christmas. After her death, the seasons blurred. As my father reflected,

> I would say that the loss of her moving out of my life has been in the structure to my life … the marking of the seasons, the jam making period, the pickle making period, the pumpkin pie making period and certainly the Christmas baking and now you partially

fill that but if you weren't here those seasons would slip right by and they'd mesh one into the other. You see, she put structure into the year (Henry and Mark Tye, Interview, 2005).

Dad goes on to describe how that "loss of structure" affects him on a daily basis. He struggles to shed the earlier scheduling of his life, which included a cooked meal every evening at five o'clock. Although he is now free to eat whatever and whenever he wants, he finds himself thinking that he should eat at five, even on those nights when he is not hungry or the time is inconvenient. Like us all, he finds continuity in a partial reproduction of an earlier, and much more elaborated, food preparation and preservation cycle. He might not make a cooked meal for himself, but he will eat at the regular time. He makes jam but does not take on the more labour-intensive task of pickle making. He has less need for pickles than jam, given that he does not prepare full-course meals. He finds his connections with the past and with the passing of time through the making of strawberry jam and the preparing of pumpkin pies. This is his journey back to the whole.

My brother reproduces none of my mother's tastes. He does not enter into jam-making unless he happens to be drafted into my father's annual effort. Nor does he bake. Like my father, he values structure more than actual tastes:

I remember Mom almost every time when I go out to eat. She loved to eat out. I'd eat out every day if I could. And so would she. Every time Dad was away in Toronto, we'd eat out ... I remember walking down to the Dairy Queen ... And I have a sweet after each meal ... and I know that she always had something ... I eat at five but I don't know if that's for her or not (Henry and Mark Tye, Interview, 2005).

For Dad and Mark, meaning is produced through particular kinds of consumption, more than through particular tastes. Consistent with gender roles, they are consumers rather than producers of food, which in speaking of my mother Dad clearly identifies as being her role. He sees it as "natural" that I now have taken over some of the organizational and production responsibilities for food.

This kind of gendered remembering parallels Leslie Bella's finding that women experience the imperative to recreate the prefect Christmas of their childhood much more deeply than their male partners (1992, 33). As Bella emphasizes, this assumption is rooted in a familialist ideology that holds women accountable for their families' happiness. When men help, but try to simplify rituals so that the work is lessened, women often feel that the integrity of the whole Christmas enterprise is threatened (Bella 1992, 35). Rather than easing the burden, women may regard men's attempts to save time or effort as diminishing, and even undermining, their efforts to reproduce the perfect Christmas for their family. Similarly, my family's uses of tastes to remember the past are heavily gendered. Whereas pumpkin pie made with prepared frozen pie crust meets my father's needs, my meaning-making depends on the reproduction of homemade pie crust. Mark is satisfied with a store-bought sweet to end his meal, but I consider *real* shortbread to be homemade. Only homemade baking communicates my ethic of care, and only homemade baking made from my mother's familiar recipes fully creates the relationality I intend it to.

NOT REMEMBERING

Of everyone in our family, my sister Cathy is the least invested in past tastes. She tells me that when she makes cookies for her daughters she does not use our mother's recipe; rather, she turns to a library book: "All my recipes come from books from the library. I got a few from Mom, maybe two or three [but I don't make them very much]" (Cathy Tye, Interview, 1999). That she does not seek meaning either in the making of Mom's recipes or in their consumption is the result of several factors in her life journey. Although personality and inclination undoubtedly play a role in determining how many, if any, family traditions a person decides to carry on, as for my father, brother, and me, Cathy's meanings, or lack of them, are shaped by her subject positions. In her case these include being a deaf person, a wife, a mother, and a second-born daughter. While the subjectivities in this combination may be Cathy's alone, they underscore how differently individuals can experience family membership and point to some of the ways that subject positions can be isolating rather than integrative.

> Last Christmas, last Christmas, did I make something? I made cake. I didn't make very many [things], no. Because I don't have the recipes, I don't know [how]. I looked for the marshmallow dessert [Mom used to make] but I didn't know what it's called … (Cathy Tye, Interview, 1999).

I am struck by Cathy's inability as a deaf person to search for recipes by name. Although she can describe varieties of squares and cookies, she doesn't know what they are called. Occasionally I track down a childhood taste. "Do you have a recipe for old-fashioned shortbread?" I ask my friend Mary Ellen, who also grew up in Nova Scotia. Another friend calls me in her search for a taste she is seeking from her youth: Spider Cookies. These reconstructive exercises, these detective searches, elude Cathy. She cannot find what she cannot name.

But Cathy's distance from the baking traditions of our youth runs deeper and stems from the life-long sense of isolation she has felt from her hearing family. When I interview Cathy, I notice how difficult it is for her to change subjects, which is one of the most challenging aspects of lip-reading. Growing up Deaf in a hearing family at a time when oral communication was emphasized at the expense of all other dimensions of Deaf education, she has a great deal of experience trying to catch up on conversations going on around her. When I comment that she was often left out as she was growing up, Cathy emphatically adds, "A LOT." That feeling of exclusion runs deep. Cathy was on the outside of many of family traditions, missing much of the texture and detail that gave them richness. Even now, she is forced to piece together the flow of information and family culture that is passed on around her.

Today, Deaf educators and activists alike strongly challenge oralism, but during Cathy's childhood it was the dominant educational philosophy. Cathy's formal education, first in the preschool classes in Charlottetown that my parents helped to organize, and then as a student at the Interprovincial School for the Deaf (later the Atlantic Provinces Resource Centre for the Hard-of-Hearing) in Amherst in the 1970s, was in spoken English, and at home we never signed. Cathy's feelings of being on the outside of family life are certainly not unusual for a Deaf person. Over 90 percent of Deaf children have two hearing parents (Benderly 1980, 12–13) or, as Benderly puts it, parents "who know nothing about deafness or deaf people" (1980, 40). Cathy tells me she has only one friend whose hearing family knows American Sign Language, or ASL. He is a man in his twenties, approximately twenty years her junior.

Although we tried to include Cathy in conversations, this was difficult when communication took place solely in speech. Despite everyone's good intentions, our experience supports Benderly's claim that "it is close to impossible to include the [Deaf] child in family discussions, if those discussions occur solely in speech" (1980, 49). We talked as Cathy lip-read and struggled to piece together what she could of the talk going on around her. When we addressed her directly, we used the simplest of words and sentences. The end result was that we, like the vast majority of families Cathy knows comprised of a Deaf child, hearing parents, and usually hearing siblings, relied on a kind of "limited communication" that got across main points but usually sacrificed details.[3] After years of being excluded from family talk, Deaf children feel more separated from, than an integral part of, the family unit.[4] Shared language symbolizes more than an ability to communicate; it signifies a shared identity, a collective heritage, and facilitates the imagining of ties (Atkin, Ahmad, and Jones 2002, 40). Some suggest that this exclusion results in many Deaf children believing that their parents favoured their hearing siblings (Atkin, Ahmad, and Jones 2002, 27). It saddens me that Cathy remembers our mother's baking as being only for our brother Mark. As she recalls it, Mom's baking and, perhaps, her nurturing more generally were for others in the family and were not meant primarily for her.

Family traditions are nuanced. Without narratives to support and reinforce them (Bennett, Wolin, and McAvity 1988, 218), they have different, and often diminished, meanings. Cathy's inability to access supporting narratives has meant that she chooses to pass on few family customs to her daughters. One exception is the custom of putting money in a birthday cake. She says that she has told her daughters about the childhood custom we had growing up of hiding money in birthday cake. "[When I make a birthday cake I never put money in it like Mom did when we were growing up]. I can't. I haven't much money" (Cathy Tye, Interview, 2005). Cathy credits her decision to tell the children about putting money in a birthday cake rather than to reproduce it to the everpresent financial stresses she faces. Carrying on traditions becomes a lower priority than meeting the daily demands of an overstretched household. This raises the question of how much family traditions are linked to privilege. She assures me that the custom has registered with her children even if they have not experienced it personally: she overheard them share it with our father. When I press for details, however, Cathy can supply only the broad strokes: "I don't know what they said to him exactly. They were talking [and I didn't understand]. Dad will tell you. You have to ask them" (Cathy Tye, Interview, 2005). I must consult a hearing member of the family to learn more.

Although tangible evidence, like money in the cake, may be important to me, Cathy values process over product. She continues traditions of women's work unselfconsciously, and feeding the family has become part of her own construction of mothering. I see how she performs feeding and other domestic work just like our mother did, quickly and without reflection. And, just like our mother and grandmother, Cathy is acutely aware of her children's food preferences. Is her emphasis on process partly a Deaf cultural adaptation of a hearing family's traditions? Today she lives bilingually, speaking to her hearing daughters. However, she is most comfortable in the Deaf world. Having a Deaf partner and access to technology such as the Internet, a webcam, and MSN, allows her to keep in touch with a large circle of Deaf friends, and she now identifies most deeply with Deaf culture.

When Cathy remembers our mother, it is by talking about her rather than by passing on her traditions: "I don't know [if I pass on any of Mom's traditions]. I don't know if I do or not ... I always talk about her ... Oh, Mom used to do this and maybe, oh I remember Mom told me to do that (Cathy Tye, Interview, 2005)." This is consistent with the emphasis placed on talk within Deaf culture. Sign language is usually regarded as the criterion for belonging (e.g., Benderly 1980, 223), and members of the Deaf community are judged on their abilities to communicate and think like a Deaf person (Lane 1992, 17, Padden and Humphries 1988, 53). I've come to appreciate how ASL represents more than an ability to communicate with the Deaf; it signifies a shared identity and a collective heritage (see Atkin, Ahmad, and Jones 2002, 40). Because so many Deaf people are from hearing families, they are socialized into the Deaf community through their talk, and in turn talk reconstitutes the community.[5] I've seen conversations in ASL go on for

hours at a time – sometimes eight or ten – only to be picked up and continued the next day for another equally long stretch. Far from
considering it a distraction from other activities, Cathy and her friends
privilege talk and often prioritize it above all else. It is not surprising,
then, that Cathy tells me what she misses most since our mother died is
talking with her. And it strikes me that Cathy's own talk about our
mother and about our family traditions may well hold different meanings within Deaf culture, where talk is so highly regarded. Within this
context, is it possible that talk about a tradition is as valued, or maybe
more valued, than the tradition itself?

TRADITION AND MARRIAGE

When Cathy searches for answers as to why she does not make any of
Mom's recipes, she looks to the first years of her marriage. She explains
how the recipes she grew up with provided her with no currency after she
got married in 1988: "No, [I don't make anything that Mom made]. I
follow the library book. All the time. I forget what Mom made … A lot
of recipes [come] from [my husband's] family because that was what he
liked"(Cathy Tye, Interview, 1999). In a later interview, she expanded:
"There were different tastes in his family than ours. For example, his
family ate things like cabbage rolls that I never ate before." (Cathy Tye,
Interview, 2009).

Around the time Cathy married, she relocated to Toronto, where her
husband drove a delivery truck; until the birth of their second child,
Cathy worked in a medical records company. When the company down-
sized, she became a stay-at-home mother to her two young daughters.
In the late 1990s the couple returned east, hoping for employment. A
year later they had added another daughter to their family, but their
marriage was over.

Because her husband preferred his mother's baking, Cathy adopted her mother-in-law's recipes. She explained that her husband "did not like Mom's recipes. He liked his mother's way. So I copied them" (Cathy Tye, Interview, 2001). When I spoke to her in 2001, Cathy indicated that "mostly all" of her recipes came from her former mother-in-law. On another occasion she added, "I have a lot of recipes from his family because that is what he liked" (Cathy Tye, Interview, 1999).

In attempting to please her husband by reproducing his mother's baking, Cathy conformed to the models she grew up with. She followed the examples of older women she knew: our mother, who prepared food according to our father's preferences, and our aunt, who equated being a "good wife" with adopting her mother-in-law's recipes. Cathy accepted the premise that feeding one's family well is central to women's caring work (see DeVault 1991 and Murcott 1982, 1983a, 1983b, 1983c, 1993) and that it defeats much of the purpose if family members dislike the food. Baking no longer clearly communicates the intended ethic of care if it is unappreciated. Given my father's disinterest in food, my mother would have had no particular motivation to seek out recipes from her mother-in-law. In fact, as far as I can tell, she did not have a single recipe that came from my father's mother. However, in Cathy's case, her husband equated "good food" with his mother's tastes, and her efforts to reproduce that food echo our mother's nurturing in form, if not in content.

Food preparation can be a site of complex power relations, however, and couples often name issues around food and food preparation as sources of conflict. According to Anne Murcott, "the sort of work women are to do to ensure the homecoming meal provides a critical instance of the juncture between the control of a worker and the (his) control of his wife" (1983b, 89). Margaret Visser also notes that power struggles between men and women are frequently expressed through the medium of food (1991, 247). This conflict can have its origin in both economic and labour relations in a family and expresses the relation of the marital partners to the means of production of domestic labour (Murcott, 1983b, 79). As McIntosh and Zey observe, "Studies of task distribution and decision making in the family do show that women make decisions about food purchases and do the actual purchasing, storing, and preparing of food, but observers have drawn the unfounded conclusion that women thus control the flow of food into the family. *Responsibility* is not equivalent to *control*" (1989, 318). They argue that "although women have generally been held responsible for these roles, men, to varying degrees, control their enactment" (1989, 318). They also contend that "this ability to control depends on the relative distribution between men and women of certain social resources. The study of who controls family food thus may tell us much about family power structure" (1989, 318). These authors reach a disturbing conclusion, given the history of women's unpaid and underpaid work: a woman's control over food is usually directly related to her income (1989, 324). They suggest that a woman's control increases if she works outside the home and earns as much or more than her husband; if she works outside the home and earns less, her control is diminished over a woman who works within the house (1989, 324). Further, they suggest that if the wife has the greater emotional stake in the marriage, she will exercise less control over the flow of food into the house (1989, 326). DeVault claims that "in addition to its constructive, affiliative aspect, the work of care – as presently organized – has a darker aspect, which traps many husbands and wives in relations of dominance and subordination rather than mutual service and assistance" (1991, 163).

In troubled marriages, mealtimes may be particularly problematic (Burgoyne and Clarke 1983, 154). For example, the findings of a British study suggest that outbreaks of domestic violence often occur when men feel that their wives fail to live up to their expectations around meal provision (see Ellis 1983 and DeVault 1991, 43). A husband's refusal of food can be an act both of control and of deep rejection. DeVault writes, "When conflict about housework does arise, it can be quite painful, at least partly because it carries so much emotional significance. Women who resist doing all of the work, or resist doing it as their husbands prefer, risk the charge – not only from others, but in their own minds as well – that they do not care about the family" (1991, 153–4).

In my sister's case, the kitchen became a site of contestation, such that eventually Cathy did very little baking or meal preparation: "[When I was married] I felt that he would rather bake ... So he baked. Most times I let him do the baking" (Cathy Tye, Interview, 2009). When food preparation becomes a source of trouble rather than pleasure for family members, women make what accommodations they can both to communicate an ethic of care to their families and to maintain their sense of self as a good wife and mother. For Cathy, these compromises led to an inevitable devaluing of our mother's recipes. Rather than offering a site of enjoyment and accomplishment for herself and her partner, the recipes eventually became a marker of inadequacy for Cathy, and by the end of her ten-year marriage she owned very few of the recipes she had grown up with. Although on the surface it might seem like a minor change to make cookies for her children from a library book rather than from our mother's recipe, which originally came from the back of a package, it represents a significant disconnection from her past. After a few years of marriage, Cathy had forgotten the tastes of her childhood. Eventually, she had difficulty remembering what and if my mother baked at all. When I asked her to recall some of the food she had grown up with, Cathy responded with hesitation: "Did Mom bake?" In contrast to the rest of us, who shared memories of many baked goods, Cathy drew a blank. According to Julian Barnes, this kind of disjunction with one's past represents a profound loss. He states, "Memory is identity ... You are what you have done; what you have done is in your memory; what you remember defines who you are; when you forget your life you cease to be, even before your death" (2008, 140). Isolated from an element of what sometimes is called matri-lineage, Cathy's memory of her own mother's nurturing has disappeared, or at least has been seriously diminished.

Elizabeth Simpson writes about the loss women experience when they are separated from their family traditions. In her study of the impact of family violence on family identity, she found that "[b]y far the deliberate destruction of items by ex-partners was raised the most frequently as the manner in which women lost tangible pieces of their history" (2001, 56). The women Simpson interviewed described violent partners destroying photographs and objects that connected them to their families of origin and their familial past (2001, 1). Repeatedly, they pointed out how grounding seemingly trivial items of family history and folklore can be, and how those items have the power to "stabilize life" (Csikszentmihalyi 1993, 463, quoted in Simpson 2001, 19). Some of the women in Simpson's study went to extraordinary lengths to preserve items they wished to hand down to children and grandchildren, hiding them in closets, locking them in trunks, or storing them with friends or parents in order to keep them safe (2001, 71). Significantly, among the frequently cited treasured objects the women protected were family recipes (2001, 61), and Simpson's work underscores the centrality of a feminine culinary genealogy to a woman's sense of who she is.[6] What Cathy cannot remember, she cannot reproduce for her children. Her daughters have also lost touch with part of the family's feminine genealogy.

MOVING FORWARD

Mark comments that he often thinks of our mother: "I remember her almost every day" (Henry and Mark Tye, Interview, 2005). His remembering is prompted by family pictures and objects that belonged to our mother, and it takes form in symbolic actions that cannot be read by others but that hold special meaning for him in that they encapsulate an aspect of her character or memorialize her in some way. When Mark runs in a charity race with his young daughter, a granddaughter my mother never met but would have doted on, he does it for Mom. When he loans out the small stash of spare change he keeps in his desk to students who have forgotten their lunch money or does some other small favour at the school where he teaches, he does it with our mother in mind. He recalls that she often helped out the students at the high school where she worked and frequently lent lunch money to those who needed it (Henry and Mark Tye, Interview, 2005). Where others see a runner supporting a cause or a teacher helping out a student, Mark understands his acts of charity as a continuation of the support our mother extended to people who needed help. Their resonance back to her provides Mark with a sense of continuity.

Cathy prefers not to remember. She recalls our mother by talking about her, but as a rule she does not like to speak of her or to share stories. Her forgetting, like Mark's remembering, goes deep into the soul. She comments, "Dad always talks about Mom. Mom, Mom, Mom, Mom. He always talks about her. Sometimes I am uncomfortable when he talks but that's okay. I let it be" (Cathy Tye, Interview, 2005). There are few visible reminders of my mother in Cathy's life. For many years she removed all photos of Mom, but lately has begun to display one again, in her bedroom. Nor does Cathy surround herself with objects that remind her of our mother. In the memories, the stories, and the symbolic acts that provide Mark, Dad, and me with a sense of connectedness, Cathy feels pain: "I don't know [at what times I'd say I remember Mom the most]. I try *not* to think about it. It's hard" (Cathy Tye, Interview, 2005). When I press Cathy to come up with times that she does remember Mom, her response is set outside the home, "Maybe if I walk into a store, I'll think, 'Oh, I remember Mom always wanted to own a store.' Mom really wanted to do that, I remember that" (Cathy Tye, Interview, 2005). This memory, of an unfulfilled desire, strikes me as very different from Mark's memory embodied in the lending of lunch money. The actions that Mark describes represent ongoing gifts from my mother both in the form of his memories of her and in the acts that symbolize them. In contrast, Cathy's memories seem unfulfilled and unfulfilling. Anthropologist Margaret Visser wrote, "Because food is such a powerful metaphor for love, and sharing it such a binding force, refusing to eat is often one of the most wounding insults one can wield" (1991, 247). How powerful, then, is not remembering? Sutton's observation that food can be used in creative forgetting (2001, 169), and that productive forgetting is as interesting as remembering (2001, 168), may well apply to my sister.

Cathy assures me, "If my mother were alive, it would be nice [to have some of her recipes but she's not.] So I think, I should forget about it. Leave it alone. So I use the library" (Cathy Tye, Interview, 2001). We remember in ways that are meaningful to us (Sutton 2001, 176) and that Cathy opts to forget raises the question of how traditions, especially those we link to a long-ago childhood or a family member no longer living, move us forward on our own individual journeys. I am beginning to recognize how my own selective reproduction of my mother's baking traditions and seasonal customs offers me advantages: it earns me appreciation, allows me to celebrate my mother, and provides affirmation of my nurturing. It provides tangible proof and moves me forward. As a middle child, Cathy can rely on my father and me to reproduce a range of family traditions. Should she ever want them, some of the tastes of her childhood are already available to her in the form of the homemade jam that my father makes and the batches of Christmas cookies I produce. Cathy does not necessarily need to undertake these endeavours on her own; she can be a consumer. Cathy's life proceeds in directions that make carrying on traditions difficult. Moving house often, she looks forward. Even saving and then finding the objects that one needs to create the kind of continuity I value (handwritten recipes, worn tin measuring cups, a familiar serving plate) may be impossible under such fluid conditions.

Baking offers me a meaningful expression of identity, while Cathy finds value in other places and practices. Tradition is a complex concept that is symbolic rather than natural, and more fluid than static (see Handler and Linnekin 1984, 276). As Richard Handler and Jocelyn Linnekin write, tradition is "an interpretive process that embodies both continuity and discontinuity" (1984, 273). What of the past we choose to remember, and how we opt to celebrate it, is the product of an ongoing process of selection and reinterpretation that has both personal and collective dimensions. Cathy did not find currency in our mother's food when she was establishing herself in her marriage, and now it does not help cement her place in the Deaf community. Like our mother, who learned new recipes when she moved into middle-class circles, and who came to take more pleasure from the recipes she learned from her friends than from those passed on by her mother, Cathy looks to her Deaf friends for recipes and other kinds of cultural information. They are her closest family, and her efforts at connection extend in their direction.[7]

My son once remarked to me, "I never met my grandmother or great-grandmother but I know what their cookies taste like," but Cathy's children are more removed from this heritage. When we get together at Christmas or other occasions, I prepare my mother's recipes for my nieces. Will these tastes that the other hearing members of the family celebrate become part of their positive identity as an extended family? Will these be some of the tastes of their childhood that they look back on happily and try to reproduce as adults? Or will these tastes, which do not hold the same meanings for their Deaf mother, contribute to their sense of exclusion? Will they symbolize feelings of partial family membership?

In part, looking back is privileged. The memories I discover in childhood recipes are warm and nurturing, whereas Cathy's are a mixed bag. I taste a peanut butter cookie and for a second I am three years old again sitting on the church pew beside my mother. For Cathy, such tastes recall isolation. As I read some of the names in Cathy's recipe collection – former in-laws and estranged friends – I realize, as she does, that the life story told in her recipes, and perhaps in other family traditions, is complex, and that not all chapters are to be celebrated or perhaps even remembered.

FROM DAUGHTERS TO MOTHERS

As is clear by now, most of the recipes my mother owned were not lov-ingly handed down through generations from mother to daughter. This seems to be true for her friends as well. Other women of my mother's age let me know that their mothers passed along very few, if any, recipes; it turns out that their families' favourite recipes are not generations old, either. My Aunt Peg, as well as my mother's friends Anne, Sadie, and Helen, all talk about getting most of their recipes from friends. And all four say that they very often turn to community fund-raising cookbooks, many of them produced by women's church groups that they've been associated with, for reliable recipes. Helen didn't have any family recipes when she married in approximately 1960: "No, no. See the recipes that I grew up with were very basic because I came from a farm. And we cooked different. My mother cooked an awful lot with cream and not shortening. Like if she made a white cake she made it with cream. And you know we didn't do any fancy cooking" (Farrow, Interview, 2003). Helen also points to changes in technology. As a young married woman, she was frustrated in her attempts to reproduce her mother's simple meals because she was no longer working on a wood stove: "Our first stove was an oil stove and that was different too ... but when I first got an electric stove, I did find it hard. It said to simmer and I'd turn it to low and well it just wouldn't do anything. I just found that it didn't do the same job" (Farrow, Interview, 2003).[8]

LAURENE WITH HER PARENTS, BELL AND FRED, CHRISTMAS, CHARLOTTETOWN, C. 1965. A SPECIAL OCCASION MARKED BY HATS AND A PLATE OF SQUARES.

A CHRISTMAS PARTY FOR THE BRIDGE CLUB, AMHERST, c. 1985

Christmas provides a striking example of how this generation of women created new baking traditions. This was the one time of year that my mother, and other women in our extended family and neighbourhood, allowed the scale of economy and abundance they so carefully managed to tip in favour of excess. Foods were exceptional in that they were of a higher register than the baking we usually had in the house. Mom used more expensive ingredients, like dried fruit and nuts; it was the one time that she baked with butter, and everything was made with white sugar. The variety was truly staggering. On Christmas Eve Mom would open boxes of cookies, squares, donuts, and cakes that she had made over the fall and then frozen. Mincemeat and apple pies sat on the top of the stove, and a frozen strawberry dessert, a favourite of my sister's, was kept cool in a refrigerator so overcrowded that things fell out when you opened the door. Delicate shortbread cookies, each decorated with a dot of icing and a piece of cherry; gingerbread men with raisin eyes; sugar cookies cut out in Christmas shapes with dobs of bright icing slopped on by children; peanut butter balls dipped in chocolate; cherry surprise cookies so rich they were hardily edible; donuts, usually so tough they were hardly edible; fudge, both chocolate and divinity; cherry squares; cherry cake; gumdrop cake; light fruit cake; dark fruit cake; mince pie; apple pie; frozen strawberry dessert: these were the Christmas foods of my childhood, and the holiday lasted until they were gone.

Although I knew that many of the traditions and foods associated with Christmas were not of ancient origin but dated back to the rise of the Victorian Christmas in the nineteenth century (see Kaufman 2004; Bella 1992), I only recently realized that the excess that marked Christmas in our household was my mother's invention, or at least that of her generation. So were the rich recipes that I associate with the holiday: sickeningly sweet creations like cherry surprise cookies and gumdrop cake. My grandmother's Christmas foods were different: mince and apple pie along with several cookies, squares, or more likely "Droppies," which I viewed as globs of various combinations of ingredients mixed together and dropped onto a baking sheet. In contrast to my mother's, my grandmother's baking was often hard and tasteless. It did not compare either in its richness or its expansiveness. Although dark Christmas cake may have its origins in the sixteenth century (see Leach and Inglis 2003), Christmas foods that I regard as traditional, such as the white fruit cake that I once imagined being passed down through generations of rural working-class Nova Scotian women, actually do not date back beyond my mother. The familiar taste of white fruit cake that for me represents Christmas is based on a recipe that Mom found in *Tested Sweet Recipes*:

White Fruit Cake

3 squares butter

2 cups white sugar

6 eggs

4 cups bread flour (sifted then measure)

1 lb white raisins

¼ lb citron

½ lb cherries

2 slices pineapple

1 cup almonds (bleached) to decorate top of cake

½ cup milk (fill cup with boiling water)

2 tsp salt

1 tsp vanilla, almond, lemon flavouring

Boil raisins 2 minutes, drain well until dry. Cream butter, then add sugar, add 2 eggs at a time, flour fruit well. Bake 275 for 2 hours. 300 for 1 hour.

Mrs. D.C. Reid

(*Tested Sweet Recipes* 39)

My mother's friends and my father's sister Peg confirm that many of the recipes that comprise the elaborated baking traditions that I grew up with – both of the everyday and of Christmas – were their generation's creation. The only older women in my family are on my father's side, but they corroborate this. Like my mother and her mother, the women on the paternal side of my family are all from northern Nova Scotia. My father's Aunt Annie, born in 1917, did not learn to bake from her mother, because as Annie puts it, "she couldn't bake" (Goodyear, Interview, 1999). She remembers only ginger snaps, oatmeal cookies, and pie from her childhood. When asked about Christmas baking, she thinks for a few moments. Then she tentatively suggests, "it might be Christmas pudding. Fruit pudding. And probably fruit cake is the only thing." But she insists, "I can't remember any special baking." Her niece, and my father's sister Peg, born in 1933, agrees. Peg begins her conversation with me by claiming that she doesn't remember her mother baking very often. After a few minutes she manages to produce a modest list of her mother's baked goods, which includes biscuits and cake bread:

> [T]he thing I remember Mom making most was tea biscuits and this cake bread ... Another thing she made every once in a while was Johnny cakes, cornmeal cakes but they were called Johnny cakes ... I remember making oatmeal cookies that she put together with a date filling ... And plain sugar cookies. And white cakes. I don't remember Mom making chocolate cakes. She might have made them once in a long while ... She used to make bread ... [and] pies, oh she could make pies (Miller, Interview, 1999).

My father adds date squares to this list; in his mind's eye he sees his mother taking a big pan of date squares out of the oven. But, like Annie, Peg can recall only fruitcake being made at Christmas time: "The fruit-cake would represent Christmas. That's all I can remember anyway." In comparison, the Christmas baking that Peg did as a wife and mother of two daughters is far more extensive and mirrors my mother's. Peg credits this to improved economics and increased sociability:

> It came with our generation more ... because the generation before us would have been right in the middle of the Depression and they wouldn't have had the wherewithal to buy the ingredients ... They would not have had the money to do that so it had to have started in my generation. And I suppose in my generation we were going out to more social things as well Diane, you know, like Church group, and all that sort of stuff. (Miller, Interview, 1999)[9]

Peg points to some of the reasons baking changed with her generation. Undoubtedly there are other, more individual, reasons why my maternal grandmother passed on only 11 recipes, or 6 per cent, of the 177 recipes in my mother's tin box but it is very difficult now for me to read the clues. I really can only wonder about these personal influences. Did my grandmother's two-year employment as a nanny in Montreal mean that she did not learn to bake from her mother? And yet, looking to one's friends and establishing networks through shared baking did not begin with my mother's generation. Perhaps women have always done this. Out of my grandmother's collection of 174 written recipes, only 7 (or 4 per cent) came from her mother.

This reminds me of how my mother writes home every Sunday. She sits at the dining room table, the ebb and flow of the household going on around her. Her writing paper is modest, just a couple of sheets of loose leaf paper from a pile on hand for children's homework. She takes a Bic pen out the blue vase that sits in the cupboard and now serves as a pencil holder and writes to her parents of the week's events. Like everything else she does, the task is quickly accomplished. In about fifteen minutes she's composed a two-page letter about the places she's gone over the week and the projects she's undertaken – the dress she is sewing, or the progress of her preserving, if it is fall. Her letters are never emotional or emotionally revealing. They chart a steady course of her life and gloss over both problems – her cancer and chemotherapy treatments, for example – and the social distance that now separates her from her parents. She does not accentuate the difference of her middle-class life in a small town from her parents' more working-class life in a more rural setting. Instead, she often underlines a commonality between her mother and herself as producers of food for church and community social events by tucking a recipe into the folds of her weekly letter. Twenty-two recipes – for Shortbread, Brownies, Pineapple Brownies, Banana Squares, Fridge Squares, Marshmallow Squares, Eagle Brand Coconut Squares, and Chocolate Treats – become part of her mother's collection.

My grandmother writes to her sister Hat (Harriet) at the end of October 1942: "Ethel Ward is having a card party tonight for the Red Cross like Kate had last week. Dell's shower came off with a *bang*. She sure was surprised." Her contributions to these events, such as Chocolate Treats, are often based on recipes she get from my mother. Mom's repertoire of finer squares and loaves made from raisins and coconut, or new products like Jell-O and graham wafers, which eased her entry into new social circles, also facilitated my grandmother's move into middle-class contexts as my grandfather progressed in his work life from labourer to manager.

Chocolate Treats

Melt in double boiler:
1 pk butterscotch chips (1 cup)
1 pk chocolate chips (1 cup)

Add:

1 cup salted peanuts

1 cup Chinese noodles.

Drop on wax paper. No baking.

The integrative functions of my mother's baking may characterize much of the folklore that is introduced to a family by younger members. Whereas we value folklore that is passed down through generations for its sense of continuity, newer items often offer synchronicity. In this case, recipes help introduce the entire family to a way of consumption that marks modernity; they represent younger family members helping elders negotiate new class-based demands. Ironically, the same factors that may interrupt the transmission of folklore from mother to daughter – a young woman's independence, her geographical or social distance, perhaps her disinterest, or even changing times and changing trends – may also facilitate the flow of traditional culture from daughter to mother. Forces can separate women intergenerationally in a family, but sometimes food is a binding agent: it reaches across generational differences and brings women together. As folklorists have already documented, commonality arises in the making and sharing of well-known, familiar dishes, but women also come together over new tastes. Through their introduction of new dishes, new narratives, and new practices, younger members ease the family's journey into an unfamiliar world and help the whole family meet changing social expectations.

This sharing of stories and customs from younger to older generations has always gone on, despite the scant attention it has been paid. I close the lid on my mother's recipe box knowing that her collection is another example of the kind of transmission that, for the most part, extended from her to her mother, from a younger member a family to an older one, rather than in the other direction. Mom did not create this collection to be any kind of heirloom or treasure to be passed down. She saw it simply as a resource required by a wife, mother, and church lady in the decades during which she lived those roles.

PAST TASTES

My mother's baking offers, as Clifford (1986) argues that all ethnographies do, "a partial truth." I study her recipes like I would a photo album or scrapbook, savouring the glimpses I find there of her life and of our family's life when she was alive. They offer me a chance to remember her through taste. And, by extension, when I make her recipes, reviving favourite tastes for others, they allow me to offer momentary connections with a particular, selective past to others who recognize these tastes and their earlier contexts. They have become part of my version of what Cashman calls "critical nostalgia" (2006, 138) in that they reflect my critical assessment of the past, present, and future. Reading the texts and subtexts of my mother's recipes helps me better understand some of the realities of her life and prevents me from confining these texts to my own personal history.

With their high concentration of sugar and packaged foods, my mother's recipes express a middle-class perspective on a particular time in history. If she had lived a longer life, her recipes would tell a different story, or at least other stories. I have no doubt that she would have gone on to make more health-conscious recipes, as her friends did in light of their aging and related health concerns. So, while I reproduce my mother's recipes selectively, and from time to time when I want to recreate a remembered or favourite taste, I would not want to recreate the cultural context that produced this kind of baking. Like Kathryn

LAURENE WITH MARK BEFORE HIS JUNIOR HIGH SCHOOL PROM,
JUNE 1985

Church, who wrote about her mother's sewing, my examination has forced me to confront "the dilemma [of] ... whether I could celebrate what my mother represented without reproducing it" (Church 2002, 252). My mother's cookies and cakes now provide me with the pleasure of a little voyeurism or culinary tourism into the past; they allow me to flirt with the idea of being the perfect 1950s mother, however unlikely the reality of that is or how little I really aspire to this unrealistic model of mothering and domesticity. These recipes thankfully do not reflect my life. The story they tell is only partly mine, as it is only partly shared by my father, my brother, and my sister. Mostly, the recipes tell my mother's story in ways that reveal many of the cultural conventions and social restrictions placed on women of her generation. They speak of the exacting expectations and heavy social obligations connected with being a church lady, the importance placed on being the right kind of mother as indicated by a full cookie jar, and the too few opportunities for women to come together purely for enjoyment, away from the demands of their social roles and family and community responsibilities. Importantly, they also point to ways in which women resisted these demands. For all these reasons, I do not mourn their passing and the type of woman's life they were part of. In fact, just as Steinberg concludes that it is necessary for his family members to lose tradition if they are to become the modern Americans they aspire to be (1998, in Sutton 2001, 125), I am resigned to the fact that my mother's recipes sit on the shelf. Despite the deep meaning I find in their occasional reproduction, they should be left behind. They are contemporary reflections of my mother's life as constructed through her social interactions, rather than vestiges of her history. In truth, my sister's move to rely on recipes she gets from her Deaf friends is in keeping with our mother's own experience and attitude, for Mom's baking and recipes reflect as much about change and how to accommodate it as they do of generational continuity. Henry

Glassie defines tradition as "the creation of the future out of the past" (1995, 395). He continues, "If tradition is a people's creation out of their own past, its character is not stasis but continuity" (1995, 396). Perhaps in an ironic twist, my sister, the family member most distanced from my mother's baking, is the one who most faithfully reproduces the tradition. In telling the story of her life, my mother's recipes shed light on the shared experiences of other middle-class women of her generation. For the family my mother left behind, and for a new generation of young women, they also underscore the importance of moving forward.

NOTES

CHAPTER ONE

1 See Anonymous (1890) for a description of Eureka, and Bliss (Unpublished, c. 1961) for an unpublished history of the community.

2 By the early twentieth century, Pictou County was heavily identified as Scottish. For example, a 1916 publication promoting the county lauded its Scottish character. It estimated that more than 26,000 of the 36,000 residents were of Scottish descent (New Glasgow 1916, 6–7).

3 Cathy was part of what Benderly refers to the "huge bulge of 'rubella babies'" born deaf during the early to mid 1960s (1980, 22). Although the association of maternal rubella with deafness had been established in 1944, the German measles vaccine was not available until shortly after the 1960s rubella outbreak (36, 38).

4 Ellis traces the use of the term "autoethnography" to Karl Heider's reference in 1975 to the Dani's own account of what people do, but she notes that David Hayano is usually credited as the originator: "Hayano limited the meaning to cultural-level studies by anthropologists of their 'own people,' in which the researcher is a full insider by virtue of being 'native,' acquiring an intimate familiarity with the group, or achieving full membership in the group being studied" (2004, 38).

CHAPTER TWO

1 Throughout the Maritime Provinces, "lunch" refers to a bedtime snack. Lewis J. Poteet includes this as one meaning of the word in his Nova Scotian, *The South Shore Phrase Book:* "lunch: an evening snack, usually tea, sandwiches, cake, squares, cookies" (1983, 45).

2 For a selection of wartime recipes from Nova Scotia, see Edwards (1998).

3 Bennett reports that a war bride she spoke to described scones as being thinner in Quebec than in Scotland; otherwise they would be what Canadians call tea biscuits or baking-powder biscuits (1998, 173).

4 Bennett indicates that baking scones was an aspect of traditional culture that, for one woman she spoke to, characterized Scottishness; this woman thought that most of her generation would view scones this way (1998, 174). Bennett also notes that scones were once a daily feature of every table in Scotland (1998, 173).

5 In the *Dictionary of Prince Edward Island English*, cake bread is described as "biscuit bread resembling bannock, leavened with baking powder or soda rather than yeast, and baked in cakes." The entry goes on to describe cake bread as bannock "dressed up a little with sugar and raisins" (Pratt 1988, 28–9).

6 Bill Casselman describes war cake as follows: "[D]uring the Second World War, amid ration coupons and scarcity, there was War Cake, a spicy, boiled, raisin cake made with no eggs, no butter, and no milk, much of which had gone overseas to the war effort" (1998, 206).

7 In *Out of Old Nova Scotia Kitchens*, Marie Nightingale writes that "[m]olasses and ginger cookies were the most widely made, since molasses was a common and inexpensive sweetener and spices were considered a staple in every household. White sugar, when it became available, was used in baking cakes and shortbreads only for such special occasions as a wedding, a christening, or when the minister came to call" (1981, 156). Nightingale goes on to note that "[t]he amount of spices used in ginger cookies was left to the individual cook's own taste"; in

equivalent amounts of cookie dough, the quantity of ginger could range from half a teaspoon to two tablespoons, and the amount of other spices, such as cinnamon and cloves, varied as well.

8 The following discussion of molasses is adapted from Tye (2008).

9 The Memorial University Folklore and Language Archive has evidence of molasses being used extensively for medicinal purposes. See the Archive's Folklore survey card collection for examples.

10 Dick Nolan recorded his "Newfoundland Good Times," on his CD of the same title (Condor label, Heritage Music, HCD 4449, 1999. Here is an excerpt:

> Well did you ever have molasses on your doughboys?
> And did you ever have molasses in your tea?
> Did you ever put molasses on your porridge?
> On fish and brewis and homemade bread and tea?
> And a great big bowl of puffs in the morning
> And toasted homemade bread enough for three
> Then you can say that you're a real true Newfie
> Remembering the way it used to be.

11 DeVault notes that Sarah Fenstermaker Berk, "using the concept of doing gender to interpret her study of household work, suggests that household tasks often become 'occasions' for 'reaffirmation of one's gendered relation to the work and to the world'" (1991, 119).

12 For a discussion of *Chatelaine* within the historical context of Canadian magazines, see Sutherland (1989).

13 For a discussion of the reluctance to notice or talk about food as masculine practice in Norwegian households, see Roos and Wandel (2005, 172–3).

CHAPTER THREE

1 When the United Church of Canada was inaugurated on 10 June 1925, it brought together the Methodists, Congregationalists, and 70 per cent of

the Presbyterians. It was an unprecedented move that made Canada the first county in which Protestant denominations opted to amalgamate.

2 Anne Bower has traced the history of the community cookbook in the United States to the Civil War, when northern women developed money-raising strategies to support the Sanitary Commission of the Union Army. She notes, "After the Civil War, other benevolent organizations, especially churches and synagogues, adopted the use of fund-raising cookbooks" (Bower 1997a, 137).

3 Here I am concentrating on add-ins rather than flavouring such as vanilla. Vanilla appears in nearly half the recipes (48%). There is also recurrent use of certain spices: cinnamon, ginger, and nutmeg, as discussed in the last chapter.

4 In 1927 General Foods purchased the company, and in 1989 merged with Kraft to form Kraft Foods, Inc. (www.kraftfoods.com). But there were also more local chocolate sources, including Ganongs of St. Stephen, New Brunswick, which began producing candy in 1876 (Folster 1990, 23).

5 For a collection of sweet recipes from African American church women, see Brenda Rhodes Miller (2001).

6 For other examples of gendered analyses, see Jenkins (2001) for a discussion of bananas as women's food and Neuhaus 2001 on gender and meatloaf recipes.

7 Popular culture played an important role in promoting ideals of daintiness and its connections with food. Inness writes:

> Cooking literature in the early 1900s taught women not only the right way to make tea sandwiches or decorate teacakes but also how to be feminine and ladylike. A woman proved herself to be a lady by preparing dainty, genteel foods for everything from bridge gatherings to tea parties. Popular cooking literature taught women lessons about the desirability of daintiness/and femininity ... In the first few decades of the twentieth century, a woman could hardly flip through a woman's magazine or cookbook without encountering scores of articles about

dainty foods, including appetizers, salads, main dishes, and desserts ... [D]ainty foods for ladies appeared everywhere, particularly in the dessert sections of cookbooks (2001c, 53–4).

8 Inness writes: "Daintiness fit perfectly into Veblen's theories about a woman's role as a conspicuous consumer of the goods that her husband bought. Daintiness in women and their food served as a visible sign of the invisible wealth that was necessary to pursue a distinctly upper-middle-class concept; after all, daintiness was not available to poor women, who could not afford to worry about such frivolity" (2001c, 58).

9 In her discussion of daintiness, Sherrie Inness identifies the aesthetic as a middle-class expression that spoke of a family's means as well as taste: "The ability to provide a wide selection of dainty and delectable dishes also served as a marker of a family's class background, as a sign of middle-class tastes, since only well-off people can afford to think about the taste and appearance of food" (2001c, 59).

10 See Mennell (1985, 112–27) for a discussion of extravagance and refinement in relation to cookery.

11 According to my father, the social status of these women generally mirrored that of the other contributors at the same time as it reflected a negotiation between the town's established elite and a rising middle class. Two of the three women came from the emergent mercantile middle class (one was married to the owner of a local grocery store, and the other's husband operated a garage), while the third woman is characterized by my father as belonging to the town's small segment of the "upper middle class," having married into "old money." Her husband's family had prospered in the town's shipbuilding and lumbering glory days.

12 It is now impossible, of course, to assess all the factors that would have influenced the women's contributions. For example, Dad mentions that the woman with the most recipes printed under her name was a free spirit with an appreciation for the arts, suggesting that she or others may have submitted recipes because they enjoyed the creativity of baking. Neither

does my father remember who initiated the cookbook, or whether there was a subcommittee of the Friendly Group who oversaw its production; clearly, these considerations might hold implications for the number of recipes each woman contributed. Some group members may have felt more responsibility for filling empty pages. My father does not mention, and perhaps never knew, the most salient piece of information for my mother and other users of the cookbook: all three of the major contributors were accomplished cooks. My mother has underscored their names and highlighted a few of their contributions as "Good" in the copy of the cookbook she gave to her mother. In turn, my grandmother marked some of their recipes, presumably to remind her of items she had tried successfully. *Tested Sweet Recipes*, then, hints at the many dimensions of membership in a small town for these women; finding their voice depended on several factors, including social status, age, personality, sense of duty, and aptitude. No doubt, these qualities came together in different combinations for each contributor.

13 For an overview of the various kinds of work involved in a Manitoban church supper, see Krotz (1993).

14 Although the poem as it appears in *Tested Sweet Recipes* is untitled and unattributed, it was available in the 1950s as a decorative kitchen plaque titled "The Kitchen Prayer," and credited to Klara Munkres.

15 Coblentz (1897–1951) was an American writer whose children's books were popular in the 1930s and 1940s.

The Housewife

Jesus, teach me how to be
Proud of my simplicity.

Sweep the floors, wash the clothes,
Gather for each vase a rose.

Iron and mend a tiny frock
Taking notice of the clock,

Always having the time kept free
For childish questions asked of me.

Grant me wisdom Mary had
When she taught her little Lad.

Catherine Coblentz

16 See Barbara Kirshenblatt-Gimblett (1987, 8) for a consideration of the complex ways in which contributors to Jewish charity cookbooks constructed Jewish identity through a rejection of dietary laws and an acceptance of culinary eclecticism.

17 Food production was a significant way in which women of this generation supported their churches and, by extension, social action initiatives from the local to the international level. For example, for many years my mother's church group supported the Brunswick Street Mission, an outreach program operated by the United Church and located in an inner city Black neighbourhood of Halifax. They collected used clothing and other items to send to the mission, and some of the proceeds of the women's teas and suppers would have gone to support this or other causes. Within the communities where we lived – Cape North, Parrsboro, Charlottetown, and Amherst – women's church groups offered direct support to local families in need of clothing, food, and other goods. And, as noted earlier, within the context of their church congregations, the women's volunteer efforts were counted on to keep clergy paid, churches maintained, and programming going. For a discussion of links between food and labour in the southern United States, see Yaeger (1992).

18 See Seymour and Short (1994) for a gendered analysis of Church of England congregations in rural England. The authors argue that the Church

reproduces, rather than challenges, traditional gender divisions of the labour market.

19 Joan Colborne explains her actions in an epilogue to her published collection of letters dating from her first years of married life as a rural minister's wife in 1949–50, "Readers will notice that I didn't write much about summer on the Island. I'm sorry, but as soon as summer started, I left, and went back home to Nova Scotia. The women in the community were beginning to plan for the big summer undertaking: a turkey supper to which every woman was expected to make six pies – and I had never made one – so I just took off ... So I went to visit my parents on the south shore of Nova Scotia" (2003, 126).

20 Although earlier research suggests that women have tended to undervalue their voluntary labour, a study by Petrzelka and Mannon suggests that some women do see their work as crucial to the social and economic vitality of their community (2006, 253).

21 Daniels writes: "Work provides a clue to a person's worth in society – how others judge and regard him or her. To work – and earn money – is also to gain status as an adult. Thus, working is an important way to develop both a sense of identity and a sense of self esteem" (1987, 404).

22 Daniels makes the point that women are expected to coordinate public and purchased services with the private requirements of the family, and that this tailoring is invisible work that women themselves don't always recognize (1987, 405).

23 This supports the findings of Meg Luxton's study, set in Flin Flon, Manitoba in 1976–77, where the majority of respondents clearly placed the responsibility for household labour in the female sphere; men merely helped out. As well, Luxton describes several common strategies that the men she interviewed relied on to avoid doing household work (or being assigned more), including not performing the task well or doing it in a way that generated even more domestic work (1986, 27).

24 For a discussion of ways in which a church supper builds community see Allen (1998).

25 Daniels writes that the work of making community arises through the efforts of many volunteers (1987, 412). Little links this kind of work to the larger cultural constructions of rural ideology, noting that "[t]he church, both as a physical structure and an institution, holds a very important place in the rural ideology" (Little 1997, 206–7). Finally, Milroy and Wismer argue the importance of women's voluntary work to the building of strong organizations and communities. However, they point out that it is difficult, if not impossible, to judge women's community work along a continuum of political action (1994, 4). First, such a classification assumes intentionality. As well, the literature shows that groups can be more or less political at different times in their history. Furthermore, there is the problem of defining "political": it can mean different things to different women, and what we define as political has typically been based on male criteria and pertains to power in the public realm (Milroy and Wismer 1994, 4).

CHAPTER FOUR

1 Radner and Lanser (1993) detail six different means of implicit coding that include appropriating or adapting to feminist purposes those forms or materials normally associated with male culture or with androcentric images of the feminine (10): juxtaposition – the ironic arrangement of texts, artifacts or performances (13); distraction – strategies that drown out or draw attention away from the subversive power of a feminist message (15); indirection – indirection or distancing that includes metaphor, impersonation, and hedging (16); trivialization – the employment of a form, mode, or genre that the dominant culture considers unimportant, innocuous, or irrelevant (19); and incompetence – demonstrating incompetence at conventionally feminine activities (20).

2 Lovegren characterized chiffon cake as "the first really new cake in 100 years": "Neither a sponge cake nor a butter cake, chiffon cake used the newly popular salad oil and was beaten rather than creamed. The cake was invented by a California salesman named Harry Baker in 1927.

Although he kept the recipe a secret for many years, the cake became famous in Hollywood where Mr. Baker made it for celebrity parties. He finally sold the recipe to General Mills in 1947 – which posted gains of 20 percent on sales of cake flour after the recipe was published" (2005, 154).

3 Although apparently the tradition is not widespread throughout North America, our family birthday cakes always contained coins, and so did many of those I encountered at friends' birthday parties when I was a child. The custom is likely related to the English tradition of putting coins in Christmas puddings.

4 The *Better Homes and Gardens* recipe was as follows:

STRAWBERRY SQUARES

Base and topping:
1 c flour
¼ c firmly packed brown sugar
½ c walnuts, chopped
¼ c (½ stick) butter or margarine, melted
pinch of salt
For the filling:
1 T gelatin
2 T lemon juice
½ c boiling water
24 marshmallows
½ c sugar
1 (10 oz) package frozen strawberries, thawed
1 c heavy cream, whipped until firm peaks form, or 1 (4 ½ oz) container Cool Whip

(Quoted in Lovegren 2005, 349).

CHAPTER FIVE

1 For a discussion of the political implications of this move to make Asian and other cuisines, see Heldke 2001.

2 Sutton refers to Proust, who is not speaking of migration. "But if the past 'is a foreign country,' then similar processes can be at work in temporal as in spatial or spatio-temporal displacement. And indeed Proust directs us once again to the power of sensory parts to return us to the whole, of the unsubstantial fragment to reveal the vast structure" (2001, 84).

3 Describing this very kind of communication, Atkin and colleagues state, "Limited communication, typical of most families, allowed them to 'get by' although, as noted, deaf young people often felt excluded, and the lack of communication with certain family members hindered the development of strong ties. Respondents specifically bemoaned their compromised ability to communicate 'deep things'. Being able to explore 'deep things' became more important with age" (2002, 30). When a hearing family communicates with a Deaf child, subtlety and qualification are lost. The example one writer offers is that a Deaf child sees "no" rather than "no because ..." (Benderly 1980, 48). Furthermore, Benderly argues, "Deaf children receive speech messages that are incomplete, ambiguous, or both. They have to speechread or understand truncated sounds in a language they barely know (impressive accomplishments even for those fluent in the language), so they miss much of the emotional overtone and even of the factual content" (Benderly 1980, 48).

4 Padden and Humphries describe the isolation that Deaf children of hearing families experience. In writing of one such child, they say, "For Tony, being deaf meant being set apart from his family and his friends; he was 'deaf' and had an 'illness'" (1988, 20). In stressing how lack of communication prevents Deaf children from becoming fully functioning members of their families and communities, Atkin and colleagues write: "The

resultant loss of social and cultural capital makes it difficult for young people to function as full members of their families and communities. This creates potential difficulties for the relationship between parent and child" (2002, 32).

5 Benderly makes the important point that "[o]nly a very small proportion of deaf people ... can learn how to be culturally deaf in their parental homes; they must learn to be the adults they become from others, in other places, and often without their parents' knowledge or approval. This strange and melancholy circumstance reverberates through the entire life and history of deaf people all over the world ... The deaf culture, there-fore, in all but rare cases recruits its new members in a very unusual way. Young people learn basic cultural identity and most social skills from contemporaries rather than elders" (1980, 12–3).

6 Marion Bishop elaborates on the concept of a feminine culinary geneal-ogy as follows:

And I believe these women also find each other – that in making the journey to their own bodies they connect themselves with the bodies of other women. I am referring here to the idea of a feminine culinary genealogy – a matri-lineage based not just on a woman's name but also on her kitchen, her act of cooking, and her body. Irigaray defines and explains the importance of the term 'feminine genealogy' in 'The Bod-ily Encounter with the Mother.' She believes that establishing such a genealogy is necessary for women to own and understand their identi-ties. In advising women to discover their heritage, the following passage begins to explain the power of the matri-lineage that is also part of my cookbooks: 'It is necessary ... for us to assert that there is a genealogy of women. There is a genealogy of women within our family: on our mothers' side we have mothers, grandmothers, and great-grandmothers, and daughters ... Let us try to situate ourselves within this female genealogy so as to conquer and keep our identity. Nor let us forget that we already have a history, that certain women have, *even if it was culturally difficult*, left their mark on history and that all too often we do not know them'"(1997, 102).

She writes about the importance of this feminine culinary genealogy to her own identity:

> Joyce Eck is not my biological mother, but her food connected me to a bodily based sense of the maternal in the community where I grew up. Today, her recipes provide me with both a linguistic and corporeally based knowledge of my culture and roots. It is this ability of a recipe to bind the experience of the body, the unwritten, into measurable amounts that can be replicated, that makes the idea of a feminine culinary genealogy not just about cataloguing names, but about literally preserving the *sense* of a woman's life. Each recipe serves as a textual token – something a woman can hold in her hands that speaks of and connects her to wor(l)ds both linguistic and corporeal (Bishop 1997, 103–4).

7 Atkin and colleagues note, "A Deaf identity is thus rarely developed through family-based socialisation. A sense of belonging and identification with Deaf culture, if it occurs, is engendered through the use of BSL [British Sign Language], peer groups and attendance at Deaf events and institutions" (2002, 35). Therefore, as many writers have observed, the Deaf must learn their traditions and culture, not from elders but from contemporaries. Of Deaf "family," Lane writes:

> 'We are all in the same family,' said one deaf leader, and, indeed, the metaphor of family is fundamental and recurrent. It is by hearing standards a heterogeneous family: the salience of deaf identity overshadows differences of age, class, sex, and ethnicity that would be more prominent in hearing society. Likewise, there is a penchant for group decision-making, and mutual aid and reciprocity figure importantly in deaf culture. Favors are more easily requested, my deaf friends tell me, more readily granted, and there is less individual accounting than in American hearing society (1992, 17–8).

8 Murcott (1983c) takes up aspects of technology in her article on cook-book images of technique and technology.

9 For a discussion of the relationship of Christmas feasting to class, see Pitts and colleagues (2007).

WORKS CITED

UNPUBLISHED SOURCES

Bliss, Edwin. c. 1961. "Chronological History of Eureka and Ferrona with Historical Introduction, Brief Biographies and other Information," PANS MG1-vol 2053#2, www.parl.ns.ca/eurekaferrona/1951_60.htm (accessed 2 March 2010).

Falconer, Fred (1934–), and Geraldine Falconer. 2003. Interview. 21 August.

Farrow, Helen. 2003. Interview. 6 February.

Friendly Group. c. 1958. *Tested Sweet Recipes*. Parrsboro: Unpublished.

Goodyear, Annie. 1999. Interview. 28 July.

Green, Anne. 2004. Interview. 19 August.

Hunter, Annie. 1986. Interview. 12 March.

Latimer, Sadie. 2000. Interview. 8 August.

Miller, Peg. 1999. Interview. 18 July.

Simpson, Elizabeth K. 2001. "Family Violence and Family Identity." MA thesis, Acadia University, Wolfville, NS.

Tye, Cathy. 1999. Interview. 16 August.

– 2001. Interview. 27 February.

– 2005. Interview. 23 July.

– 2009. Interview. 2 July.

Tye, Diane. 2005. "'Did Mom Bake?': Participating in Tradition." Paper presented to the American Folklore Society, Atlanta, Ga.

Tye, Henry. 1999a. Interview. 3 July.

– 1999b. Unrecorded interview. 14 June.

– and Mark Tye. 2005. Interview. 20 August.

Tye, Laurene. 1984. Interview. 8 May.

– 1986. Interview. 19 March.

Tye, Mark. 1999. Interview. 18 July.

Ward, Helen. 2004. Interview. 23 August.

PUBLISHED SOURCES

Abarca, Meredith E. 2001. "*Los Chilaquiles de mi 'ama*: The Language of Everyday Cooking." In *Pilaf, Pozole, and Pad Thai: American Women and Ethnic Food*, ed. Sherrie A. Inness, 119–44. Amherst: University of Massachusetts Press.

– 2006. *Voices in the Kitchen: Views of Food and the World from Working-Class Mexican and Mexican-American Women*. College Station: Texas A&M University Press.

Abrahams, Naomi. 1996. "Negotiating Power, Identity, Family, and Community: Women's Community Participation." *Gender & Society* 10 (6):768–96.

Abu-Lughod, Lila. 1993. *Writing Women's Worlds: Bedouin Stories*. Berkeley & Los Angeles: University of California Press.

– 1990. "The Romance of Resistance: Tracing Transformations of Power through Bedouin Women." *American Ethnologist* 17:41–55.

Allen, Patricia, and Carolyn Sachs. 2007. "Women and Food Chains. The Gendered Politics of Food." *International Journal of Sociology of Agriculture and Food* 15 (1):1–23.

Allen, Terese. 1998. "Goodness Gracious! For Local Flavor and Fellowship, You Can't Beat a Church Supper." In *Wisconsin Folklife: A Celebration of Wisconsin Folklore*, ed. Marshall Cook, 43–9. Madison: Wisconsin Academy of Sciences, Arts and Letters.

Anderson, Jay Allan. 1971. "The Study of Contemporary Foodways in American Folklife Research." *Ethnolgia Europea* 5:56–63.

Anderson, Robert. 1968. "I Never Sang for My Father." In *The Best Plays of 1967–1968,* ed. Otis L. Guernsey, Jr., 277–98. New York: Dodd, Mead.

Anonymous. 1890. "Eureka." *Presbyterian Witness* (March 15):85.

– 1948. "Molasses Pool." *Newfoundland Journal of Commerce* 15:30.

Atkin, Karl, Waqar I.U. Ahmad, and Leslie Jones. 2002. "Young South Asian Deaf People and their Families: Negotiating Relationships and Identities." *Sociology of Health and Illness* 24 (1):21–45.

Avakian, Arlene Voski, ed. 1977. *Through the Kitchen Window: Women Explore the Intimate Meanings of Food and Cooking.* Oxford: Berg.

– and Barbara Haber, eds. 2005. *From Betty Crocker to Feminist Food Studies: Critical Perspectives on Women and Food.* Amherst: University of Massachusetts.

Bacchi, Carol Lee. 1993. *Liberation Deferred? The Ideas of the English-Canadian Suffragists, 1877–1918.* Toronto: University of Toronto Press.

Baldock, Cora V. 1983. "Volunteer Work as Work: Some Theoretical Considerations." In *Women, Social Welfare and the State in Australia,* ed. Cora V. Baldock and Bettina Cass, 279–97. Sydney: George Allen & Unwin.

Barnes, Julian. 2008. *Nothing to be Frightened of.* Toronto: Random House Canada.

Barthes, Roland. 1997. "Toward a Psychology of Contemporary Food Consumption." In *Food and Culture: A Reader,* ed. Carole Counihan and Penny Van Esterik, 20–7. New York & London: Routledge.

Bateson, Mary Catherine. 1989. *Composing a Life.* New York: Grove Press.

Beagan, Brenda, Gwen E. Chapman, Andrea D'Sylva, and B. Raewyn Bassett. 2008. "'It's Just Easier for Me to Do It': Rationalizing the Family Division of Foodwork." *Sociology* 42 (4):653–71.

Behar, Ruth. 1996. *The Vulnerable Observer: Anthropology that Breaks your Heart.* Boston: Beacon Press.

Bella, Leslie. 1992. *The Christmas Imperative: Leisure Family and Women's Work.* Halifax, NS: Fernwood.

Benderly, Beryl Lieff. 1980. *Dancing Without Music: Deafness in America*. Washington, DC: Gallaudet University Press.

Bennett, Linda A., Steven J. Wolin, and Katharine J. McAvity. 1988. "Family Identity, Ritual and Myth: A Cultural Perspective on Life Cycle Transition." In *Family Transitions: Continuity and Change over the Life Cycle*, ed. Celia Jaes Falicov, 211–34. New York: Guilford Press.

Bennett, Margaret. 1998. *Oatmeal and Catechism: Scottish Gaelic Settlers in Quebec*. Edinburgh & Montreal: John Donald & McGill-Queen's University Press.

Bentley, Amy. 2002. "Islands of Serenity: Gender, Race, and other Gendered Meals during World War II." In *Food in the USA: A Reader*, ed. Carole M. Counihan, 171–92. New York: Routledge.

Berger, Leigh, and Carolyn Ellis. 2002. "Composing Autoethnographic Stories." In *Doing Cultural Anthropology: Projects for Ethnographic Data Collection*, ed. Michael V. Angrosino, 151–66. Prospect Heights, Ill.: Waveland.

Berkeley, Ellen Perry, ed. 2000. *At Grandmother's Table: Women Write about Food, Life, and the Enduring Bond between Grandmothers and Granddaughters*. Minneapolis: Fairview Press.

Berzok, Linda Murray. "My Mother's Recipes. The Diary of a Swedish American Daughter and Mother." 2001. In *Pilaf, Pozole, and Pad Thai: American Women and Ethnic Food*, ed. Sherrie A. Inness, 84–101. Amherst: University of Massachusetts Press.

Bishop, Marion. 1997. "Speaking Sisters: Relief Society Cookbooks and Mormon Culture." In *Recipes for Reading: Community Cookbooks, Stories, Histories*, ed. Anne L. Bower, 89–104. Amherst: University of Massachusetts Press.

Black, Sarah. 2006. "'Kiddies' Delight': Children and Community Cookbooks in Australia, 1900–2000." *Food, Culture & Society* 9 (3):345–54.

Blend, Benay. 2001. "'In the Kitchen Family Bread Is Always Rising!': Women's Culture and the Politics of Food." In *Pilaf, Pozole, and Pad Thai:*

American Women and Ethnic Food, ed. Sherrie A. Inness, 145–64. Amherst: University of Massachusetts Press.

Bloom, Lynn Z. 2001. "Writing and Cooking, Cooking and Writing." In *Pilaf, Pozole, and Pad Thai: American Women and Ethnic Food*, ed. Sherrie A. Inness, 69–83. Amherst: University of Massachusetts Press.

Bourdieu, Pierre. 1984. *Distinction: A Social Critique of the Judgement of Taste*, trans. Richard Nice. Cambridge, Mass.: Harvard.

Bower, Anne. 1997a. *Our Sisters' Recipes*: Exploring "Community" in a Community Cookbook." *Journal of Popular Culture* 31 (3):137–51.

– 1997b. "Cooking Up Stories: Narrative Elements in Community Cookbooks." In *Recipes for Reading: Community Cookbooks, Stories, Histories*, ed. Anne L. Bower, 29–50. Amherst: University of Massachusetts Press.

Brettell, Caroline B. 1997. "Blurred Genres and Blended Voices: Life History, Biography, Autobiography, and the Auto/Ethnography of Women's Lives." In *Auto/Ethnography: Rewriting the Self and the Social*, ed. Deborah E. Reed-Danahay, 223–46. Oxford: Berg.

Brown, Linda Keller, and Kay Mussell, eds. 2001 [1984]. "Introduction." *Ethnic and Regional Foodways in the United States: The Performance of Group Identity*, 5th ed., 3–15. Knoxville: University of Tennessee.

Brunvand, Jan Harold. 1996. "Occupational Folklore." In *American Folklore: An Encyclopaedia*, ed. Jan Harold Brunvand, 519–23. New York & London: Garland Publishing.

Buchan, David. 1972. *The Ballad and the Folk*. London & Boston: Routledge & Kegan Paul.

Burgoyne, Jacqueline, and David Clarke. 1983. "You Are What you Eat: Food and Family Reconstitution." In *The Sociology of Food and Eating: Essays on the Sociological Significance of Food*, ed. Anne Murcott, 152–63. Aldershot, England: Gower.

Cameron, James M. 1983. *A Century of Industry: The Story of Canada's Pioneer Steel Producer*. Trenton: Trenton Centennial Commission.

Camp, Charles. 1989. *American Foodways: What, When, Why and How We Eat in America*. American Folklore Series. Ed. W. K. McNeil. Little Rock, Ark.: August House.

– 1996. "Foodways." *American Folklore: An Encyclopaedia*. Ed. Jan Harold Brunvand. New York: Garland, 299–302.

Cashman, Ray. 2006. "Critical Nostalgia and Material Culture in Northern Ireland." *Journal of American Folklore* 119:137–60.

Casselman, Bill. 1998. *Canadian Food Words*. Toronto: McArthur and Company.

Castillo, Debra A. 1992. *Talking Back: Strategies for a Latin American Feminist Literary Criticism*. Ithaca: Cornell University Press.

Charles, Nickie, and Marion Kerr. 1988. *Women, Food and Families*. Manchester: Manchester University Press.

Chatelaine magazine. 1954. Various issues. Toronto: MacLean-Hunter Publishing.

Christensen, Paul. 2001. "The Cup of Comfort." In *Cooking Lessons: The Politics of Gender and Food*, ed. Sherrie A. Inness, 1–17. Lanham, Md.: Rowman & Littlefield.

Church, Kathryn. 2002. "The Hard Road Home: Toward a Polyphonic Narrative of the Mother-Daughter Relationship." In *Ethnographically Speaking: Autoethnography, Literature, and Aesthetics*, ed. Arthur P. Bochner and Carolyn Ellis, 234–57. Lanham, Md.: Altamira Press.

Clifford, James. 1986. "Introduction: Partial Truths." In *Writing Culture: The Poetics of Ethnography*, ed. James Clifford and George E. Marcus, 1–26. Berkeley & Los Angeles: University of California Press.

Colborne, Joan Archibald. 2003. *Letters from the Manse*. Charlottetown, PEI: Island Studies Press.

The Concise Oxford Dictionary. 1976. 6th ed. Ed. J.B. Sykes. Oxford: Clarendon Press.

Conrad, Margaret. 1993. "The 1950s: The Decade of Development." In *The Atlantic Provinces in Confederation*, ed. E. R. Forbes and D. A. Muise, 382–420. Toronto: University of Toronto Press.

Counihan, Carole M. 1999. *The Anthropology of Food and Body. Gender, Meaning, and Power*. New York: Routledge.

– 2004. *Around the Tuscan Table: Food, Family, and Gender in Twentieth-Century Florence*. New York: Routledge.

Crawford, Elaine, and Kelly Crawford. 1996. *Aunt Maud's Recipe Book: From the Kitchen of L. M. Montgomery*. Norval, Ont.: Moulin Publishing.

Csikszentmihalyi, Mihaly. 1993. "Why We Need Things." In *History From Things: Essays on Material Things*, ed. S. Lubar and W. D. Kingery. Washington, DC: Smithsonian Institution Press, 20–9.

Daniels, Arleen Kaplan. 1987. "Invisible Work." *Social Problems* 34 (5): 403–15.

Davidson, Alan. 2002. *The Penguin Companion to Food*. New York & London: Penguin.

Davis, Gayle R. 1997. "Women's Quilts and Diaries: Creative Expression as Personal Resource." *Uncoverings: The Research Papers of the American Quilt Study Group* 18:213–29.

Davy, Shirley, Project Coordinator. 1983. *Women Work & Worship in the United Church of Canada*. [Toronto:] United Church of Canada.

DeVault, Majorie L. 1991. *Feeding the Family: The Social Organization of Caring as Gendered Work*. Chicago: University of Chicago Press.

Dictionary of Newfoundland English Online. 1999. 2nd ed. with supplement. Ed. D.G.M. Story, W.J. Kirwin, and J.D.A. Widdowson. Toronto: University of Toronto Press. www.heritage.nf.ca/dictionary/(accessed March 8, 2008)

di Leonardo, Micaela. 1987. "The Female World of Cards and Holidays: Women, Families, and the Work of Kinship. *Signs* 12 (3):440–53.

Dietler, Michael. 1996. Feasts and Commensal Politics in the Political Economy: Food, Power, and Status in Prehistoric Europe. In *Food and the Status Quest: An Interdisciplinary Perspective*, ed. Pauline Weissner and Wulf Schiefenhovel, 87–126. Providence, RI: Berghahn Books.

Diner, Hasia R. 2001. *Hungering for America: Foodways in the Age of Migration*. Cambridge, Mass: Harvard University Press.

Dorson, Richard M., ed. 1972. *Folklore and Folklife: An Introduction*. Chicago & London: University of Chicago Press.

Dorst, John. 1989. *The Written Suburb: An American Site, an Ethnographic Dilemma*. Philadelphia: University of Philadelphia Press.

Douglas, Mary. 1997. "Deciphering a Meal." In *Food and Culture: A Reader*, ed. Carole Counihan and Penny Van Esterik, 36–54. New York & London: Routledge.

Edwards, Devonna. 1998. *Wartime Recipes from Nova Scotia 1939–1945*. Privately printed.

Eichler, Lillian. 1940. *The New Book of Etiquette*. New York: Garden City Publishing.

Ellis, Carolyn. 1995. *Final Negotiations: A Story of Love, Loss, and Chronic Illness*. Philadelphia: Temple University Press.

– 2004. *The Ethnographic I: A Methodological Novel about Autoethnography*. Walnut Creek & New York: Altamira.

Ellis, Carolyn, and Arthur P. Bochner. 2000. "Autoethnography, Personal Narrative, Reflexivity: Researcher as Subject." In *Handbook of Qualitative Research*. 2nd ed. Ed. Norman K. Denzin and Yvonna S. Lincoln, 733–68. Thousand Oaks, London & New Delhi: Sage Publications.

– eds. 1996. *Composing Ethnography. Alternative Forms of Qualitative Writing*. Ethnographic Alternative Series No. 1. Walnut Creek & New York: Altamira.

Ellis, Rhian. 1983. "The Way to a Man's Heat: Food in the Violent Home." In *The Sociology of Food and Eating: Essays on the Sociological Significance of Food*, ed. Anne Murcott, 164–71. Aldershot, England: Gower.

Elstad, Åsa. 1999. "Changing Labour Roles in North Norwegian Fisherman-Farmer Households." In *Global Coasts. Life Changes, Gender Challenges*, ed. Siri Gerrard and Randi Rønning Balsvik, 19–29. Kvinnforsk Occasional Papers 2. Kvinnforsk: University of Tromsø Press.

Endrijonas, Erika. 2001. "Processed Foods from Scratch: Cooking for a Family in the 1950s." In *Kitchen Culture in America: Popular Representations of Food, Gender, and Race*, ed. Sherrie A. Inness, 157–73. Philadelphia: University of Pennsylvania Press.

Everett, Holly. 2009. "Vernacular Health Moralities and Culinary Tourism in Newfoundland and Labrador." *Journal of American Folklore* 122:28–52.

Farmer, Fannie Merritt. 1941. *The Boston Cooking School Cook Book*. Toronto: McClelland & Stewart, 1896.

Ferguson, Bruce. 1967. *Place Names and Places of Nova Scotia*. Halifax: Public Archives of Nova Scotia.

Fishman, Pamela M. 1978. "Interaction: The Work Women Do." *Social Problems* 25:397–406.

Folster, David. 1990. *The Chocolate Ganongs of St. Stephen, New Brunswick*. Toronto: Macmillan.

Friedan, Betty. 1974. *The Feminine Mystique*. New York: Dell, 1963.

Gabaccia, Donna R. 1998. *We Are What We Eat: Ethnic Food and the Making of Americans*. Cambridge, Mass.: Harvard University Press.

Gantt, Patricia M. 2001. "Taking the Cake: Power Politics in Southern Life and Fiction." In *Cooking Lessons: The Politics of Gender and Food*, ed. Sherrie A. Inness, 63–85. Lanham, Md.: Rowman & Littlefield.

Glassie, Henry. 1995. "Tradition." *Journal of American Folklore* 108: 395–412.

Goffman, Erving. 1959. *The Presentation of Self in Everyday Life*. Garden City, New York: Doubleday.

Gold, Doris B. 1971. "Women and Volunteerism." In *Woman in Sexist Society: Studies in Power and Powerlessness*, ed. Vivian Gornick and Barbara K. Moran, 384–400. New York: Basic Books.

Goody, Jack. 1982. *Cooking, Cuisine and Class: A Study in Comparative Sociology*. Cambridge, England: Cambridge University Press.

Grant, Gail. 1993. "Starting Out: Outfitting the Bride in Seaside." *Canadian Folklore Canadien* 15 (2):69–82.

Greenhill, Pauline. 1997. "'The Handsome Cabin Boy': Cross-Dressing Ballads, Sexualities, and Gendered Meanings." In *Undisciplined Women: Tradition and Culture in Canada*, ed. Pauline Greenhill and Diane Tye, 113–30. Montreal & Kingston: McGill-Queen's University Press.

– 2005. "Making the Night Hideous: Death at a Manitoba Charivari, 1909." *Manitoba History* 52:3–17.

– and Diane Tye. 2001. "Resistance and Popular Theory: Folklore, Feminism, and Women's Studies in the 1990s." *Journal of Canadian Studies* 36 (2):191–205.

– and Diane Tye. 1994. "Critiques from the Margin: Interdisciplinary Perspectives on the Place of the Feminine in Canadian Folklore Studies." In *Canada: Theoretical Discourse*, ed. Terry Goldie, Carmen Lambert, and Rowland Lorimer, 167–86. Montreal: Association for Canadian Studies.

Gutierrez, C. Paige. 1984. "The Social and Symbolic of Ethnic/Regional Foodways: Cajuns and Crawfish in South Louisiana." In *Ethnic and Regional Foodways in the United States: The Performance of Group Identity*, ed. Linda Keller Brown and Kay Mussell, 169–84. Knoxville: University of Tennessee Press.

Hall, Edward T. 1983. *The Dance of Life*. New York: Anchor.

Handler, Richard, and Jocelyn Linnekin. 1984. "Tradition, Genuine or Spurious." *Journal of American Folklore* 97:273–90.

Heldke, Lisa. 1992. "Recipes for Theory Making." In *Cooking, Eating, Thinking: Transformative Philosophies of Food*, ed. Deane W. Curtin and Lisa M. Heldke, 251–65. Bloomington & Indianapolis: Indiana University Press.

– 2001. "Let's Cook Thai: Recipes for Colonialism." In *Pilaf, Pozole, and Pad Thai: In American Women and Ethnic Food*, ed. Sherrie A. Inness, 175–98. Amherst: University of Massachusetts Press.

Hollis, Susan Tower, Linda Pershing, and M. Jane Young, eds. 1993. *Feminist Theory and the Study of Folklore*. Urbana & Chicago: University of Illinois Press.

Hook, Jennifer L. 2004. "Reconsidering the Division of Household Labor: Incorporating Volunteer Work and Informal Support." *Journal of Marriage and Family* 66:101–7.

Humphrey, Theodore C., and Lin T. Humphrey, eds. 1988. 'We Gather Together': Food and Festival in American Life. Ann Arbor, Mich.: UMI Research Press.

Inness, Sherrie A. 2001a. "Introduction: Of Meatloaf and Jell-O ..." In Cooking Lessons: The Politics of Gender and Food, ed. Sherrie A. Inness, xi–xvii. Lanham, Md.: Rowman & Littlefield.

– 2001b. "Introduction. Thinking Food/Thinking Gender." In Kitchen Culture in America: Popular Representations of Food, Gender, and Race, ed. Sherrie A. Inness, 1–12. Philadelphia: University of Pennsylvania Press.

– 2001c. Dinner Roles: American Women and Culinary Culture. Iowa City: University of Iowa Press.

– 2006. Secret Ingredients: Race, Gender, and Class at the Dinner Table. New York: Palgrave Macmillan.

Innis, Harold A., ed. 1948. The Diary of Simeon Perkins 1766–1780. Toronto: Champlain Society.

Ireland, Lynne. 1981. "The Compiled Cookbook as Foodways Autobiography." Western Folklore 40 (1):107–14.

Jeffries, Giovanna Miceli. 2005. "Introduction." In Keeping House: A Novel in Recipes, by Clara Sereni, trans. Giovanni Miceli Jeffries and Susan Briziarelli, 1–19. New York: State University of New York.

Jelinek, Estelle. 1980. Women's Autobiography: Essays in Criticism. Bloomington: Indiana University Press.

Jenkins, Virginia S. 2001. "Bananas: Women's Food." In Cooking Lessons: The Politics of Gender and Food, ed. Sherrie A. Inness, 111–28. Lanham, Md.: Rowman & Littlefield.

Jesperson, Ivan F., ed. 1974. Fat-Back and Molasses: A Collection of Favourite Old Recipes from Newfoundland and Labrador. St. John's, Nfld.: Jesperson Publishing.

Jones, Michael Owen. 2007. "Food Choice, Symbolism, and Identity: Bread-and-Butter Issue for Folklorists and Nutrition Studies." American Folklore Society Presidential Address, October 2005. Journal of American Folklore 120:129–77.

Jones, Suzi. 1976. "Regionalization: a Rhetorical Strategy." *Journal of the Folklore Institute* 13:105–20.

Julier, Alice, and Laura Lindenfeld. 2005. "Mapping Men onto the Menu: Masculinities and Food." *Food & Foodways* 13:1–16.

Kaminer, Wendy. 1984. *Women Volunteering*. New York: Anchor Doubleday.

Kass, Leon. 1994. *The Hungry Soul: Eating and the Perfecting of Our Nature*. New York: Free Press.

Kaufman, Cathy. 2004. "The Ideal Christmas Dinner." *Gastronomica: The Journal of Food and Culture* 4 (4):17–24.

Kirshenblatt-Gimblett, Barbara. 1987. "Recipes for Creating Community: The Jewish Charity Cookbook in America." *Jewish Folklore and Ethnology Review* 9 (1):8–12.

– 1989. "Objects of Memory: Material Culture as Life Review." In *Folk Groups and Folklore Genres*, ed. Elliott Oring, 329–38. Logan: Utah State University Press.

Kraft Foods. www.kraftfoods.com (accessed 20 September 2009).

Krotz, Larry. 1993. The Church Supper ... Food for the Soul." *Reader's Digest* 143 (858):43–8.

Labov, William, and Joshua Waletzky. 1967. "Narrative Analysis: Oral Versions of Personal Experience." In *Essays on the Visual and Verbal Arts*, ed. June Helm, 12–44. Seattle: University of Washington Press.

Lane, Harlan. 1992. *The Mask of Benevolence: Disabling the Deaf Community*. New York: Alfred A. Knopf.

Lawless, Elaine J. 2001. *Women Escaping Violence: Empowerment through Narrative*. Columbia, Missouri: University of Columbia Press.

Leach, Helen M., and Raelene Inglis. 2003. "The Archaeology of Christmas Cakes." *Food & Foodways* 11:141–66.

LeBesco, Kathleen. 2001. "There's Always Room for Resistance: Jell-O, Gender, and Social Class." In *Cooking Lessons: The Politics of Gender and Food,* ed. Sherrie A. Inness, 129–49. Lanham, Md.: Rowman & Littlefield.

Leonardi, Susan J. 1989. "Recipes for Reading." *PMLA* 3:340–7.

Levenstein, Harvey A. 1988. *Revolution at the Table: The Transformation of the American Diet*. New York & Oxford: Oxford University Press.

– 1993. *Paradox of Plenty: A Social History of Eating in Modern America*. New York & Oxford: Oxford University Press.

Lewis, George H. 1989. "The Maine Lobster as Regional Icon: Competing Images over Time and Social Class." *Food and Foodways* 4:303–16.

Little, Jo. 1997. "Constructions of Rural Women's Voluntary Work." *Gender, Place and Culture* 4 (2):197–209.

Locher, Julie L., William C. Yoels, Donna Maurer and Jillian Van Ells. 2005. "Comfort Foods: an Exploratory Journey into the Social and Emotional Significance of Food." *Food & Foodways* 13:273–97.

Lockwood, Yvonne R., and William G. Lockwood. 1998. "Pasties in Michigan's Upper Peninsula: Foodways, Interethnic Relations, and Regionalism." In *A Taste of American Place: A Reader on Regional and Ethnic Foods*, ed. Barbara G. Shortridge and James R. Shortridge, 21–36. Lanham, Md.: Rowman & Littlefield.

Long, Lucy M. 2000. "Holiday Meals: Rituals of Family Tradition." In *Dimensions of the Meal: The Science, Culture, Business, and Art of Eating*, ed. Herbert L. Meiselman, 143–59. Gaithersburg, Md.: Aspen.

– 2009. "Introduction." *Journal of American Folklore* 122:3–10.

– ed. 2004. *Culinary Tourism*. Lexington: University Press of Kentucky.

Lord, Alfred B. *The Singer of Tales*. New York: Atheneum, 1965.

Lovegren, Sylvia. 2005. *Fashionable Food: Seven Decades of Food Fads*. Chicago & London: University of Chicago Press.

Lupton, Deborah. 1996. *Food, the Body and the Self*. London: Sage.

Luxton, Meg. 1986. "Two Hands for the Clock: Changing Patterns in the Gendered Division of Labour in the Home." In *Through the Kitchen Window: The Politics of Home and Family*, ed. Meg Luxton and Harriet Rosenberg, 17–36. Toronto: Garamond.

MacDonald, Rev. D[onald]. 1980. *Cape North and Vicinity*. n. p.: n. pub. 1933.

MacKenzie, A.A. 2003. *Scottish Lights: Robust Reflections on Celtic Nova Scotia*. Wreck Cove, Cape Breton: Breton Books.

McAlpine Directory Co. 1898. *McAlpine's Maritime and Newfoundland gazetteer for Nova Scotia, New Brunswick, Prince Edward Island, and the island of Newfoundland*. St. John, NB: McAlpine Directory Co.

McCann, L. D. 1981. "The Mercantile-Industrial Transition in the Metals Towns of Pictou County, 1857–1931." *Acadiensis* 10 (2):29–64.

McCarl, Robert S. 1986. "Occupational Folklife." In *Folk Groups and Folklore Genres: An Introduction*, ed. Elliott Oring, 71–89. Logan: Utah State University Press.

McIntosh, William Alex, and Mary Zey. 1989. "Women as Gatekeepers of Food Consumption: A Sociological Critique." *Food and Foodways* 3 (4):317–32.

McNeil, W. K. 1989. "Introduction." In *American Foodways: What, When, Why and How We Eat in America*, ed. Charles Camp, 11–19. American Folklore Series, ed. W. K. McNeil. Little Rock, Ark.: August House.

McWilliams, Mark. 2007. "Good Women Bake Biscuits: Cookery and Identity in Antebellum American Fiction." *Food, Culture & Society* 10 (3):388–406.

Mace, David, and Vera Mace. "Marriage Enrichment for Clergy Couples." 1982. *Pastoral Psychology* 30:151–9.

Mäkelä, Johanna. 2000. "Cultural Definitions of the Meal." In *Dimensions of the Meal: The Science, Culture, Business, and Art of Eating*, ed. Herbert L. Meiselman, 7–18. Gaithersburg, Md.: Aspen.

Mennell, Stephen. 1985. *All Manners of Food: Eating and Taste in England and France from the Middle Ages to the Present*. Oxford: Basil Blackwell.

Meyers, Miriam. 2001. *A Bite off Mama's Plate. Mothers' and Daughters' Connections through Food*. Westport, Conn.: Bergin & Garvey.

Miller, Brenda Rhodes. 2001. *The Church Ladies' Divine Desserts. Heavenly Recipes and Sweet Recollections*. New York: HP Books.

Miller, Daniel. 1998. *A Theory of Shopping*. Ithaca, NY: Cornell University Press.

Miller, Nancy K. 1996. *Bequest and Betrayal: Memoirs of a Parent's Death.* Oxford: Oxford University Press.

Miller, Vincent J. 2004. *Consuming Region: Christian Faith and Practice in a Consumer Culture.* New York: Continuum.

Milroy, Beth Moore, and Susan Wismer. 1994. "Communities, Work and Public/ Private Models." *Gender, Place & Culture: A Journal of Feminist Geography* 1 (1):71–90.

Mintz, Sidney W. 1985. *Sweetness and Power. The Place of Sugar in Modern History.* New York: Viking.

Montaño, Mario. 1997. "Appropriation and Counterhegemony in South Texas: Food Slurs, Offal Meats, and Blood." In *Usable Pasts: Traditions and Group Expressions in North America*, ed. Tad Tuleja, 50–67. Logan: Utah State University Press.

Montgomery, Lucy Maud. 1985. *The Selected Journals of L. M. Montgomery. Volume 1: 1889–1910.* Ed. Mary Rubio and Elizabeth Waterston. Toronto: Oxford University Press.

– 1987. *The Selected Journals of L. M. Montgomery. Volume II: 1910–1921.* Ed. Mary Rubio and Elizabeth Waterston. Toronto: Oxford University Press.

– 1992. *The Selected Journals of L. M. Montgomery. Volume III: 1921–1929.* Ed. Mary Rubio and Elizabeth Waterston. Toronto: Oxford University Press.

Murcott, Anne. 1982. "On the Social Significance of the 'Cooked Dinner' in South Wales." *Social Science Information* 21:677–96.

– 1983a. "Cooking and the Cooked: A Note on the Domestic Preparation of Meals." In *The Sociology of Food and Eating*, ed. Anne Murcott, 178–85. Aldershot, England: Gower.

– 1983b. "'It's a Pleasure to Cook for Him': Food, Mealtimes and Gender in Some South Wales Households." In *The Public and the Private*, ed. Eva Garmarnikow, David Morgan, June Purvis, and Daphne Taylorson, 78–90. London: Heinemann.

– 1983c. "Women's Place: Cookbooks' Images of Technique and Technology in the British Kitchen." *Women's Studies International Forum* 6 (1):33–9.

– 1993. "Talking of Good Food: An Empirical Study of Women's Conceptualizations." *Food and Foodways* 5 (3):305–18.

Narváez, Peter, and Martin Laba. [1988]. "Introduction: The Folklore-Popular Culture Continuum." In *Media Sense: The Folklore-Popular Culture Continuum*, ed. Peter Narváez and Martin Laba, 1–8. Bowling Green, Ohio: Bowling Green State University Popular Press.

Nestlé. "History of Nestlé Toll House." www.verybestbaking.com/products/tollhouse/history.aspx (accessed 3 March 2010).

Nestlé. "Original Nestlé Toll House Chocolate Chip Cookies." www.verybest baking.com/recipes/specialty/nth-detail-occc.aspxhttp://nestle.ca/en/articles/Toll_House (accessed 3 March 2010).

Neuhaus, Jessamyn. 1999. "The Way to a Man's Heart: Gender Roles, Domestic Ideology, and Cookbooks in the 1950s." *Journal of Social History* 32:529–55.

New Glasgow, Stellarton, Westville & Trenton Councils. 1916. *Nova Scotia's Industrial Centre: The Birthplace of Steel in Canada.* n. p.: n. pub.

Newton, Sarah E. 1992. "'The Jell-O Syndrome': Investigating Popular Culture/Foodways." *Western Folklore* 51:249–67.

Nightingale, Marie. 1981. *Out of Old Nova Scotian Kitchens.* Halifax, NS: H.H. Marshall, 1970.

Nolan, Dick. 1999. "Newfoundland Good Times." Condor label HCD 4449. Heritage Music.

Oakley, Ann. 1974. *The Sociology of Housework.* New York: Pantheon.

Oden, Marilyn Brown. 1988. "Stress and Purpose: Clergy Spouses Today." *The Christian Century* (20 April):402–4.

Off, Carol. 2006. *Bitter Chocolate: Investigating the Dark Side of the World's Most Seductive Sweet.* Toronto: Random House Canada.

Oldenburg, Ray. 1997. *The Great Good Place: Cafés, Coffee Shops, Community Centers, Beauty Parlors, General Stores, Bars, Hangouts and How They Get You through the Day.* New York: Marlowe.

Omohundro, John T. 1994. *Rough Food: The Seasons of Subsistence in Northern Newfoundland*. Social and Economic Studies 54. St. John's, NL.: Institute for Social and Economic Research.

Oring, Elliott. 1986. *Folklore Groups and Folklore Genres: An Introduction*. Logan: Utah State University Press, 1986.

O'Sullivan, Grace, Claire Hocking, and Valerie Wright-St. Clair. 2008. "History in the Making: Older Canadian Women's Food-Related Practices." *Food and Foodways* 16:63–87.

Padden, Carol, and Tom Humphries. 1988. *Deaf in America: Voices from a Culture*. Cambridge: Harvard University Press.

Parrott, Lora Lee. 1953. *Christian Etiquette,* Grand Rapids, Mich.: Zondervan Publishing House.

Petrzelka, Peggy, and Susan E. Mannon. 2006. "Keepin' this Little Town Going: Gender and Volunteerism in Rural America." *Gender & Society* 20:236–58.

Pitts, Martin, Danny Dorling, and Charles Pattie. 2007. "Christmas Feasting and Social Class: Christmas Feasting and Everyday Consumption." *Food, Culture & Society* 10 (3):407–24.

Pocius, Gerald L. 2000. *A Place to Belong: Community Order and Everyday Space in Calvert, Newfoundland*. Montreal & Kingston: McGill-Queen's University Press.

Poteet, Lewis J. 1983. *The South Shore Phrase Book*. Hantsport, NS: Lancelot Press.

Pratt, T. K. 1988. *Dictionary of Prince Edward Island English*. Toronto: University of Toronto Press.

Radner, Joan Newlon, ed. 1993. *Feminist Messages: Coding in Women's Folk Culture*. Urbana & Chicago: University of Illinois Press.

Radner, Joan, and Susan Lanser. 1993. "Strategies of Coding in Women's Cultures." In *Feminist Messages: Coding in Women's Folk Culture*, ed. Joan Newlon Radner, 1–29. Urbana & Chicago: University of Illinois Press.

Radway, Janice A. 1984. *Reading the Romance: Women, Patriarchy and Popular Culture*. Chapel Hill: University of North Carolina Press.

Reed-Danahay, Deborah E. 1997. "Leaving Home: Schooling Stories and the Ethnography of Autoethnography in Rural France." In *Auto/Ethnography: Rewriting the Self and the Social*, ed. Deborah E. Reed-Danahay, 123–43. Oxford: Berg.

Reeves, Maud Pember. 1999. *Round about a Pound a Week*. London: Virago.

Rich, Adrienne. 1976. *Of Woman Born: Motherhood as Experience and Institution*. New York: W. W. Norton.

Robertson, Marion. 1991. *The Chestnut Pipe: Folklore of Shelburne County*. Halifax, NS: Nimbus.

Roos, Gun, and Margareta Wandel. 2005. "'I Eat Because I'm Hungry, Because It's Good, and to Become Full': Everyday Eating Voiced by Male Carpenters, Drivers, and Engineers in Contemporary Oslo." *Food & Foodways* 13:169–80.

Rozin, Elisabeth. 2000. "The Role of Flavor in the Meal and the Culture." In *Dimensions of the Meal: The Science, Culture, Business, and Art of Eating*, ed. Herbert L. Meiselman, 134–42. Gaithersburg, Md.: Aspen.

Sack, Daniel. 2000. *Whitebread Protestants. Food and Religion in American Culture*. New York: St. Martin's Press.

Scott, James C. 1990. *Domination and the Arts of Resistance: Hidden Transcripts*. New Haven & London: Yale University Press.

Seid, Roberta Pollack. 1989. *Never Too Thin: Why Women Are at War with Their Bodies*. New York: Prentice Hall.

Sereni, Clara. 2005. *Keeping House: A Novel in Recipes*. Trans. Giovanni Miceli Jeffries and Susan Briziarelli. New York: State University of New York.

Sewell, Jessica. 2008. "Tea and Suffrage." *Food, Culture & Society* 11 (4):487–507.

Seymour, Susanne, and Christopher Short. 1994. "Gender, Church and People in Rural Areas." *Area* 26 (1):45–56.

Shapiro, Laura. 1986. *Perfection Salad: Women and Cooking at the Turn of the Century*. New York: Farrar, Straus and Giroux.

– 2001. "'My Problem is Watery Custard.' Reading the Confidential Chat." *Gastronomica: The Journal of Food and Culture* 1 (4):48–55.

– 2004. *Something from the Oven: Reinventing Dinner in 1950s America.* New York: Viking.

Shortridge, Barbara G., and James R. Shortridge, eds. 1998. *The Taste of American Place: A Reader on Regional and Ethnic Foods.* Lanham, Md.: Rowman & Littlefield.

Shuman, Amy. 1981. "The Rhetoric of Portions." *Western Folklore* 40 (1): 72–80.

Smith, Dorothy E. 1987. *The Everyday World as Problematic: A Feminist Sociology.* Toronto: University of Toronto Press.

Smith, Robyn. 2008. "Exploring the Ethical Limitations and Potential of Aesthetic Experiences of Food and Eating in Vegetarian Cookbooks." *Food, Culture & Society* 111 (4):420–48.

Smith, Sidonie, and Julia Watson, eds. 1996. *Getting a Life: Everyday Uses of Autobiography.* Minneapolis: University of Minnesota Press.

Sokolow, Jayme A. 1983. *Eros and Modernization: Sylvester Graham, Health Reform, and the Origins of Victorian Sexuality in America.* Rutherford, NJ: Fairleigh Dickinson University Press.

Stanley, Della. 1993. "The 1960s: The Illusions and Realities of Progress." In *The Atlantic Provinces in Confederation*, ed. E.R. Forbes and D.A. Muise, 421–59. Toronto: University of Toronto Press.

Steinberg, Stephen. 1998. "Bubbie's Challah." In *Eating Culture*, ed. Ron Scapp and Brian Seiz, 295–7. Albany, NY: SUNY Press.

Stevinson, Jean. 1935. "The Minister's Wife." *Chatelaine* (February): 26.

Storace, Patricia. 1986. "Repasts Past: Delicious Memories from Antique Cookbooks." *House and Garden* June: 62.

Sutherland, Fraser. 1989. *The Monthly Epic: A History of Canadian Magazines.* Markham, Ont.: Fitzhenry & Whiteside.

Sutton, David E. 2001. *Remembrance of Repasts: An Anthropology of Food and Memory.* Oxford & New York: Berg.

Sydner, Ylva Mattsson, Christina Fjellström, Margaret Lumbers, Birgitta Sidenvall, and Monique Raats. 2007. "Food Habits and Foodwork: The Life Course of Senior Europeans." *Food, Culture & Society* 10 (3):367–87.

Symons, Michael. 1982. *One Continuous Picnic: A History of Eating in Australia*. Adelaide, Australia: Duck Press.

Szwed, John. 1966. "Gossip, Drinking and Social Control: Consensus and Communication in a Newfoundland Parish." *Ethnology* 5:434–41.

Telfer, Elizabeth. 1996. *Food for Thought: Philosophy and Food*. London & New York: Routledge.

Theophano, Janet. 2001. "Home Cooking. Boston Baked Beans and Sizzling Rice Soup as Recipes for Pride and Prejudice." In *Kitchen Culture in America: Popular Representations of Food, Gender, and Race*, ed. Sherrie A. Inness, 139–56. Philadelphia: University of Pennsylvania Press.

– 2002. *Eat My Words: Reading Women's Lives through the Cookbooks They Wrote*. New York: Palgrave.

Thomas, Jeannie B. 1997. *Featherless Chickens, Laughing Women, and Serious Stories*. Charlottesville: University Press of Virginia.

Toelken, Barre. 1996. *The Dynamics of Folklore. Revised and Expanded Edition*. Logan: Utah State University Press.

Tuleja, Tad, ed. 1997. *Usable Pasts: Traditions and Group Expressions in North America*. Logan: Utah State University Press.

Turner, Jack. 2004. *Spices: The History of Temptation*. London: Harper Perennial.

Tye, Diane. 1995. "Katherine Gallagher and Women's World of Folksong." *Atlantis* 20 (1):101–12.

– 1996. "The Great Amherst Mystery: Linking Folk Belief and Female Experience," *Collections of the Royal Nova Scotia Historical Society* 44:105–19.

– 1997. "Contributions from Undisciplined Ethnography: The Case of Jean Heffernan." In *Undisciplined Women: Tradition and Culture in Canada*, ed. Pauline Greenhill and Diane Tye, 49–64. Montreal & Kingston: McGill-Queen's University Press.

– 2001. "The Traditional Craft of Christmas Form Letters." *Fabula* 42:201–12.

– 2002. "Tales of Whose Village? Legend as Female Countermemory."

Contemporary Legend: The Journal of the International Society for Contemporary Legend Research. New Series 5:1–23.

– 2008. "'A Poor Man's Meal.' Molasses in Atlantic Canada." *Food, Culture & Society* 11 (3):335–53.

– and Ann Marie Powers. 1998. "Gender, Resistance and Play: Bachelorette Parties in Atlantic Canada." *Women's Studies International Forum* 21 (5):551–61.

Visser, Margaret. 1988. *Much Depends on Dinner*. Toronto: McClelland & Stewart.

– 1991. *The Rituals of Dinner*. Toronto: Harper Collins.

Walker, Nancy. 1985. "Humor and Gender Roles: The 'Funny' Feminism of the Post-World War II Suburbs." *American Quarterly* 37:99–113.

Wansink, Brian, and Collin R. Payne. 2009. "The Joy of Cooking Too Much: 70 Years of Calorie Increases in Classic Recipes." *Annals of Internal Medicine*. 150 (17 February):291–2.

Weale, David. 1992. *Them Times*. Charlottetown: Institute of Island Studies.

Weedon, Chris. 1994. *Feminist Practice and Poststructuralist Theory*. Cambridge, Mass. & Oxford, England: Blackwell.

Weismantal, Mary J. 1988. *Food, Gender, and Poverty in the Ecuadorian Andes*. Philadelphia: University of Pennsylvania Press.

Welch, Wendy. 1997. "Pouring Out their Hearts: A Study of How Women Use Coffee." *Culture & Tradition* 19:69–86.

Wheaton, Barbara. 1998. "Finding Real Life in Cookbooks: The Adventures of a Culinary Historian." In *Food, Cookery and Culture*, ed. Leslie Howsam, 1–11. Working Papers in the Humanities, Humanities Research Group. Windsor, Ont.: University of Windsor Press.

Wilk, Richard. 2006. "Serving or Helping Yourself at the Table." *Food Culture & Society* 9 (1):7–12.

Wyman, Carolyn. 2001. *Jell-O: A Biography. The History and Mystery of 'America's Most Famous Dessert.'* San Diego, New York & London: Harcourt.

– 2004. *Better than Homemade. Amazing Foods that Changed the Way We Eat*. Philadelphia: Quirk Books.

Yaeger, Patricia. 1992. "Edible Labor." *Southern Quarterly* 30:150–59.

Yoder, Don. 1972. "Folk Cookery." In *Folklore and Folklife*, ed. Richard M. Dorson, 325–50. Chicago: University of Chicago Press.

Zafar, Rafia. 2002. "The Signifying Dish: Autobiography and History in two Black Women's Cookbooks." In *Food in the USA: A Reader*, ed. Carole M. Counihan, 249–62. New York: Routledge.

INDEX